# Letters from Ghana
# 1968-1970

*Canadian volunteer Nestor Kwasnycia (left) and U.S. Peace Corps volunteer Dave Fitzjarrald (right) among Ghanaian students, with the reflecting telescope donated by Cap Thiem, Acherensua, 1970-71; Courtesy of David Fitzjarrald.*

# LETTERS FROM GHANA 1968-1970

## A Peace Corps Chronicle

Compiled and Edited by Jon Thiem

A PEACE CORPS WRITERS BOOK

An Imprint of Peace Corps Worldwide

*Letters from Ghana 1968-1970: A Peace Corps Chronicle*
A Peace Corps Writers Book
An Imprint of Peace Corps Worldwide

Copyright © 2013 Jon Thiem
All rights reserved.

Printed in the United States of America
by Peace Corps Writers of Oakland, California.
No part of this book may be used or reproduced in any manner whatsoever without written permission except in the case of brief quotations contained in critical articles or reviews.

For more information, contact peacecorpsworldwide@gmail.com
Peace Corps Writers and the Peace Corps Writers colophon are trademarks of PeaceCorpsWorldwide.org

Cover photo: front row. L. to R.: "Ohene's" parents, Mr. and Mrs. Owoahene, and Jon Thiem. Behind them, holding a movie camera is "Ohene," Mr. Owoahene-Akyampong, August 1969.

Cover background: detail of a Kente cloth, *Adwini Asa* "the exhaustion of all designs," purchased by Jon Thiem in Bonwire, Ghana, May 1970.

Book and cover design by Natalie Bolton.

ISBN: 978-1-935925-39-2
Library of Congress Control Number: 2013954505

First Peace Corps Writers Edition, November 2013

Dedicated to Mike Moynihan

In memoriam

"Cap"—John R. Thiem (1922-2004)

Ralph Slotten (1926-2007)

"Ohene"—E. W. Owoahene-Akyampong (1943-2008)

# EPIGRAPHS

*The native who knows English is the one who tells the white man whom to praise.*

Ashanti Proverbs (1916). Translated by R. S. Rattray, revised by Jon Thiem.

*You were expecting maybe romance . . . glamour? Then forget about the Peace Corps. Glamorous it's not. You're going to be right in there with monotony, illiteracy, and an army of bloodthirsty mosquitoes. [. . .] And you will see one fraction of the results you'd hope for. But it's worth it when a kid in Nigeria understands what an alphabet is and some day will be able to use it.*

Peace Corps advertisement. 1964.

[The Climate of Acherensua]: *North East Trades, alias the Harmattan, in the dry season have . . . much influence on the school. It is very hot in the day . . . . As the rate of evaporation is very rapid because of the lowness of the relative humidity, students' skins crack, especially the lips. In the morning the temperature is so cool that people feel reluctant to bathe, in effect. However, the temperature encourages much sleep.*

Antwi Nimako, fifth-form student, Acherensua Secondary School, for *The Achiscodian Times* (November 1970).

*Somehow we must even pledge not to publish one another's letters or ever mention such a ridiculous idea again.*

Jon Thiem in Acherensua to Mike Moynihan in East Lansing, Michigan. June 7, 1969.

*The destruction of the past, or rather of the social mechanisms that link one's contemporary experience to that of earlier generations, is one of the most characteristic and eerie phenomena of the late twentieth century.*

Eric Hobsbaum. *The Age of Extremes: A History of the World, 1914-1991* (1994).

CONTENTS

List of Illustrations

Map

Preface                                                    1

Acknowledgments                                           12

Introduction                                              15

Notes to the Preface and Introduction                     46

Editorial Guidelines                                      54

Letters from Ghana: Texts and Commentaries I              55

A Ghanaian Portrait Gallery 1968-1970                    140

Letters from Ghana: Texts and Commentaries II            146

"Post Script"                                            233

Addendum: Apaeɛ for Owoahene                             237

Works Consulted                                          239

Timeline                                                 243

Glossary                                                 247

# LIST OF ILLUSTRATIONS

Cover Photo: front row. L. to R.: "Ohene's parents, Mr. and Mrs. Owoahene, and Jon Thiem. Behind them, holding a movie camera: "Ohene" Owoahene-Akyampong, August 1969.
Frontispiece: Canadian volunteer Nestor Kwasnycia (left) and U.S. Peace Corps volunteer Dave Fitzjarrald (right) among Ghanaian students, with the reflecting telescope donated by Cap Thiem, Acherensua, 1970-71; Courtesy of David Fitzjarrald.
Map: Ghana and the Ahafo area of the Brong Ahafo region (c.1969); courtesy of Natalie Bolton.
The Okyenhene during an adjudication, Kibi (Kyebi), September 1968. | 68
View of the campus, Acherensua Secondary School, 1968-69. | 72
Two students and Jon examine a cocoa pod, near Acherensua, 1968. | 81
Two Muslim boys, Tamale, Northern Region, December 1968. | 95
Lawrie Altrows, Canadian volunteer, with the staff of *The Achiscodian Times*, 1968-69; Courtesy of Lawrence Altrows. | 103
Jon, McClure, Kwasi Dum, and Ohene, Sebedie, June 1969. | 161
Presentation of ceremonial sword to Cap Thiem in Acherensua. L. to R.: Mrs. Owoahene, Mr. Baiden (Music Master), Ohene, Cap, Gene Katona & Mrs. Boakye, July 28, 1969. | 169
Ohene & Jon harvest a cassava root on Ohene's farm plot near Acherensua, July 1969. | 170
Black Rhinoceros and Oxpecker Bird, Ngorongoro Crater, August 1969. | 175
Cap Thiem and Kilimanjaro, August 1969. | 176
Kwasi Dum recites apaeε, Sebedie, June 1969. | 193
Fisherman on a wooden plank, Lake Bosumtwi, December 1969. | 198
Kente cloth weaver, Bonwire, April 1970. | 206
At the Beer Bar in Acherensua: Jon, Nestor Kwasnycia, and Dave Fitzjarrald, with two women friends from Hwidiem, 1969-1970. | 223

A GHANAIAN PORTRAIT GALLERY 1968-1970 | 140-146

Barber and client, Kumasi, September 1968.
Shoemaker, Kumasi, September 1968.
Stool carver, Kumasi, November 1968.
Motorcyclist next to a lorry, northern Ghana, December 1968.
Fetish vendor, Kumasi, no date.
Children at play, Kokofu or Sebedie, June 1969.
Drummer, Sebedie, June 1969.
A princess of Kokofu (standing next to a traditional Asante stool), August 1969.
The Kokofuhene with members of his court, Kokofu, August 1969.
Farm woman bringing plantains and yams to Acherensua, September 1969.
Cocoa farmer near Asiwa, December 1969.
Women at a funeral, December 1969.
Woman, Kokofu, 1970.


Jon in East Africa, August 1969. | 253

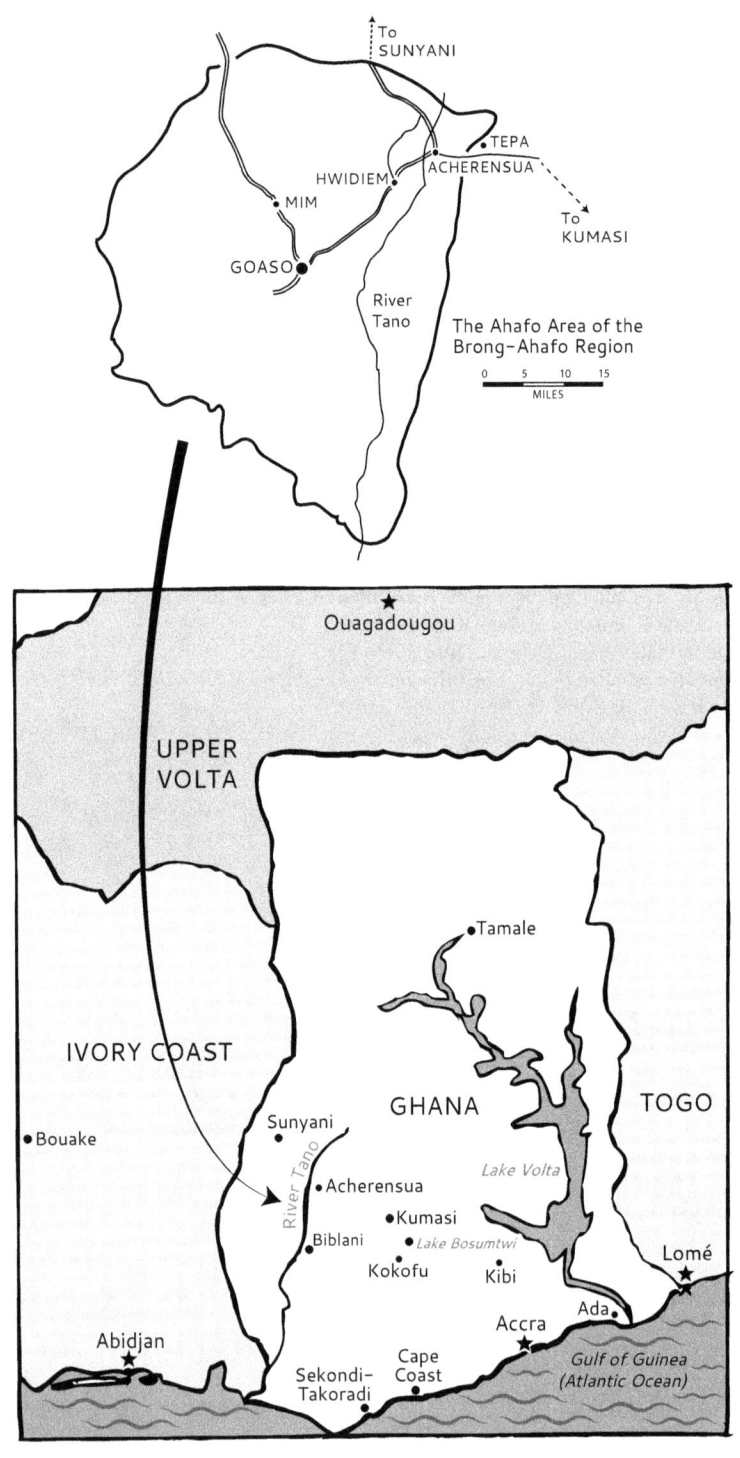

# PREFACE

Several years ago, I mentioned to a young woman (with a Ph.D.) that I had served with the Peace Corps in Ghana during the late 1960s. She thought I was referring to a U.N. Peacekeeping Force! Taken by surprise, I laughed. I thanked her for the alternative biography she had bestowed on me. Then I told her about the Peace Corps. I also explained that Ghana had never been the object of a U.N. Peacekeeping mission, but that Ghanaian soldiers had contributed to such missions in other countries.

This incident made me think again about the legacy of Peace Corps, and it made me wonder at the frailty of collective memory, in which important events of the recent past quickly fade away and become incomprehensible to the next generation. The incident, trivial as it seems, moved and inspired me to put together this collection of letters.

From August 1968 to June 1970, I was a Peace Corps volunteer living in a village in the rain forest of southern Ghana. There I taught English at the district secondary school. The village, called Acherensua, is on the River Tano, in the Brong-Ahafo region. Every two weeks or so, I sent letters or audiotapes to the States. These described my day-to-day impressions of Ghana—the miseries and splendors of life in the tropics.[1]

I was in my early twenties during the years of 1968, 1969, and 1970. An argument could be made that they were the most fateful and breathtaking three years of the later 20th century. Most of my present-day readers will have been born in that century, and yet the deep influence that period still exerts over current realities is not widely understood.[2]

The massive Peace Corps engagement during the 1960s, 70s, and 80s resulted in the dispersal of thousands of U.S. volunteers throughout the world—a dispersal that generated, in its turn, a large corpus of letters, some unknown percentage of which survives. This legacy may equal in human significance the letters written as a result of other historical occurrences of the 20th century: prolonged wars, migrations of people seeking work, and the forced expatriations of ethnic and political groups.

# PREFACE

The 1960s, the first decade of the Peace Corps, was a turbulent time shaped by the ongoing Cold War, the hot war in Vietnam, and student rebellions worldwide. The conflicts in Southeast Asia caused massive destruction of human life. Hundreds of thousands of civilians in Vietnam, Cambodia, and Laos were killed. The Soviet invasion of Czechoslovakia crushed the emerging democratic government. Martin Luther King, Jr., and Robert F. Kennedy were assassinated within months of each other in 1968. At Kent State University, in May 1970, a National Guard unit shot and killed four unarmed students. Government misconduct and the ill-advised military schemes of the Vietnam War years inspired a significant minority of young people to rise up against the authorities in a rebellion whose scope was as much cultural as political—a rebellion that was both a catalyst and channel for youthful idealism.

It was in this context that Peace Corps emerged as a symbol of hope—a desperate hope that peace and progress might replace government-imposed violence. The letters of the three Peace Corps teachers included in this collection offer windows into an extraordinary period of "on the ground," non-military intervention in a developing country. They bear witness to the ambivalent missions, harsh living conditions, and cross-cultural labyrinths faced by young American volunteers.

While it is true that the Peace Corps is still an active presence in the world, some commentators today wonder if it is not "the remnant of a bygone era," as Karen Rothmyer wrote in *The Nation* (March 21, 2011). Few will deny, however, that in its heyday the Peace Corps was a highly visible organization that set in motion an energetic and far-reaching humanitarian campaign. Its efforts were at the time denounced by both the political right and left (for reasons discussed in my Introduction and in the letters included in this collection), and its mission and effectiveness remain controversial to this day.

Because they represent the views of outsiders, the letters written by me and the two other Peace Corps volunteers are unable to do justice to the complex realities of Ghana in the 1960s and 1970s. The texts I

## PREFACE

myself wrote offer instead the chronicle of a young American's changing perspective on the country and on himself. They reveal how his preconceptions and expectations changed under the influence of daily contact with Ghanaians and the pressures of work. The letters chart the tribulations, discoveries, and friendships that arose out of a disconcerting new environment.

If my own texts highlight traditional culture and folk beliefs—as opposed to the more modern side of Ghana—this is in part because I was writing from "the bush," not from the city. In those remote and rural parts of the country, tradition played a major role. Its vital presence decisively shaped my responses to Ghanaian life. I saw tradition as an obstacle to rational thinking and progress, especially in health care, sanitation, and child development. At the same time, I found the oral Akan culture a fascinating area of study.

My letters and those of the two other volunteers record particular instances of what it was like to be a young, single, white male teaching in a West African country. The original texts were mainly handwritten, jotted down in haste. They reveal the freshness, naiveté, and stereotyping that typify new impressions in a foreign land. My own thinking at the time was quickened by the heat of atrocious events, by keen enthusiasms and bitter aversions. If some of the positions taken—or poses struck—in these texts seem extravagant, it is because they reflect the moral revolt, political tumult and cultural ferment of the times.

In the mid 1960s, when I attended college, I belonged to a radical political organization, Students for a Democratic Society.[3] As a political science major, I had developed an interest in the distinctive cultures of "Third World" countries—and in their struggles to achieve real independence, overcome poverty, and create modern institutions and infrastructures. I also became intensely curious about worldviews different from the one I grew up in.

I decided to become a Peace Corps English teacher in Ghana for three reasons. First, Peace Corps service offered an alternative to participation in the U.S. military campaign in Vietnam, which I opposed on moral and pragmatic grounds.[4] Secondly, I wanted to live in West Africa and observe firsthand the people and customs. I wanted to explore

# PREFACE

a different way of life. And finally, I hoped, as an English teacher, to assist in the economic and social development of Ghana.

Signing up with the Peace Corps marked a shift in my political stance. On the one hand, I continued to believe that the U.S. intervention in Vietnam was both wrong and wrong-headed. But I turned away from confrontational political action as a means to end the war. Hence my confession to Mike Moynihan: "I could no longer pretend to be a radical after I joined the Peace Corps" (Jan. 11, 1969).[5]

The reader might well ask, why yet *another* book about Peace Corps experiences. Around the time of the 50th anniversary of Peace Corps in 2011, there appeared an outpouring of such books.[6]

Several features distinguish *Letters from Ghana* from those recent books. This collection offers what few others do: the voices of host country nationals. These are represented both in writing and in cassette tape transcripts. The words of my colleague "Ohene" Owoahene, in particular, add an eloquent Ghanaian note to the epistolary chorus. Another feature here, seldom found in Peace Corps letter collections, is the extensive interpretive apparatus. The general introduction and individual commentaries situate the letters and other writings in their historical, geographical, and personal contexts. (To help readers navigate unfamiliar material about Ghana and the United States, the book also includes a map, a glossary, and a timeline.)

A third feature of *Letters from Ghana* is its awareness of recent scholarship that contests the goals and methods of assistance organizations like the Peace Corps. *Doing Bad by Doing Good: Why Humanitarian Action Fails* (Stanford University Press 2013) is the trenchant title of a recent study. Though not mentioning Peace Corps, the author, Christopher Coyne, draws on economic research and official reports to argue that most humanitarian programs are not only ineffective but also harmful. From a different angle, social historians have called into question the value of national literacy campaigns, such as the one Peace Corps teachers in Ghana contributed to in the 60s and 70s. In *Literacy Myths, Legacies & Lessons* (2011), for instance, Harvey Graff takes to task the familiar axiom that reading and writing ability is "a

# PREFACE

necessary precursor to and invariably results in economic development, democratic practice, cognitive enhancement and upward social mobility"(6).

Other recent studies examine the ulterior political motives behind well-intentioned assistance programs and argue that liberal-minded Westerners, who in the 1960s and 1970s sought to make African societies emulate Western institutions and ways of thinking, were in fact "secular missionaries" (to use Immanuel Wallerstein's term).

Julius Amin entitled his illuminating study of Peace Corps volunteers in Ghana "The Perils of Missionary Diplomacy" (1999). And Larry Grubbs in *Secular Missionaries: Americans and African Development in the 1960s* (2009) presents evidence of how U.S. government officials, area specialists, and development experts were zealous modernizers in the service of imperialism (8). Grubbs argues that modernization programs are tainted by their origins in colonialism and racist ideologies.

These studies tend to underrepresent both the achievements of the modernizers and the strong desire of African leaders and their constituents to become modern. For rural Ghanaians modernity meant (among other things) getting access to books, Western medicine, health care, clean water, and good nutrition for children.

Present-day criticism of humanitarian action in developing countries is one of the contexts in which *Letters from Ghana* was compiled. The book holds to an awareness of this climate of opinion and responds to it in different ways. The letters I have selected, for example, inevitably reveal the ethnocentric views and frustrations of three young "secular missionaries."

In my own letters, readers will find a passionate modernizer, but a modernizer who is *also* collecting traditional poems of the Asante court. He is, in other words, working at cross-purposes—endeavoring to preserve a kind of "magical thinking" that he hopes his Ghanaian students will learn to reject. This is one of the many paradoxes that a modernizer working "on the ground" experiences. It is true that the letters at hand offer examples that reinforce the arguments of skeptics. The letters show the troubling contradictions that arise when a

# PREFACE

humanitarian program intervenes in a society whose purposes and norms differ from the project of modernity. At the same time, however, the letters undermine and complicate some of the easy generalizations made in these arguments.

The title *Letters from Ghana* should not be taken too literally. First of all, a number of documents are not letters. There are journal entries, transcripts of audio tapes, articles written by students in the Acherensua school newspaper, and excerpts from the manuscript *Apaeε: Ashanti Praise Poems. Recited from Oral Tradition by Kwasi Dum* (1969), edited by me and Mr. E. W. Owoahene. Secondly, the reader will find here not just letters sent by me *from* Ghana, but letters sent *to* me by friends and relatives from the States. Other letter writers include a handful of Ghanaians, foremost among them my late colleague E. W. Owoahene, and two other Peace Corps volunteers, John McClure and Dave Fitzjarrald, who were, at different times, assigned to the school in which I taught. Although these two volunteers knew me, they did not know each other, and their letters present contrasting views of Ghana and the Peace Corps.[7]

I had access to a cornucopia of audio tapes, letters (some over twenty pages long), and other writings. Most of the texts that made the "final cut" have been shortened. They have been shortened for the usual reasons: readability, constraints on manuscript length, and the need to spare the feelings of others. The passages chosen mainly focus on living and teaching in Ghana. But I also give weight to two other topics that run through the letters. First of all, my literary and intellectual passions of the time—for postmodern writers, such as Barth, Mailer, and Borges, and for Marshall McLuhan, whose theory of communication explored the interplay of oral cultures and writing cultures. I used McLuhan's theory as a tool to make sense of things I had difficulty understanding: the learning styles of Ghanaian students, the nature of Akan culture, and the significance of the elusive poetry I was collecting.

The second topic is the disturbed political situation in the U.S.—a result of the unpopular war in Vietnam. Lacking television and radio, the Peace Corps volunteers in faraway Acherensua struggle to understand

# PREFACE

the violence roiling their native land. They brood over their draft status and the life-changing decisions they will face if they are called up.

I cannot make the claim that these letters represent a whole generation. Even within this collection, the letter writers interpret things according to their own lights. Nevertheless, many of the texts reflect the political and cultural changes that American youth of the time experienced in common. Most of these changes did not endure, yet they marked and defined the collective memory of a generation.

Through a happy set of circumstances, I was able to draw on two complete exchanges of letters from the Ghana period. Letters get lost, especially after forty years. It is a rare and lovely thing to have *both* sides of a correspondence.

The first set is between me and Mike Moynihan. I met Mike when I was five years old; soon thereafter we became the best of friends. He grew up across the street. As kids we roamed the southern Delaware woods together. In our teen years we were avid readers and talked about books. When I lived in Ghana, Mike was at Michigan State University. His letters to me were a solace, for in them I recognized the voice of someone as alien to the world as I was, though in different ways. The letters I wrote Mike take up inchoate feelings and ideas and turn them into a discourse through which I was able to reflect on my own thinking. In this way I began to formulate how I wanted to be in the world—exactly at a time when, in the midst of personal and cultural uncertainties, I felt the pressing need of self-definition.

The second set of letters is between me and Ralph Slotten. He was my professor of comparative religions at Dickinson College (in Pennsylvania), and my mentor. "Dr. Slotten," as I addressed him then, belonged to my father's generation, which came of age in the 1930s and 1940s. Like my father, Cap Thiem, Slotten was a World War II veteran. Like my father, he opposed sending U.S. troops to Vietnam. My interest in various kinds of Ghanaian religious behavior—traditional, Christian and Muslim—owed a great deal to the inspired teaching of Slotten.

For forty years the letters I wrote lay comatose—in boxes and manila envelopes. Some got hauled around from state to state; some were

# PREFACE

at my mother's; some were in the hands of correspondents. Two years ago, I took another look at these neglected texts, and decided to resuscitate them. With this publication I am "sending" the letters out a second time—now to a public of *anonymous* readers (though many will be known to me).

*Re*reading is a distinctive experience, very different from first reading, especially when the act of rereading occurs four decades later. In the case of these letters, "first reading" was the actual writing of them, when letter production was very much a day-to-day affair. At that time, I couldn't look back on a letter—as I do now—from the vantage point of knowing what happened in the years that followed its writing. The future was uncertain—however much I tried to mold it in accordance with my own purposes. In the flux of events, I, the letter writer, was in the dark, continually shifting and adapting.[8]

What at the time were *extemporaneous* texts have now taken on a weight and significance greater, perhaps, than the sum of the parts. The act of *rereading* the letters, especially viewed as a coherent body, transforms their meaning. The rereader's present knowledge of the past, which was then an uncertain future, yields the benefits of a long view. The daily concerns, feelings, and vexations, expressed in all their raw immediacy through the letters, rise up to become part of larger stories, both historical and personal.

When the letters I wrote are read in sequence, several narratives coalesce out of the miscellany of topics addressed. First is a story of changing responses to a new and exotic culture—a cycle of engagement, disillusionment, and reconciliation. Second is my effort to bring into harmony the conflicting selves that inevitably emerge from living in one culture while being from another. Third, there is an existential quest for meaning in a world I perceived as absurd and impossible to live in. And finally, there is my search for a suitable calling in life—a tough assignment for someone whose usual reactions to middle class values were scorn and alienation. The letters build up between myself and others a discussion about what I value, and, no less important, what I disdain.

# PREFACE

As a Peace Corps volunteer, I believed that peace, justice, and progress could be reached by restructuring society. Before joining Peace Corps, I acted on that principle in the United States. Thus, even within my own culture, I was a "secular missionary." The letters from Ghana, however, document a loss of faith in political change.

Long before my Peace Corps service ended, I realized that an aesthetic approach to the world was the one most meaningful to me. The letters show how, out of that recognition, I took the necessary steps to join an establishment I had earlier wished to overthrow.

Who will want to read this book? Who, that is, besides people who delight in perusing other people's private mail? I had in mind a rather diverse audience. There is much here to hold the attention of readers interested in Africa, in Peace Corps, in the repercussions of the Vietnam war, and in the youth movements of the 1960s. Other potential readers are Peace Corps volunteers and early "Baby Boomers." For present-day Ghanaian readers, especially those living abroad, the letters provide impressions of life in Ghana during what must now seem a bygone era —a time of great events, including the abdication of the military junta that felled Nkrumah and the election of a civilian government.[9]

I want to recognize here three other collections of letters from Ghana that I have read, all written by North Americans. Each compilation has its own merits. Together, they present the experiences of westerners in Ghana, extending (with very large gaps) through five decades, from 1957 to 2010.

Richard and Gertrude Braun's *Letters from Ghana* (1959) is the first collection. Braun was a Presbyterian physician working in a mission hospital in eastern Ghana from 1957 to 1958, and his wife was a nurse. The letters give an intriguing glimpse of conditions in rural Ghana before the arrival of the first Peace Corps volunteers in 1961. The second collection compiles Peace Corps letters by Mary Rugh, published in *Report from Molly* (1964). Mary taught science and math at a secondary

# PREFACE

school in Cape Coast, Ghana. Her well-crafted, witty letters, which cover the first year of her service (1963-64), are rich in detail. The third and most recent collection is by Heather Johnston, the wife of a Canadian diplomat. It is entitled *Please Be Upstanding: Letters from Ghana.* (2013). The letters are in fact "group emails" sent out from 2007 to 2010. The letter written for one individual has been superseded by a different technology, intensely collective—one that has transformed the content, tone and structure of personal communication.

The existence of these works makes me feel that I belong to a special line: that of North American correspondents who publish their letters from Ghana. Thanks to these earlier collections, my book will become part of—even as it modifies—a worthy tradition.

Many books that recount Peace Corps experiences are memoirs, another valuable form of testimony. Letters, however, have one advantage over memoirs: they are documents *written in the time.* Memoirs provide a stronger narrative, but their value as history is lessened by the unavoidable constructedness of personal memory. Memoirs are by definition retrospective. The memoirist must call back experiences from a distant past, a transaction governed by selective recall, forgetfulness, nostalgia, hindsight, and so forth.

Letters are fresh and immediate testimonies. They bear the living marks of their own genesis. They are also naive, for they possess no certain knowledge of the future, which is always full of surprises. That is their value. Old letters are not skewed by the overriding concerns and passions of our present time, of 2013. Even so, every *edition* of letters, through editorial selection, deletion, and commentary, will be shaped by present-day knowledge and obsessions. This collection is no exception. Yet the core of the letters remains. Because of this dialectic, every edition of letters preserves a fascinating tension between voices from the past and the voices of the present.

In the introduction and commentaries that follow, I refer to myself in the third person. This may strike some readers as artificial, though it

## PREFACE

seems quite natural to me. I will not deny that I recognize in the epistolary Thiem (of the 1960s) aspects of my present self. In several ways, though, my past self seems unlike me. (Or at least I want to think so.) I am not entirely the person I was then. In those days I spoke a different language. One example will serve to illustrate this point. In Acherensua, I made audio cassette tapes in which I recorded conversations between myself and Ghanaians, conducted in Asante Twi. At that time, I spoke this language with some degree of fluency. Today, I can barely understand a word I am saying in those conversations. This example stands for the many discontinuities that have made it more comfortable for me to deal with my old self—paradoxically, young at the time—in the third person.

Jon Thiem
Boulder, Colorado

jonthiem.com

# ACKNOWLEDGMENTS

Many friends and family members contributed to this project. They supplied letters and photographs, critiqued drafts, gave copyright permissions, answered questions, listened when I read the text, and spurred on my work.

I am most indebted to Natalie Bolton. She has lent a kind and untiring ear to my thoughts (and doubts) about the project. In addition, she took on the map, cover, and book design, and she advised me on photo reproduction.

For keeping in contact over the years and visiting me in Boulder in 2012, my heartfelt gratitude extends to fellow Acherensua volunteers John McClure, Lawrie Altrows, Dave Fitzjarrald and Nestor Kwasnycia. McClure and Fitzjarrald generously gave permission to quote from their letters. Altrows and Fitzjarrald kindly gave permission to reproduce photos. I am also grateful to two Ghanaian friends. First, Festus Osei Owoahene-Akyampong (Ohene's son), who kindly gave permission to print his late father's letters. Secondly, Kofi Ampofo (once the Peace Corps cook's assistant and now director of a junior high school) who answered various questions.

Many thanks to my patient writing group friends: Deborah Dimon, Mateo Pardo, Alfonso Rodriguez, and Fernando Valerio-Holguin. Thanks also go to Darrell Fargo and John Chamberlin who read early versions of the manuscript and gave me encouragement. I am indebted to John Doyle for his astute critique of the Introduction.

Barbara Thiem and my sister Judy Barker were helpful in a number of ways, for which I am grateful.

My former student Theresa Spangler, who now manages the Interlibrary Loan Department of Colorado State University, kindly arranged to have books I needed sent to me. My thanks go to Martha Slotten for her permission to reprint Ralph's letters, and for so many stimulating telephone conversations.

Janet Thiem has been most helpful in filling in gaps in Cap Thiem's life.

# ACKNOWLEDGMENTS

Two evenings with John Chamberlin, a returned volunteer from Malaysia, gave me a different perspective on the Peace Corps in the late 1960s. Thanks go to Mike Moynihan for permission to use his letters to me, and for his friendship over many decades.

It is, alas, too late to thank Ginny Thiem, my mother, who saved the bulk of my letters and tapes. She would have enjoyed this compilation.

*Every effort has been made to locate potential copyright holders. If there are any copyright holders who are not acknowledged because they could not be found, I, the editor, would appreciate hearing from them through jonthiem.com.*

# INTRODUCTION

A TELESCOPE COMES TO ACHERENSUA

The goal of the Apollo 11 space mission was to land U.S. astronauts on the moon. The landing was scheduled for July 1969. Ghanaians were curious about this imminent turning point in the history of human exploration. At Jon Thiem's secondary school in Acherensua, the physics course included astronomy, yet there was no telescope. John McClure, the other Peace Corps volunteer, taught physics. In May 1969, McClure went by "mammy wagon" to the closest city (three hours away) to borrow a telescope so that his first-form class could see the craters of the moon.

Several months before Apollo 11 took place, Thiem and McClure visited the elders of Acherensua (McClure 4/5/69). The volunteers asked the *opanyin:* What is your idea of the moon? How big is it? One elder pointed to a white enameled basin lying in the compound of the house. The moon is that big, he said.

Jon asked students what they thought of the enterprise. One said that Onyame, the supreme god of Akan religion, would kill any men who intruded into his realm. Another said the added weight on the moon would make it fall from the sky onto the village of Acherensua. Other students, however, held less apocalyptic views.

On July 20th, the astronauts succeeded in walking on the moon. Jon missed the "live" event; there was no television and no adequate radio in Acherensua. Within a week of the landing, Jon's father, "Cap" Thiem, visited Acherensua. It was late July. Cap met the Headmaster, who asked him if he could acquire a telescope for the school (the Headmaster to John R. Thiem 5/26/70). Cap said he would do what he could. After finding a telescope in the States, he told Jon on a cassette tape:

*I just hope that maybe one or two of the boys over the years would be inclined to pick up a scientific career based on the interest you could show through this. [. . .] So the telescope will*

# INTRODUCTION

*come. I sit here and ask myself, was it worth all the work? But I guess it is.* (February-mid March 1970)

In May 1970, the telescope arrived. It was a beautiful instrument—a reflecting telescope with a six-inch mirror.

With the help of volunteers Dave Fitzjarrald (U.S.) and Nestor Kwasnycia (Canada), Jon learned to use the telescope. On clear nights, he set up the instrument in the grassy school compound and invited students to observe the heavens. There, with their own eyes, they saw what few of them had seen: the rings of Saturn, lunar topographies, the satellites of Jupiter, spiral nebulae, the multiform galaxies of the stars. These young Ghanaians caught a glimpse of the universe—a vision of worlds strewn through the wide darkness of space.

Just as the telescope offered students a larger view of the cosmos than they had previously known, so too did Peace Corps expand Jon's worldview. The experience of living in West Africa introduced him to a variety of mentalities and belief systems. Many of those ways of looking at the world were in conflict: local views versus national; rural versus urban; magical versus scientific; communal/socialist versus capitalist; religious versus secular; traditional versus modern. Jon experienced a collision of worlds—of nations, ethnicities, and mentalities.

The unfolding of new perspectives created a different view of his own country. Jon saw the United States through Ghanaian eyes, through Ivoirian eyes, through Canadian eyes, through British eyes.

At the same time, he witnessed Ghana's halting attempts to advance itself. This raised in him doubts about the possibility of progress. Jon's objectivity—his desire to transcend a Western view of things—was put to a severe test by local lifeways, religious beliefs and by the power of oral tradition in rural Ghana. Often, he did not pass the test.

## KWAME NKRUMAH

Had there been no Peace Corps in Ghana in 1969, it is doubtful Acherensua would have gotten a telescope.

# INTRODUCTION

The Peace Corps was the inspiration of President John F. Kennedy. In March 1961, he established the agency by executive order. Then in April, Sargent Shriver, the first director, flew to Ghana. There he met Kwame Nkrumah, president of the new republic of Ghana and the major architect of independence. Shriver wanted Ghana to be the *first* nation in the world to host Peace Corps volunteers, in large part because the country was the first black African colony to win its freedom. As a result, Ghana had a high profile and President Nkrumah was seen everywhere as a leader (Amin 35).

From 1935 to 1945, the future president of Ghana had been a student in the United States. He worked his way through college in Pennsylvania and earned several graduate degrees. In the United States, the young Ghanaian first encountered racism and segregation. At the same time he came to admire the country's educational system (Hoffman 151-52).

As president, Nkrumah mistrusted the United States because of its immense power, and he was wary of its neo-colonial intentions. On a state visit to the country in 1958, he delivered an address to the U.S. House of Representatives. There he explained his philosophy of non-alignment—a refusal to declare allegiance either to the United States or the Soviet Union in the superpower conflict.

> *Non-alignment can only be understood in the context of the present atomic arms race and the atmosphere of the cold war. There is a wise African proverb: 'When the bull elephants fight, the grass is trampled down.' When we in Africa survey the industrial and military power concentrated behind the two great powers in the cold war, we know that no military or strategic act of ours could make one jot of difference to this balance of power, while our involvement might draw us into areas of conflict which so far have not spread below the Sahara. Our attitude, I imagine, is very much that of America looking at the disputes of Europe in the 19th century. We do not wish to be involved. In addition, we believe the peace of the world in*

# INTRODUCTION

*general is served, not harmed, by keeping one great continent free from the strife and rivalry of military blocs and cold wars.*

Nkrumah, *I Speak of Freedom* (1961) 143.

There is pathos in Nkrumah's recognition of Ghana's powerlessness in the world. Although the "great powers" were not to be trusted, Ghana's non-alignment did not extend to refusing assistance from the United States and the Soviet Union. In 1961, Nkrumah and Shriver hammered out an agreement so that Peace Corps volunteers could work in the country, which urgently needed teachers to fulfill the government's ambitious education and literacy programs. Thus Ghana became the first nation in the world to accept the Peace Corps. In August 1961, the new volunteers arrived in the capital, Accra.

A month later, in September 1961, Acherensua Secondary School in the Brong-Ahafo region first opened its doors to students—a result of Nkrumah's passionate commitment to modernization.

When Ghana was a colony, the English called it "the Gold Coast." The country, though small, possessed valuable resources, chief among them cocoa, gold, and timber. If in the 1950s and 1960s Ghana held a place in world affairs disproportionate to its size, this came about largely through the persistence and political savvy of its young leader Nkrumah. Through him, Gold Coast became the first black colony of the sub-Saharan continent to gain independence from a colonial power. This climactic event broke open the path to independence for other colonies in Africa. In 1957, the newly independent state renamed itself Ghana.

In 1966, Nkrumah wanted to broker a peace agreement to end the escalating war between North Vietnam and the Viet Cong, on the one hand, and the United States and South Vietnam on the other. To that end, he made a state visit to China in February, with the intention of going on to Hanoi at the invitation of Ho Chi Minh. Nkrumah had achieved global stature as a leader, not only for his policy of non-alignment, but also for his efforts to create pan-African unity.

At home, however, he had become unpopular. Nkrumah's reputation began to sink because of the government's repression of peaceful dissent, and its detention or deportation (without trial) of opponents to the one-party state's policies (Rathbone 151-154). The new nation-state also faced deepening economic problems. Ghana's main export was cocoa, upon which depended the prosperity of its people and the funding of ambitious development projects. In the mid 1960s the world price of cocoa dropped sharply. Other difficulties arose from poor financial decisions by Nkrumah, from widespread corruption, and from the unscrupulous economic exploitation of the fledgling nation by the United States, Great Britain, and Russia (Birmingham 66-68, 91, 111-12). As a volunteer in Brong-Ahafo Jon witnessed the extensive felling of old-growth hardwood trees by a European logging company.[10]

While Nkrumah was on his peace mission to China, Ghanaian army officers seized power in a coup d'état. It is likely they received support from the U.S. Central Intelligence Agency.

Nkrumah went into exile. This coup, along with the one in Nigeria a month earlier (in January 1966), set a precedent for the series of military takeovers that undermined stable government in Ghana and Africa throughout the rest of the century.

In August 1968, seven years after the first U.S. volunteers entered Ghana, and two and a half years after Kwame Nkrumah's fall, Jon Thiem came to Ghana as a Peace Corps English teacher. The land was still under military rule.

PEACE CORPS IN A TIME OF WAR

War is the dark matter looming behind the *Letters from Ghana*. The writers are keenly aware of the war in "Indochina," although the letters themselves do not dwell on the subject. That the war recast the lives of large numbers of young American men, or brought those lives to an untimely close, was self-evident. By November 1968, when Jon began teaching in Ghana, thirty-two thousand U.S. soldiers had died in Vietnam (McWilliams 219). Hundreds of thousands had been wounded.[11]

The life courses of men who refused military service also took unexpected directions. Some went to prison; others into exile in Canada

## INTRODUCTION

and Sweden. Still others changed their occupations to get private-sector jobs offering military deferment. Or they signed up for Peace Corps and Vista.

In the letters at hand, there is not much discussion of the war itself, even though Jon, Fitzjarrald, and Moynihan fret a good deal about their draft status. They wonder what they will do if conscripted for service in a war they reject. Their general reticence may reflect prudence in the face of the widespread belief that draft boards used conscription to punish draft age men who openly opposed the U.S. war effort. Reticence may also have come from the difficulty of fathoming the magnitude of death and destruction caused by the war.

Among the methods employed by United States armed forces were aerial bombardment, which killed large numbers of civilians; shooting of non-combatants in "free fire zones"; use of a carcinogenic chemical (Agent Orange) to defoliate millions of acres of rainforest (McWilliams 224); and dropping of napalm on villages. The correspondents heard about what was going on. These measures raised doubts even in the mind of Robert McNamara, the U.S. Secretary of Defense at the time. In a private memorandum, dated May 19, 1967, he wrote to President Johnson: "The picture of the world's greatest superpower killing or seriously injuring 1,000 non- combatants a week, while trying to pound a tiny backward nation into submission on an issue whose merits are hotly disputed, is not a pretty one" (McNamara 269).[12]

War was a large factor in the high name recognition of the *Peace Corps*, both in the U.S. and worldwide. Vietnam and Peace Corps were antitheses, and yet oddly interdependent. In the 1950s and 1960s, Third World nations existed under the threat of U.S. military intervention. Countries were routinely invaded. One thinks of the U.S troops sent into Lebanon in 1958. Of the CIA-sponsored invasion of Cuba in 1961. Of the military occupation of the Dominican Republic in 1965-1966 by the U.S. Marines. It is worth noting here that during the latter incident, in-country Peace Corps volunteers, largely opposed to the invasion, exposed themselves to danger by aiding wounded Dominicans (Hoffman 69).

# INTRODUCTION

As this episode indicates, Peace Corps offered a striking contrast to military intervention, especially at a time of global protests against the U.S. policy in Vietnam. In the bloody years, 1964-1973, Peace Corps was the most visible and charming face of a foreign policy otherwise associated in people's minds with military force, or, at best, with foreign aid given "with strings attached."

The idea of the Peace Corps was to send college graduates abroad to help others help themselves. It was a "corps" whose purpose was not to wage war but to achieve peace by peaceful means, providing educational and technical help requested by developing countries. Like Jon, the volunteers in the 1960s were mainly college-educated and middle class. By and large, they wanted to avoid the war in Vietnam. Peace Corps provided men with military deferment during the period of service.

Peace Corps was nonetheless an instrument of the United States' Cold War strategy. Whether it was effective as such is another question. U.S. policy makers firmly believed that the modernization of developing countries (such as Ghana) on an American or Western model would make them better able to resist a Communist takeover (Grubbs 8-11, 14-15). Jon agreed with this viewpoint, though with reservations. Another underlying assumption was that countries hosting volunteers would look more favorably on the United States and its political system.

It is no wonder that Peace Corps was suspect in many quarters. When, after his two years of service in Ghana, Jon met up with an Italian friend in Bologna, the latter quipped that Peace Corps was "the Boy Scouts of American imperialism." (He apparently did not know about the women volunteers.) The argument went that Peace Corps gave U.S. neo-colonialism a human face. Which is in a sense true. In the eyes of many people, Peace Corps offered a counter-image to the pattern of U.S. belligerence and Cold War bullying. Another argument against Peace Corps was that its presence buttressed and gave legitimacy to military dictatorships supported by the United States—such as the one that ruled Ghana in 1968.[13]

# INTRODUCTION

Two letters written by volunteer John McClure to relatives in the States call into question the United States' policy of sending out volunteers. In the first letter, he writes of Peace Corps:

*You might say that this [is] a good part of a generally rotten U.S. foreign policy and should be supported. But the fact that the U.S. would never tolerate an internationalized (say under the U.N.) PC shows that it springs not from humanitarian motives but rather [from] a desire to convince people that our [foreign] policy really isn't as obnoxious as it is. [. . .] . . . Peace Corps in Accra has had to take a lot of crap from the government which it wouldn't take if it wasn't under a lot of pressure from the State Dept. to remain here regardless of the desires and needs of Ghana.* (4/18/69)

In a second letter, McClure further develops his earlier position:

*I believe [I] wrote you a few months ago about why PC is doing no good here. What Ghana needs is someone to (ruthlessly if necessary) root out their outmoded and backward ideas toward tribalism, superstition, corruption, subsistence agriculture, old age, etc. This is exactly what PC cannot do because it would offend vested interests and give Ghana an excuse (which it and many other W. African countries including Nigeria and Liberia according to [the] New York Times and my own observations [are looking for]) to kick out PC. This would be a tragedy for the U.S. since it is the U.S. which really gains from PC because we fool people into thinking all Americans are such friendly tolerant people.* (6/1/69).

A year later, Dave Fitzjarrald, the Peace Corps volunteer who replaced McClure in Acherensua, offered a different take on this controversy in a letter to a friend in the States:

*Both the Congressmen and the PC overestimate the effectiveness of PC. First of all, we couldn't do much for*

# INTRODUCTION

*American foreign policy if we tried. Granted, our mere presence means something. But out "in the field" one doesn't get the feeling he's working for Uncle Sam. [. . .]*
*I don't know about other places, but I think that the idea that Volunteers are helping a lot is wrong. At the same time . . . the experience for the Volunteer and the new perspective about the States you get is probably worth it. The Committee for Returned Volunteers is pretty radical. They're always saying the PC is an extension of US imperialism and should be abolished. Congressmen say all PC volunteers are draft-dodgers and it's a waste of money. One damning for one action and the other damning for none of that action.*
*[. . .]*
*Here in Acherensua we have a well-defined role as a teacher to fill. (6/26/70)*

From a Ghanaian perspective, the mission of Peace Corps teachers was to give young people an education, to build up literacy in English and basic knowledge in science and math. In December 1960, President Nkrumah had announced in the town of Sunyani (fifty miles by road north of Acherensua) that elementary education in Ghana would henceforth be free and universal (Hoffman 149). Nkrumah, as well as his military successors, recognized the need for Peace Corps volunteers to fulfill this ambitious goal. There was a serious shortage of teachers in the country, especially in science. In September 1968, when Jon took up his teaching duties, Acherensua Secondary School had twenty-three teachers, but, according to the Headmaster, it needed thirty. Ghanaian teachers as a rule tried to avoid rural postings. Peace Corps volunteers—Jon was one of them—took on these unwanted assignments (Hoffman 150). Thus Peace Corps helped supply instructors to secondary schools "in the bush." A major role of these secondary schools was to prepare students so that they themselves could become teachers in the new primary and middle schools essential to Nkrumah's program of national literacy (Amin 42, 43). It is significant that although Nkrumah believed that CIA agents had infiltrated the Peace Corps, he did not expel volunteers from the country. Ghana's need for instructors was too great.[14]

Many volunteers felt they had become effective teachers only as their term of service in Ghana came to an end. One of the main challenges of teaching English was language. (Another was a curriculum poorly adapted to Ghanaian needs and interests.) For volunteers, Ghanaian English was almost like another language. The accent and intonation made it hard for volunteers to understand students. It took several terms to develop an ear for Ghanaian English. Students in turn struggled with North American English. The transcripts of conversations between volunteers and Ghanaians included in the book give concrete evidence of this.

Another difficulty was that volunteers were coming from a print/reading culture, whereas their students, though they had attended elementary and middle school, were raised in a predominantly oral culture. Students had grown up in families and communities where literacy rates were very low. The reason the government sent these kids to secondary schools in the first place was to increase their competence in reading and writing.[15]

As an English master, Jon was assigned to teach literature, a task he gladly undertook, although he often wondered why Ghanaian high school students should have to gain a mastery of difficult British literary works of the 15th, 16th, and 17th centuries, works whose archaic vocabulary made them a challenge even for readers whose native tongue was English.

Teaching these works to Ghanaian students created several paradoxes which illustrate the complexities of integrating, at the level of instruction, an oral culture and a reading/writing culture. During his two years of service, Jon taught *The Canterbury Tales,* two Shakespeare plays, *Gulliver's Travels, She Stoops to Conquer* by Oliver Goldsmith, and contemporary works by two West African writers, Ama Ata Aidoo (Ghana), *The Dilemma of a Ghost,* and Chinua Achebe (Nigeria), *Things Fall Apart.* Before teaching *Gulliver's Travels,* Jon assumed that the book's comic spirit and its fables of giants and tiny people (also found in

# INTRODUCTION

Akan myth), would engage student interest. It did not—even though Ghanaians have a strong sense of humor. In spite of Jon's patient instruction, or maybe because of it, students were by and large immune to Swiftian irony.

When the course syllabus reached Shakespeare, it turned out that the texts for *Macbeth* had not arrived. Jon decided it was futile to teach until students had the books in hand. The Headmaster called him on the carpet, saying, in effect, that it was not essential that students *read* the play. The instructor should perform it aloud to them or give oral summaries. Yet Jon knew full well that students, despite their oral background, needed to *read* the text—to be able to understand the language and pass the state exams. He was fully aware of the irony of his position: Shakespeare wrote the plays for oral presentation, *not* for reading.

At last, *Macbeth* arrived. Jon's Ghanaian students read the play. They loved it. They knew about kings, witches, and dynastic conflicts from their own culture. Reveling in the rhetoric of rule and royal usurpation, they quickly turned *Macbeth* into a kind of oral tradition. They strutted about the campus reciting to each other lines and passages from the play. This happy and unexpected development gave Jon an idea. When he taught *Twelfth Night* during the next semester, he somehow got hold of a compact cassette recording of the comedy and played it to the class as a supplement to reading. Perhaps the convoluted love-intrigues of the play were not to students' taste, or they may have had trouble following the recording. In any case, the wonderful effect Jon anticipated was not realized.

However debatable the benefits for Ghanaians of Peace Corps instruction, the agency did enable a significant number of U.S. graduates to satisfy their thirst for knowledge about other nations and other cultures. This was a gain for the United States. Thousands of returning volunteers helped counteract American ignorance of the larger world.

The U.S. government wanted volunteers to be goodwill ambassadors. At the most basic level, speaking Asante Twi, eating local food, being colleagues and friends and lovers of Ghanaians, contributed to this mission and helped dispel the widespread (and not entirely mistaken) image of America as a racist society. Yet goodwill efforts by rural teachers in Ghana were impeded by their work, living conditions, and the equatorial climate. The Peace Corps urged volunteers to take on projects during vacations and make contacts with Ghanaians outside the schools, but most instructors lacked the time and energy needed for this (Amin 44; Rice 203).

Even so, the Ghanaians who experienced Peace Corps volunteers as *teachers* got another perspective on the United States. And there was indeed a lot of contact between Ghanaians and volunteers in the schools. Between 1961 and 1991, 675,000 Ghanaians had Peace Corps teachers (Amin 46; Hoffman 179). Volunteers were not representative of the United States as a whole, but, by and large, they did show its "friendly, tolerant" side.

Like McClure and Fitzjarrald and many others, Jon had doubts about the value of his teaching for Ghanaians. After one term as a master, he offers the following self-assessment: "I guess I'm a shitty volunteer. Lazy, ineffectual, over intellectual. I just sort of get on and am not unhappy. While I despise the educational system + incompetence etc. I like many of the ways and ideas of African culture" (to Mike Moynihan, January 11, 1969). Idealists that they were, many volunteers underrated their contributions to Ghanaian education. From 1970 (the year Jon left Ghana) to 2010, the ability to read and write among Ghanaians evidently rose from less than a third of the population to over two-thirds—an astonishing increase. In those four decades, Peace Corps volunteers played an important role in boosting national literacy (Hoffman 158; Amin 41-45).[16]

Jon, however, persisted in thinking that for Ghana the benefits of his service lay outside the classroom. In his view, the significant things he did were recording Asante oral poems with his friend Ohene; sending a Ghanaian student to spend a year in a California high school (through AFS); and serving as patron of the Debate Society. He thought it important that he was able to get out of Acherensua and make himself known to a wide range of people in the Akan towns and villages he visited, in Kokofu, Sebedie, Asiwa, Kumasi, and Kibi (Kyebi).

# INTRODUCTION

In later years he often thought about the telescope. He remembered the excitement and wonder it aroused when he showed its use to students and colleagues. To many of them the instrument exemplified the particular and beneficial kind of magic that westerners practiced— that is, science. In March 1983, thirteen years after the telescope arrived in Ghana, Jon's friend Ohene wrote to him about a visit he had made the year before to Acherensua Secondary School: "I was happy to learn that astronomy was still being learnt because of the device [the telescope] given by your father."

## MISERIES AND SPLENDORS

The array of expectations and hopes Jon brought to Ghana shaped the discoveries and defeats of his two-year sojourn there. The unfulfillment of anticipations was part of an ongoing, difficult learning process. Experience was a crucible in which expectations, like hypotheses, were rigorously tested, then recast or rejected.

The letters provide an archive of the preconceived notions and cultural biases that inevitably accompany a foreigner entering an exotic society. Jon's candor and self-consciousness as outsider, as modernizer *and* as curious observer, make the letters a helpful source for understanding the intricate interplay between cultural expectations and real experiences.

Undergraduate studies in politics, history of religion, and sociology of art made him eager to experience, firsthand, a pre-modern agricultural society (Jon to Ralph Slotten 11/24/68). He wanted to trek through a rainforest. He wanted to witness indigenous religious practices. During a junior year abroad in Bologna, Italy (1966-67), he had traveled extensively in Europe and visited the Soviet Union. Having experienced life on two continents, he was now keen on exploring a third—a continent in which society was less directly molded by modern technology, literacy, and western political institutions.

The shifting horizons of Jon's expectations in Ghana fell into four stages, often overlapping. First was a romantic engagement with the

# INTRODUCTION

Asante culture. Second came disillusionment with the conditions of rural life and with teaching "in the bush." In the third stage, Jon reconnected with Asante society through friendship with his Ghanaian colleague Ohene. The last stage, before Jon's departure, was marked by fatigue and a longing to go home.

Unlike most volunteers, Jon had some knowledge of Ghana prior to joining the Peace Corps. He had studied the politics of developing countries and, in one course, written a seminar paper on modernization in Ghana. With this background, Jon asked Peace Corps to assign him to Ghana, which they did. He also asked to be posted to a village rather than to a town or city.

Jon's attitudes towards Ghana in his first months were affected by the fact that he, like a significant minority of students in the postwar generation, saw himself as a refugee from the American Dream—an ideal his parents had enthusiastically embraced. Not sharing the middle class preoccupations with work, money, and consumer entertainments, he felt like an outsider in his own country. The flip side of this alienation was an exceptional openness to other cultures, an openness that accounts in part for his early romanticization of the Akan way of life during his first three months in Ghana—which was stage one.

For "in-country" training, Jon was sent to the town of Kibi (Kyebi), sixty miles northwest of Accra. There he was heartily welcomed by the people and royally received by the Okyenhene, the most important Akan king in Ghana after the Asante king himself (the titular head of the Asante people). From journal entries written in August and September of 1968, we learn that Jon is struck by the attractiveness of the Akan people. He enjoys the slow pace of life, and admires the society, where commerce and success, though important, are less zealously pursued than in North America. In Kibi, Jon discovers a kind of grace among the residents, an ease of life, a warm humanity.

Half a year into his posting as English teacher at Acherensua Secondary School, Jon's idyllic view of Akan life turns to disillusion. Peace Corps administrators recognize intense disappointment as a normal part of a volunteer's cycle of experience. They call it "cultural fatigue"

# INTRODUCTION

(Rice 203-205). For Jon, a major cause was the implacable resistance of rural Akan culture to the unfamiliar goals and methods of a foreign teacher. His letters now express disenchantment with the narrow attitudes of students and with the widespread belief in magic (even among fellow instructors). His attempts to instill in students the principles and practices of critical thinking are not effective. Students seem unreceptive. Encouraged by an antiquated version of British pedagogy, they rely on rote memorization (which, in fact, serves them well for passing the state examinations).

Jon finds teaching more valuable to himself than to his students. In a letter to Mike Moynihan, he addresses this issue:

> *I've come to love teaching, even para-literate Africans. Perhaps it's the vanity I feel in being forced to present something in a related, clear and dramatic manner. I've learned Shakespeare only insofar as I've taught him. At times the bizarre responses of African students enter into the enjoyment. You can't conceive how remote anything written is to them. Marshall McLuhan is about the only writer who gives an honest analysis of the difference between the oral-tribal and the literate industrial modes.* (April 1969)

Jon's disappointment with his Ghanaian students comes out in his use of the word "para-literate." He knew his students were able to read the words of texts, but his expectations were higher. He had set himself the impossible task of turning Ghanaians into junior literary critics who would interpret texts as he did. Hence his disillusionment.

Jon expected to be a modernizer, a catalyst for enlightenment, but he realized that at the rural posting where he taught, he could be neither. Did he lack the maturity and persistence needed to accomplish the goals he set, or were the goals themselves mistaken and finally unattainable at that time?

Another source of estrangement was the tedium of rural life. Jon himself had chosen a "bush" school, but his preconceived idea of the

# INTRODUCTION

rainforest as an earthly paradise was overturned by the realities of isolation and the lack of urban resources and intellectual stimulus. Entering into the social life of the village and the school proved difficult. He found it hard to connect with Ghanaian instructors in his age group. The common pastime of drinking palm wine "in the bush" grew wearisome. Moreover, his ability to speak Twi improved very slowly—the tonal structure of the language was a real stumbling block. Volunteers were supposed to mingle with Ghanaians, but during this period of "cultural fatigue," Jon kept company mainly with the other two North American volunteers at the school. In his isolation he turned more and more to books. Authors became like close friends.

Unfamiliar food did not help the situation. An obsessive motif in the letters of volunteers is the search for food suitable to a westerner used to eating lots of meat. Jon enjoyed a number of Ghanaian foods, especially kontumerey (a bit like spinach), plantain in its various forms, pineapples, bananas and oranges. By the end of his second year he began to relish the national dish of Ghana—foo foo, a gooey ball of pounded yam and plantain eaten with a fiery sauce. Yet like other volunteers, he craved protein. Care packages from the States and trips to Kumasi for canned goods helped, but the rural diet was a drag on his vitality.

Frequent illness lowered one's mood a notch or two. The pampered organism of a middle-class volunteer was not built to fight off tropical fevers and stomach infections. Yet Jon was lucky. He did not get malaria. He did not get hepatitis, dysentery or the clap—the scourges of a volunteer's body. He did not go out of his mind. A friend of his stationed not far from Acherensua nearly died of malaria. A Canadian volunteer up the road died of acute hepatitis. Another friend went temporarily insane and had to be sent home.

Like many volunteers, Jon was at odds with his own society, and yet he did not know how to present himself in a West African one. One result of this was a bewildering fluidity of self. The new roles he had to play in Ghana stood in uneasy relation to past ones he had known in life.

It was not a simple thing to sort out the parts he felt he had to play: exemplary white man in Africa, U.S. goodwill ambassador, Peace Corps

# INTRODUCTION

teacher, modernizer, amateur folklorist, apprentice scholar, poet, colleague, friend, son, brother, lover, and misanthrope.

Symbolic of Jon's condition is the procession of names that trail along with him through his sojourn in Ghana, and even after. To fellow volunteers, he is Jon. To close Ghanaian friends, "Kofi" (his Akan name). To students and colleagues, Mr. Thiem. People in the village streets cry out to him with gleeful irreverence, "Kwasi Obroni, Kwasi Obroni" (Kwasi White Man, Kwasi White Man). As if to reconcile these several selves through a single formula, he signs one of his letters "Jon Edgar Africanus Thiem."

There were few white-skinned people (Obroni) in rural Ghana. Whiteness excited attention, mainly favorable. Yet Jon found the attention burdensome. A white volunteer in the bush is forever on stage. In a visit to the village of Asiwa, people told him he was the first white man who had come there. He was treated like a royal personage—rather than as himself. Rural Ghanaians liked to believe whites were wealthy and possessed of uncanny mental powers. Peace Corps volunteers, however, earned little money by American standards. They were paid roughly what Ghanaian teachers were paid. (Even so, they had more discretionary income than their Ghanaian colleagues.) Volunteers had high status, in spite of only being in their twenties. In Ghana teachers of any color were (in the words of one Ghanaian master) regarded as "gods." The contradiction between such illusions and the reality of one's limitations was troubling to Jon.

In a letter to Mike, Jon frames the problem in a curious way. Whiteness makes the volunteer a kind of involuntary hero:

*The one annoyance is having to be a hero. Necessarily a teacher has to be a hero and here a white is a hero. I wouldn't mind the ticker tape parades, they're short. The next issue of Time sports someone else's face on the cover. Relief. But here the adulation is constant. Hundreds of them imitate every fetish of my dress and gesture. [. . .] I sit at my desk swamped with papers, requests for my shirts, or my autograph or my person. Letters have to be written to refuse speaking engagements (I'm not joking, dammit). The superlative ungrammatical feelings of female-admirers must be assuaged.* [. . .] *Will never this end* [sic]? *How I envy Achilles his heel, Adam his fall!! O Moynihan . . . how superior is the anonymity of the tribesman to the loneliness of the Hero.* (June 7, 1969)

One unsettling discovery that came from living in Akan society was that much of what Jon regarded as distinctive to his own individuality turned out to be the result of pure social conditioning—of his middle-class American upbringing. Fitzjarrald pungently expresses a similar epiphany when he writes: "You get over into another culture and discover how American you really are. Ironically enough, it means you see how much you have in common with Tricky Dick [President Nixon]." (6/26/70).

Life in the Brong-Ahafo region was, however, not without its pleasures. Jon's teaching schedule gave him time to read, especially literature, history, and works on Ghanaian culture. Peace Corps sent each volunteer a trunk of books, which Jon supplemented with trips to the University of Ghana bookstore in Legon.

Another compensation was that Asante women were often eager to strike up relationships with foreign volunteers. Jon found Asante women beautiful, and he welcomed their attentions. They did not seem to have an expectation of marriage or a shared household. For a young unattached man this was ideal.

Travel was a great escape. Jon visited Ghana's neighboring countries—all of them former French colonies. Weary of rural life, he savored trips to the cities of Kumasi and Accra, and to Ghana's coastal towns. After his father Cap Thiem visited Jon in Acherensua, the two flew out to East Africa where they climbed Kilimanjaro and observed the wildlife of the region. These trips offered a wider experience of the human presence in Africa.

THE ORAL POETRY PROJECT

# INTRODUCTION

By the end of his first year of teaching, Jon's interest in Asante society underwent a revival. This came about through his friendship with Mr. E. W. Owoahene-Akyampong, affectionately known as "Ohene."

Three years older than Jon, Ohene was the Bible master at Acherensua Secondary School. He was able to move easily between the world of tradition, where he felt completely at ease, and the modern world, where he also felt at home. This was an unusual ability. Secondary education often alienated Ghanaians from their agricultural roots, and yet did not sufficiently qualify them to achieve their aspirations in the modern, urban sector of society, where salaried jobs were hard to find. Unlike Ohene, they ended up in a kind of economic limbo. Ohene embraced tradition, maintained a farm plot, and felt at one with his ancestors. At the same time, he was an active Christian, a Presbyterian. He wrote and spoke English with eloquence. Jon never fully understood how his friend managed to navigate through these disparate worlds. After Jon left Ghana, Ohene earned the Diploma in Religious Studies from the University of Ghana (1973). Towards the end of his life, he was Director of Education in Kenyasi, Brong-Ahafo region.

In June 1969, Ohene and Jon began collecting oral praise poetry, called "apaeɛ." The poems focus on the historical (yet no less legendary) founder of the Asante state, King Osei Tutu I (ca. 1660-1717). It turned out that Ohene was related to the royals of Kokofu—members of the same clan as Osei Tutu. Ohene introduced Jon to the Kokofuhene and the king's court, and Jon became a regular house guest of Ohene's kinfolk.

What induced him to collect apaeɛ? As a mythology student of Ralph Slotten, Jon had become curious about how warrior heroes were presented in different kinds of narrative and national settings. In Ghana he read through a series of European epics: *The Odyssey, The Aeneid, The Song of Roland, The Poem of El Cid*. About them, he wrote to Mike: "All this shit about the glories of war and heroism. But when you read them and get suspended in them you start to wish you were Aeneus or Roland or the great Cid or one of them. The comfort of sacrificing yourself to something completely. They appeal to potential suicides, people who want to scuttle themselves whilsts [sic] straining for the noble shore . . . ." (April 1969).[17]

Jon's fascination with European epic led him to search for a hero narrative in verse among the Akan peoples. He did not find anything that was lengthy. Instead, he stumbled on the wonderful apaeɛ. Short as they are, he saw in them the lyric crystallizations of legends that had an epic scope.

The two teachers made numerous trips to Kokofu and neighboring communities during the next eight months. In the nearby village of Sebedie, they taped a series of apaeɛ recited by Kwasi Dum—priest of the god Ta Kora. They transcribed and eventually translated these oral poems into English. Kwasi Dum had learned the apaeɛ from his father, also priest of the god Ta Kora. Both Dum and his father chanted apaeɛ at the court of the Asantehene. The reciter, or *abrafo,* typically points his ceremonial sword towards the Asantehene, and with a cry of "He is the one!" exclaims the verses.

The poems refer to, and are the products of, an ancient legacy. They are the distinctive genre of a courtly milieu, expressing the values of the Asante military confederation which emerged in the late seventeenth century under Osei Tutu's leadership. The spirit of that martial age breathes through the poems.

The verses portray Osei Tutu as a warrior, liberator, protector, and provider. He frees the Asante people from their subjection to the Denkyiras, whose leader, Ntim Gyakari, he kills in battle. He preserves the nation from faction and revolt. He succors the weak. The darker side of his nature also appears. He inspires terror. He is unscrupulous. There emerges the picture of a warrior king who is majestic and unfathomable, charitable and merciless, magnaminous and lascivious. The animals and demons that populate the metaphorical world of the poems signal that Osei's character transcends human descriptive categories. In the apaeɛ, he belongs to a mythic realm.[18]

The style of the panegyric verses is terse, their meaning often obscure even to modern Asante speakers. The imagery is striking; the alliterations (in the original) intricate; the message wrapped in riddles.

# INTRODUCTION

Here follow several of the Thiem/Owoahene translations. They endeavor to convey the metaphorical vitality of the apaeɛ :

*He is the one!*
*Oprekese tree who from the outskirts of town*
*Casts his smell into every house.*
*Osei Tutu who from the outskirts of town*
*Casts his smell into every house.*
(apaeɛ 7)

*He is the one!*

*Kokote kwaako, the wild bush pig,*
*Where you and he are neighbors,*
*You will eat unripe plantain.*
(apaeɛ 15)

*He is the one!*
*Mighty Agyetakyi bird,*
*You loiter at crossroads, your fists ready to strike.*
*Osei, we say you love war.*
*You say you do not love war.*
*But aren't you the mighty Agyetakyi bird*
*Who loiters at crossroads, your fists ready to strike?*
*Osei Tutu, the spinster ghost says she thanks you.*
(apaeɛ 11)

Why does the spinster ghost thank Osei? It is because Osei, by sending legions of warriors to their death, improves her chances of marriage in the afterworld.

Jon was thrilled to learn about a poetic tradition unknown to him. He delighted in the vivid tropes and arcane allusions of the heroic lines. Ohene and Jon believed they were preserving a vanishing tradition and thereby doing Ghana a cultural service. Kwasi Dum told the collectors that his son had refused to learn the apaeɛ.[19]

The ironies of the project were not lost on Jon. Here he was, peace activist and Peace Corps volunteer, translating poems that glory in the bloody deeds of war. Moreover, Jon saw himself as an advocate of secular values—yet he was now working to preserve a tradition rooted in a "magical" worldview. Jon wrote to Slotten about his ambivalence towards traditionalism:

> *I think personally I'm more past oriented* [than most Americans] *but living in quasi tribal surroundings has made me despise the practical, dismal effects of traditionalism. As an aesthetic oriented person I find tradition indispensable to the game of art; my objection is that tradition in Africa stultifys* [sic] *creativity in doing things, in relieving the burdens of ignorance and suffering.* (November 22, 1969)

Most of all, however, Jon's absorption in the apaeɛ project reflects the shift in his interests—away from politics towards the "game of art," that is, the aesthetic side of existence. He had indeed become an "aesthetic oriented person." This realignment mirrors Jon's sense of hopelessness about political change, and his disenchantment with human beings in general—with their irrationality, ignorance, and self-destructiveness. In an earlier letter Jon explained his changed outlook to Mike Moynihan:

> [Robert] *Kennedy's death, McCarthy's defeat and apostasy, Humphrey's shittiness and Nixon's election combined to screw any idealism and radicalism I once had. Politics is only boring now. It's even worse in Africa (political digression: there is no hope for African development . . . ).* (January 11, 1969)

Aesthetic values, unlike political commitment, offered Jon an ordered world, a world that redeemed the absurdities and terrors of history, turning them into something worthy of contemplation.

# INTRODUCTION

The Institute of African Studies at the University of Ghana showed interest in publishing the apaeɛ. The manuscript was formally submitted by the Peace Corps office in Accra, in May 1970, two months before Jon left Ghana. For reasons unknown, it was never published. After Jon's return home, he let the matter drop.

The apaeɛ themselves, however, took on a life of their own in the United States. Jon and Owoahene's unpublished manuscript was a source for Esther Smith's pioneering study: "Apaeɛ: Praise Poetry of Akan Kings" (1975). In 1979, the journal *Translation* (Columbia University) published half of the poems (in English). Other apaeɛ came out in an anthology produced by Jon and two other poets (*Nine Waves,* Sutter House, 2003). Throughout his university career, Jon recited apaeɛ at public readings and in literature classes. Ohene and Jon were pleased that their translations introduced Americans to a strange and resplendent tradition.

What would the 17th-century warlord Osei Tutu have thought had he known his deeds were being sung in the 21st-century, in a strange tongue and on a faraway continent, to a classroom of young Americans? Jon wondered if some of the African American students who heard the poems were descendants of Asante slaves forcibly transported to North America from their homeland.

During his last six months in Ghana, Jon felt increasingly worn out. He was sometimes in low spirits. Sick of Acherensua, he welcomed the trips he had to undertake in this period: to Legon for a University conference on Ghanaian development; to Kokofu to see the Kokofuhene again; to Cape Coast for a teachers conference; to Takoradi for the Peace Corps termination meeting; to Kumasi for the Asantehene's permission to publish the apaeɛ; to Bonwire to order a Kente cloth for himself; to Accra three times: first, to receive and store the telescope his father sent over; second, to pick up the telescope for transport back to Acherensua; and third, to undergo the mandatory medical exam before leaving Ghana.

The style of the late letters from Ghana hint at his state of mind: the writing is often fragmentary, the language marked by curtness of

INTRODUCTION

expression. Prepping his fifth form students for their exams exhausted him. More and more, he thought about "life after Ghana." He planned to spend several weeks in Italy and France on his way back to the States. He was eager to go home and see family and friends. And he looked forward to starting graduate work at Indiana University, where he had been accepted into the Ph.D. Program in Comparative Literature.

GHANA IN TRANSITION

In the two years that Jon lived in Ghana, there occurred three events of national importance: the abdication of the military rulers (who overthrew Nkrumah) in favor of an elected civilian government (1969); the mass expulsion of foreign workers (1969-1970); and the death of the Asantehene (1970), who had reigned since 1931. Each event reverberated in Acherensua. Jon had a personal connection to all three. Yet not until years after his return to the States, and in some cases decades later, was Jon able to weigh accurately the significance of these occurrences and see them in the larger flow of time.

The first of the events in Ghana was the peaceful transfer of power by the military regime to a democratically-elected government in September 1969, at the beginning of Jon's second year in Ghana. This event inaugurated the Second Republic.

The election was quickly felt in Acherensua because the former Assistant Headmaster of Acherensua Secondary School, Mr. Badu Nkwansah, had been elected to the National Assembly.[20] (The cassette tape transcription of April 4, 1969, records a conversation about local politics between him, Jon, and McClure.) When the new government appointed Badu Nkwansah "Ministerial Secretary for Labour and Social Welfare," he became a member of Ghana's governing elite. Not long after the election, the new Ministerial Secretary used his influence to initiate an investigation of Acherensua's Headmaster, under whom he had earlier served. Thus the return to civilian government had an immediate and electric effect on school affairs. According to rumors, the Headmaster intended to set fire to the school administration building in order to destroy documents. Students got wind of the supposed plot and created a human cordon around the administration building. Jon happened to be one of two masters whose rooms were in the building.

These local effects of the election eclipsed in Jon's mind the larger import of the return to civilian government. His understanding was also limited by the fact that he could not know that two years later, in January 1972, this elected government would be toppled by the military, putting an end to the Second Republic. Only with a grasp of Ghana's later political history was Jon able to see that the free election of 1969 was the upside of an up-and-down pattern of alternating civilian governments and military dictatorships, a pattern which became the norm in sub-Saharan Africa.

The second event resulted from an early decree of the newly elected government: the Aliens Compliance Act of November 1969. By means of this act, 150,000 foreigners who lacked work permits, largely Nigerians, were rounded up and expelled from the country. The expulsions took place between December 1969 and April 1970. The motives for the Act were economic and political: At a time of high unemployment, the government wanted to demonstrate its ability to create jobs for *Ghanaians*. Jon was appalled by the xenophobia that lay behind the measure. As an alien himself, he felt sympathy for the foreigners. Kofi Ampofo, the young man who assisted the Peace Corps cook, was in danger of deportation. He had no work permit. Jon wrote about the matter: "Kofi (whom Dad met) is an alien (his parents are from Ivory Coast) and under the new Aliens decree he is supposed to be deported. I think he'll be able to stay, however, with our support" (December 11, 1969). For whatever reason, Kofi was not deported. At the time, Jon did not realize that the expulsions reflected a deeper national crisis connected with the grim state of the economy and the willingness of the new government to use dictatorial methods—both of which were later used to justify the military coup of 1972. He also did not know, until much later, that the shortage of laborers created by the expulsions would throw Ghana's economy into such dire straights that in the early 1980s, over a million Ghanaians emigrated to Nigeria in search of work, including his friend Ohene. Most of these Ghanaian migrants

# INTRODUCTION

were then expelled by the Nigerians, creating major problems for Ghana's already crippled economy (Adepoju 32).

The third national event was the death, in May 1970, of the Asantehene, Osei Agyeman Prempe II, who was born in 1892.[21] The Asantehene leads the Asante people, the largest ethnic group in Ghana. The length of Prempeh II's reign, nearly forty years, first as paramount chief of Kumasi in 1931, and then as Asante king from 1935, made him an imposing figure. Jon never met him, but made contact with his personal secretary in order to get royal permission to publish the apaeɛ. The fact that apaeɛ were recited in praise of the Asantehene at his court was a circumstance that made the king's death especially moving to Jon. When word of the death reached Acherensua, the three North American volunteers were advised not to leave their quarters at night. Rumor was that "attendants" would be captured and sent along with the king into the next world. Ohene was especially wary of going out. Related to Asante royals, he was evidently well qualified to "attend" the deceased king.

Twenty-first century Ghana, however much its roots lie in the 20th century, is in some measure a different place than the country Jon knew in the late 1960s. Ghanaians are now more connected to the larger world through emigration to other countries and through the spread of electronic communications, especially television, the Internet, and cell phones. The educational projects of the second half of the 20th century have borne fruit and been extended, even though rural education still lags behind. Some advances have been made in girls' secondary education. Traditional chiefs are more educated and progressive than they were in the 1960s and 1970s.[22]

Does Ghana now have better prospects? Although serious problems persist, the pessimism Jon expressed in the late 60s (which was perhaps justified by developments in the 70s, 80s, and early 90s) seems less applicable today. Compared to other Western African countries, Ghana has in recent years been blessed with many good things. It has not been wracked by the civil wars and inter-ethnic violence that have set back the prospects of most other West African societies. In the last two decades Ghana has been led by democratic governments, and there have been no

# INTRODUCTION

military coups. Ruling political parties have handed over power to their opponents peaceably, abiding by the results of free elections. The price of gold has skyrocketed. Offshore oil reserves were discovered in 2007. The globalization of chocolate addiction is a favorable development.

## ABOUT THE LETTERS AND CASSETTE RECORDINGS

Many of the letters in this collection are workaday texts of the kind typically sent home by Peace Corps volunteers. The letters do the jobs required of them. They channel requests—for magazines, books, food, film, application forms. They convey the teeming impressions and annoyances that attend the life of a westerner in an uncanny environment. They alleviate feelings of cultural isolation. And finally, they re-imagine and sentimentalize ties to familiar things at home—even to things the writer would have disdained, had he been there.

The longer letters, however—especially the ones to Mike—are less typical. In one text, for example, Jon takes on the voice of a disturbed man obsessing over drinking water during an outage in Acherensua (Jon to Mike, April 1969):

*(I don't understand any of this ↑ either but it flows does it not?) If it flows let it flow. (I just stopped flowing). Is this a passage of lighter moods? Parentheses are the finest (I mean to say handiest) of literary crutches.*

*All this business about flowing is probably subconsciously nostalgia for running water. (As the stoppages are for solid feces.)*

*The running water stopped two days ago and my bowels began to flow about the same time. Now water is dear. It is a curious thing that when the water stops running and becomes rarer, and you start using impure water, that soon you get a flowing in the bowels, your ass gets to be a fountain and as a result your body crys [sic] for more and more water to replenish that which it has so irresponsibly flushed out. I had Kofi boil ten bottles of river water.*

# INTRODUCTION

The atypical letters are suffused with the iconoclasm and anger of the times, with what later came to be called "the spirit of '68." This was a spirit of revolt that took dramatic form in the events of that year, events which were vividly presented on television screens throughout the developed world. One of those events was the Democratic National Convention in Chicago at the end of August 1968. It was marked by antiwar protests and by the unforgettable televised spectacle of Chicago police beating unarmed demonstrators. Volunteer John McClure captures the mood of the time in a comment on Norman Mailer's book *Miami and the Siege of Chicago*. McClure writes: "It is good to read some of the hate and derision that was piled on [President] Johnson" (June 1, 1969).

While the youth rebellions of 1968 were in large part a response to the shocks and unexpected reversals of that year (beginning with the first Tet military offensive launched by Vietnamese revolutionaries, in January and February), the winds of revolt had begun to rise in the late 1950s and early 1960s. When the first "postwar" children reached adolescence, an unprecedented number went on to university. Among them there emerged colorful coteries of beatniks, hipsters, existentialists, folk singers, civil rights activists, and political visionaries. These non-conformist students were in fact a very small minority, but unlike the majority they were outspoken; their words, artistic tastes, and styles of dress generated media attention and animosity. They raised unsettling questions about the American Dream. They wanted a reckoning of the social and cultural costs of the postwar affluence in which most of them grew up. A critical mass of these rebels reached out for alternative values and adopted life styles that went against the common grain. They denounced the secure material world their middle class parents had with so much fervor constructed around them. Jon was one of their number.[23]

Awareness of this is useful to understanding (if not accepting) the rancor and scurrility that bursts forth in some of the letters collected here.

Jon connected with the cultural revolution in other ways that find expression in the letters to Mike or Slotten. First of all, he was an advocate of "sexual freedom" (the 'right' to engage in sex independent of religious, romantic and domestic constraints). Secondly, he was a partisan of the postmodern revolution in literature. He writes at some length about his devotion to innovative writers like John Barth, Norman Mailer, Jorge Luis Borges, and Vladimir Nabokov. In a number of letters he emulates, or parodies, their styles.

"I think the letter is at the nadir of literary forms." Thus Jon to Slotten in a letter dated May 15, 1969. He goes on to say: "You can convey the spectacle of your own mind but you cannot communicate because there is no [immediate] reply."

Here Jon rejects the commonplace that letters are conversations carried on by other means. For him, written correspondence cannot replace real talk and all that goes with it: ambiance, the back and forth of repartee—above all, *hearing* a friend's voice.

Reading Marshall McLuhan, the renowned communications theorist, gave Jon a vocabulary for thinking about the letter as a problematic genre. McLuhan's writings made Jon conscious of the technical and sensory distinctiveness of various media, and sharpened Jon's ambivalence towards both oral culture and print culture.

Three theses set forth by McLuhan helped Jon frame and interpret his cross-cultural experience in Ghana. The first thesis is that a communication medium is *in itself* more culturally transformative than the *message* or content it conveys. The medium *is* the message. Secondly, the power of oral discourse is inversely proportional to the prevalence of print (or writing) culture. Finally, the rise of electronic media (like TV and compact cassettes) will turn the world into a "global village." This virtual "global village" certainly did not extend to the real village of Acherensua; even so, Jon's life in Acherensua gave him a visceral sense of what McLuhan meant by oral culture. Every time Jon walked into the village or went to drink palm wine, he experienced immersion in an intensely aural/vocal world.

The tension between oral and written forms of communication was for Jon more than an academic question. It figured in his teaching, and,

INTRODUCTION

as we have seen, in the apaeε transcription project. As an English master, Jon was helping to pull a select group of Ghanaians away from oral tradition into print culture. In the apaeε project, Jon and Ohene recorded oral recitations on compact cassettes in order to put them into written form. They were well aware of the considerable loss involved in this transfer from oral performance to cold print. It is telling that the name Jon gave his compact cassette recorder was "Mac," after McLuhan.

The then-recent technology of compact cassette recording proved useful in another way. Jon and his parents sent tapes to each other by airmail. These served as a substitute for letters. Because Jon's parents' letters are lost, the tape transcriptions included in this collection help make up for a gap in the correspondence.

A look at this new tool of oral exchange highlights some of the features and limitations of the written letter for which it served as a novel surrogate. It is odd to realize that cassette recordings are now nearly as obsolete as the letters they were (in part) superseding in the late 1960s.[24]

The collection at hand includes a number of spoken excerpts transcribed from cassette recordings. So, once again, I am turning an oral medium into print. This conversion is not entirely effective. Transcription robs the tapes of many essential things, like intonations, pauses, and the sounds of laughs and gasps. Shifting the medium changes the message. Not only do the printed texts leave out mumbled words and the distortions of faulty recording, they also leave out the "background music" pouring out of the compact cassettes—shouts, choruses of voices, drumming, High Life songs, and roosters.

The portability of cassette recorders and their ease of operation enabled Jon to capture the sound world of rural Ghana. In one recording (April 4, 1969) we hear Jon and Lawrie Altrows walking through the village. "Mac" is turned on. That day, Jon runs into a lot of people on the street and at a bar. Among them are Mr. Badu Nkwansah (Assistant Headmaster and member of Ghana's Constituent Assembly), the village Okyeame, John McClure, the Sports Master of Acherensua Secondary School, several other Ghanaian masters, and a Ghanaian WWII veteran. "Mac" picks up conversations in the street and at the akpeteshie bar,

# INTRODUCTION

along with a symphony of collateral noise. "Mac" itself becomes an object of conversation (duly recorded) when a Ghanaian discovers the machine is on. Ginny Thiem called these recorded rambles "Jon's documentaries." They gave his parents, sister, and relatives a palpable sense of village life.

Cap and Ginny, in their turn, sent Jon around forty cassettes containing messages from themselves, friends, and relatives. These cassettes include hours and hours of TV programs in which Walter Cronkite, Eric Sevareid, and others report or comment on the war, the draft, demonstrations, the killings at Kent State, and protests by blacks against racial discrimination. The cassettes became a vital source of information in news-starved Acherensua.

Jon's distaste for the written letter did not prevent him from firing off twenty-page epistles to Mike Moynihan and Ralph Slotten. The letter genre is the mainstay of his writing in Ghana, otherwise limited to lecture notes, poems, and translations. The only longer prose piece is the introduction to the apaeɛ manuscript he and Ohene put together.

Like every letter writer, Jon fashions a persona adapted to the individual he addresses. At times he pushes the convention to an extreme, deliberately inventing a fictional self, the better to play up—or play with—the emotional and personal sides of his thinking. In the letters to Slotten, Jon presents himself as Scholar and Aesthete.[25] In the letters to Mike, Jon the Misanthrope presents his darkest sentiments. Yet for all the tirades against his fellow humans, Jon does not stop rubbing shoulders with them. He spends a lot of time with Ghanaians and with the two North American volunteers in Acherensua. In a letter to Mike, he hints that his misanthropy is a pose: "Think of me: scholar, lover, misanthrope, a killer of wild elephants—a madman who writes letters to Mike Moynihan" (April 1969). The comic juxtaposition of "misanthrope" and "killer of elephants" is significant.

And yet the pervasive mood of refusal and doubt that informs Mike and Jon's correspondence also spills over into their view of the letters

INTRODUCTION

themselves. When Mike imagines what will happen to the letters in the future, he asserts:

> *I agree completely that no one is going to care one bit about our correspondence, now or any time. It all reeks of insanity, dis-illusion, meandering and nothingness.* [. . .] . . . *I'm sure no one wants us immortalized by publication for future generations to savor.* [. . .] *Our sporadic correspondence is really ridiculous, you know it.* (Feb. 10, 1969)

Although the two friends protest that their correspondence will have no future life, this dismissal itself is built on a telling assumption: that private letters may indeed have a public dimension.

Neither friend got around to discarding the other's letters. Inertia perhaps played a role. Ginny Thiem certainly played a role. Her high regard for old letters assured the preservation of Jon's. A large number (though not all) have come down to the present. Only in this minimal sense have these letters stood the test of time. Now with their publication they have the chance to do so in other ways.

### NOTES to the Preface and Introduction

1. In 1968, Acherensua had a population of about 800. The secondary school employed around 23 teachers. There were probably two hundred or more students. The language of instruction was English. Campus occupied a square-mile tract of land adjacent to the village, and was surrounded on the other sides by forest. Acherensua Secondary School was conceived in 1960 by the Ghana Education Trust Fund, an initiative of the Nkrumah government—and first opened in September 1961, as an all-boys boarding school. In 1969, it began admitting girls, a first step toward gender parity at the secondary level. In 1968, I was one of 242 Peace Corps volunteers in Ghana (Amin 43) and one of 13,823 volunteers and trainees in the field worldwide (Hoffman 262). At the present time, Acherensua Senior High School is still going strong. In 2006, it received from the government a new Information Communication Technology Centre—

# NOTES

to further computer literacy among students. See "Brief History of the School" and "ICT Centre for Acherensua Secondary School Inaugurated."

2. Two other periods are candidates for the most intense years of the second half of the twentieth century: 1961-63 (Cuban missile crisis, assassination of John F. Kennedy) and 1988-91 (collapse of the Soviet empire, the end of communism in Russia).

3. My earliest public protest against the escalation of U.S. military operations in Vietnam took place in October 1965—a month of worldwide protests (see DeBenedetti 125-27). With Larry Warner, my political science professor at Dickinson College, and a handful of other students, I demonstrated in front of the draft board in Carlisle, Pennsyvlania. Some people drove by and threw tomatoes. During my junior year abroad in Italy (1966-67) I attended a large Vietnam war protest in Bologna. In October 1967, I was at the Lincoln Memorial rally (about 70,000 protesters) in Washington, D.C., and the next day I marched on the Pentagon along with 30,000 other demonstrators. That protest is the subject of Norman Mailer's *Armies of the Night* (1968), which won the Pulitzer Prize and a National Book Award. In the mid 1960s, a number of different organizations and age groups opposed the war. The young people engaged in rebellion were largely college students, yet college students themselves were only a minority within their age group. Among college students the rebels were also a distinct minority, although they stood out because of their dress, their manners (or lack thereof), and their eloquence, often expressed in music. Similarly, the number of young Americans who went to other countries (except as soldiers) was very small in absolute numbers, but large relative to those who had gone overseas in previous decades. Study abroad programs offered 1960s students the opportunity, and the affluence of their middle class parents gave them the means, to live in other countries.

4. When I was in Ghana, my parents urged me to apply to the White House Fellows program, which would have exempted me from conscription *after* my volunteer service. But I was no longer interested in civic endeavors. I wrote back: "Avoiding the draft. I'm not willing to do something I don't want to do just to avoid the draft. I wanted to join the Peace Corps not just to avoid the draft. If it had been only to avoid the draft I probably wouldn't have joined or if I had I would not have stayed" (11/17/69).

5. For example, I did not approve of those protesters at the Chicago Democratic Convention (August 1968) who courted violent confrontation with the police. For all my interest in Marshall McLuhan and the power of electronic communications, I rejected violence as a method of gaining media publicity, even for what I thought was a just cause. I wanted to end the war using other means: rational persuasion, refusing the draft, and passive resistance.

# NOTES

6. In December 2012, I made a rough and probably incomplete survey of letter collections and memoirs by volunteers assigned to West Africa in the 60s, 70s, and 80s, and first published as books in the 2000s. Besides one letter collection (Nigeria), there were eight memoirs (four for Nigeria and one each for Ivory Coast, Sierra Leone, Cameroon, and Gambia). All nine books were self-published.

7. Canadian University Service Overseas (CUSO) posted two Canadian volunteers successively, to Acherensua Secondary School in the same period I was there: Lawrence ('Lawrie') Altrows (1968-69) and Nestor Kwasnycia (1969-71). Unfortunately, neither was able to locate letters they wrote in that period. Their pictures and doings, however, appear in *Letters from Ghana*.

8. Further reflections on rereading can be found in Thiem, "Reading and *Rereading:* A Twenty- First-Century Perspective."

9. Since the 1960s, profound political and demographic changes have transformed Ghana, and thousands of Ghanaians have left their native land and gone forth into the wider world, creating a grand diaspora. Demographer K. A. Twum-Bah estimated that 1.5 million Ghanaians were living abroad in 2001, with about 150,000 in the U.S. and Canada and about 310,000 in Europe (Twum-Bah 67-68). The Ghanaian diaspora is part of the West African migrations that took place in the 1980s and 90s, and which continue to this day. These migrations began as a result of economic hardship, civil strife, and political repression throughout the region. Migrations away from West Africa were enabled when developed nations introduced more liberal immigration policies. See the studies of Adepoju 24-54, and Takyi "Africans Abroad: Comparative Perspectives on America's Postcolonial West Africans" 236-254. On Ghanaians of Asante origin living in Canada and the U.S., see Manuh "Ghanaians, Ghanaian Canadians, and Asantes" 481-494 and Amoako 107-119. Isidore Okpewho's "Can We 'Go Home Again'?" (3-14) is a personal account that exposes the identity paradoxes, confusions, and opportunities arising out of the new African diaspora.

10. The company was Belgian and worked out of Mim. Big trucks hauling trees of phenomenal girth were a daily sight on the unpaved Tepa-Goaso road, which went by Acherensua. As a result of such operations, along with illegal cutting and burning by Ghanaians, around 80% of Ghana's equatorial forest canopy has been destroyed. On the deforestation of Ghana and on the remnants of closed canopy forests that remain, see Amy Corbin. On the history of the forest in the Ashanti region, from the 15th to the 19th century, and on its transformation through intensive farming, see Wilks 41-63.

11. All told, the war ended the lives of between one and three million people. For the range of figures and the sources of estimates, see: "Vietnam War Casualties" and for U.S. casualties, American War Library. For other statistics,

# NOTES

see McWilliams and Piotrowski 224 and Calvocoressi 467, who estimates two million deaths. By January 1973, when the U.S. military involvement came to an end, a total of 58,191 U.S. personnel had died in action (McNamara 321). In spite of the enormous sacrifice of human life, the United States did not achieve its objective in the war, which was to keep Vietnamese revolutionaries from taking power in South Vietnam. In the mid 1960s, the "domino theory" was used to justify the increase of U.S. military involvement in Vietnam. The theory maintained that if South Vietnam went Communist, so too would the other states of Southeast Asia. If South Vietnam could be saved, the "dominoes" would not fall. In 1966, at the beginning of the U.S. escalation, George F. Kennan (the major architect of the U.S.'s Cold War strategy to contain Communism) presented his arguments *against* the domino theory to President Johnson. Kennan said that recent events in Indonesia showed that the domino theory was false. Johnson did not heed Kennan's arguments (Langguth 419). The irony is that after the North Vietnamese takeover of South Vietnam, the Communist victors invaded Laos and deposed the Communist rulers there. Communist Vietnam was in turn attacked by Communist China. These developments confirmed that the insurgencies in Southeast Asia were more driven by national independence movements than by a monolithic Communist program (McWillams and Piotrowski 226). By the end of the twentieth century, "Communist" Vietnam, in emulation of China, was rapidly putting its economy on a capitalist footing. On the persistence of the war in American collective memory and on recent ground-breaking scholarship that presents Vietnamese points of view and voices, see Barbier's Introduction and Masur's review essay.

12. The context of McNamara's memorandum to President Johnson is McNamara's rejection of General Westmoreland's proposal in 1967 to increase the number of U.S. troops in Vietnam by 200,000. McNamara argued the increase would lead to an escalation of the war, more bombing, more noncombatant deaths—to the tune of a thousand a week. This figure hints at how high noncombatant fatalities must have really been, given the actual military force levels at the time.

13. Karen Rothmyer in "The Peace Corps at 50" (2011), argues that the employment of Peace Corps teachers in present-day Kenya has the unfortunate effect of taking jobs away from Kenyan graduates, among whom unemployment rates are high. The author is a former Peace Corps teacher in Kenya.

14. In the Brong-Ahafo region during the late sixties, the vast majority of adults could not speak English (Dunn 213). In 1970, 56.8% of the Ghanaian population six years and older had never attended school (Ghana Statistical Service 69). The figures would be higher for rural areas. In 1971, only 30.2% of the population age 15 or over was literate, and only 18.4% of women (U.S. Department of Commerce, Table 11, p. 9); again, the figures for rural areas

# NOTES

would be lower. It was difficult to attract teachers to rural areas. On March 3, 1983, Ohene wrote Jon that of all those masters who were teaching at Acherensua Secondary School in the 1968-70 period, only one remained at the school. This is a very high turnover rate, especially considering that the 1968-70 staff had been rather young. (The one teacher who had stayed in the school was from a nearby village.) The problem of retaining teachers in rural schools persists (see Casely-Hayford).

15. Ghanaian officials and educators counted on Peace Corps English teachers to bolster the ongoing national literacy campaign initiated by Nkrumah. Since Jon's Peace Corps service, scholars have raised serious questions about the assumptions made about literacy in the 1960s (and earlier) and its socio-economic effects. Here are some of the the findings of the new scholarship: literacy is very hard to define and differentiate from illiteracy; literacy may be a by- product, rather than a cause of social and economic development (as was believed in the 60s); traditional literacy advocates overvalue reading and writing; literacy programs can be seen as ethnocentric, as the imposition of Western, post-Enlightenment values on other cultures. For a summary of the new research on literacy and literacy campaigns, see Harvey J. Graff, *The Labyrinths of Literacy* (Rev. ed. 1995) xviii-xxvi, 270-298. In the same volume, Graff and Robert Arnove make the point that African leaders and political elites accepted and propagated "myths of literacy" to promote the legitimacy of their regimes and gain popular support (292). In Ghana, the push for education and literacy, however much shaped by Western thinking, already had strong support among the people, who believed that education was the road to wealth.

16. In 1971, the literacy rate of Ghanaians 15 or older was only 30.2% (U.S. Department of Commerce 9); by 2010 it had risen to 67.3% of the population 15 and over ("List of countries by literacy rate"). These statistics refer to basic literacy. They do not indicate ranges of writing skills —or for reading, the types of materials and degree of comprehension. Many Ghanaian literacy numbers are based on censuses or surveys in which individuals are asked to identify their own level of literacy—a method subject to considerable error.

On the efforts of Peace Corps instructors in Africa, even the wary Grubbs concludes: "Education received a modest but symbolic boost from American teachers" (176). Julius Amin (one of Grubbs' main sources) is critical of "missionary diplomacy," and yet he underscores the contributions of Peace Corps teachers in Ghana, especially in science (43, 45-46).

17. The comparison of traditional heroes with the "anti-heroes" of modernist and postmodern literature was an undertaking Jon intended to pursue in graduate school. The letters from Ghana show Jon's penchant for applying the concepts of hero and anti-hero to his own life (e.g. Jon to Mike 6/7/69).

# NOTES

18. There are now a number of important studies of apaeɛ, their uses, their reciters. See especially Lange, Yankah, Sutherland-Addy, and Anyidoho.

19. Widespread familiarity with apaeɛ (in Ghana) and their distinctive characteristics, such as concision and martial metaphors, have led to their successful adaptation to modern political and religious purposes. Kwame Nkrumah, for example, engaged Okyeame Boafo Akuffo to recite heroic praise epithets in his honor; they are essentially apaeɛ (see Yankah). These epithets lent to Nkrumah's charisma a traditional Akan note. Here is an example, translated by Yankah. It strongly resembles one of the apaeɛ (# 7) collected by Jon and Ohene (and quoted in the Introduction, above):

*Osagyefo, the fearsome Gyan Ada,*
*Whose presence is sniffed in the entire village,*
*Even though he was sighted at the outskirts.*
(Yankah 49)
Osagyefo, or Redeemer, was a common epithet for Nkrumah.

Father "Kofi" Ron Lange has investigated the adaptation of apaeɛ by a Christian Pentacostalist. Madam Afua Kuma composed a cycle of heroic epithets for Jesus (*Jesus of the Deep Forest*). See also the study of Kuma by Anyidoho. One example:

*Jesus blockades the road of death*
*with wisdom and power.*
*He, the sharpest of all great swords,*
*has made the forest safe for the hunters.*
*The* mmoatia [dwarves] *he has cut to pieces;*
*he has caught* sasabonsam [the tree demon]
*and twisted off its head!*
(tr. Kofi Ron Lange and Jon Kirby, ll. 366-372)

20. The early political career of Mr. Badu Nkwansah, and the context of his victory in the 1969 parliamentary elections, is discussed in John Dunn's essay "Politics in Asunafo." For Ghanaian political history in the 1960s and 1970s, I found the work of the following scholars particularly useful: Kwame Arhin Brempong, Dennis Austin "Introduction," David Birmingham, Naomi Chazan, Roger S. Gocking, and David Owusu-Ansah, *Historical Dictionary of Ghana.*

21. In April 1970, Jon and Ohene tried to see the Asantehene to get formal permission to publish the apaeɛ. Because the king was quite ill, they were received instead by the king's personal secretary, who stated there would be no royal objection to publication. The Asantehene, Prempeh II, died not long afterwards, in May 1970. Shortly before leaving Ghana, Jon attended the large durbar (in Kumasi) to celebrate the enstoolment of the new Asantehene. The successor of Prempeh II was Opoku Ware II. He occupied the Golden Stool from 1970 until his death in 1999. He was succeeded by Barima Kwaku Dua

# NOTES

Bonsu, who took the name King Osei Tutu II. Ohene and Jon were pleased that the new Asantehene linked himself to the hero celebrated in the apaeε recited by Kwasi Dum.

22. In 2005, primary school education, though extensive, was still not universal in Ghana; it encompassed 82% of eligible children (Takyi-Amoako 198). Since the late 1960s, however, great strides have been made in school attendance (which explains the rise of the national literacy rate —see note 16 above). Figures for people six years or older who *never* attended school dropped from 56.8% in 1970 to 38.8% in 2000 (Ghana Statistical Service 69). Comparable figures of non- attendance for girls are 66.2% in 1970, and 44.5% in 2000 (Ghana Statistical Service 69). While more girls now go to school, gender parity remains a distant goal (Takyi-Amoako 204). In 2003, in the Brong-Ahafo region (where Acherensua Secondary School is located), for every 833 boys who completed secondary school, only 100 girls did (Takyi-Amoako 202). A vivid account of the difficult teaching and living conditions in rural Brong-Ahafo (and other regions) in 2000-2001 is found in Casely-Hayford 146-161. On the decline of those living below the poverty line in Ghana between 1992 and 2001, from 51.7% to 39%, see Annin 66. On the role of the chiefs in Ghana, past and present, see Arhin Brempong, "Chieftaincy, An Overview." Richard Rathbone discusses the trend of educated professionals to become chiefs (164). Kwame Boafo-Arthur summarizes the benefits that have accrued to Ghana from the long spell of uninterrupted democratic government and stable leadership (17-18).

23. Important recent work on the spirit of 1968 includes the essays in Fink, Gassert and Junker, and the book by Horn. Although the antiwar demonstrators were mainly young people, the overwhelming majority of people in their twenties supported the war (unlike the age cohort of people over fifty). For the statistics, see Gordon L. Bowen.

24. By 1966, audio compact cassettes were widely available in the U.S. market, having been introduced by the Philips corporation. They were initially used for oral dictation, later for music. By the late 1990s, they were becoming obsolescent in western countries, except for certain specialized uses, as in audiobooks. See "Audio Cassette." Interestingly, many diaspora Ghanaians send compact cassettes, rather than letters, to communicate with relatives in their native land.

25. Slotten, in his poem "Giles Goat Boy in Africa," mischievously endorsed Jon's favorite personas. Giles Goat Boy is the student protagonist of John Barth's 1968 novel of the same name. Jon had recommended the work to Slotten.

# NOTES

*Giles Goat Boy in Africa*

*Far in Africa tonight*
*he pours over Rattray*
*and Ashanti history,*
*or listens to his tapes*
*of Akan poetry with nervous*
*fingers.*

*His bed is piled*
*with the improbable and*
*mocking stories of Borges,*
*and he imagines himself*
*The Giles Goatboy of Dickinson*
*College . . . . he writes*
*that he plans to return*
*with a new literature.*

*HE is the ONE! HE is the ONE,*
*ordained to break heads.*

(Written after November 22, 1969 and sent to Jon in Ghana.)

# EDITORIAL GUIDELINES

This book presents a selection from the extant letters and journal entries that Jon wrote and received. It also includes letters and writings by others not addressed to him. Of the compact cassette tapes that Jon sent or received, fifty-eight are extant, representing, very roughly, as many hours of playing time. The number of excerpts included out of this huge body of aural material is, however, relatively small.

If only a part or parts of a text or transcript are included, this is indicated by the word Excerpt or Excerpts at the head of the text. Where the editor omits part of a sentence, this is indicated by an ellipsis (. . .) ; where a sentences or paragraphs in a text are omitted, there is an ellipsis in brackets [. . .]. An ellipsis with double dots (.. .. ..) indicates an ellipsis that the letter writer wrote in the original manuscript. Words that are illegible or inaudible (on a cassette tape) are denoted by a line: _____ .

Punctuation errors have been silently corrected and capitalization regularized. Misspelled words, on the other hand, have been left as they stand in the original texts, but the correct spelling is given in brackets [ ] or is identified with a *sic* in brackets. Errors in grammar have been allowed to stand, but a correction in brackets sometimes follows in order to make the sentence more intelligible.

The editor has also used brackets [ ] to insert clarifications and emendations. Parentheses ( ), as opposed to brackets, enclose comments made *by the letter writer.* Longer notes and explanations are in *italics,* usually placed at the end of a letter.

# LETTERS FROM GHANA 1968-1970

## Texts and Commentaries

*The following texts are ordered chronologically—with the exception of several articles published in the November 1970 issue of* The Achiscodian Times. *These articles, written by Ghanaian students, are usually placed near letters they share common material with (though the articles themselves may have been written later than the letters).*

**August 16, 1968.** Jon to his draft board in southern Delaware. Probably written at Columbia University, New York City. Typed. Excerpts.

Selective Service Local Board No. 2
State Armory
Georgetown, Delaware 19947

Re: Jon Edgar Thiem
Selective Service No. . . .

Gentlemen:
    This letter is to request reconsideration of the board's recent decision to classify me 1-A. If no reconsideration is to be given, please consider this my notice of appeal to the state appeal board.
    I have just successfully completed eight weeks of Peace Corps training at Teachers College, Columbia University. My group is scheduled to depart the territorial United States on August 20, 1968, for four weeks of additional training in Accra, Ghana. Upon successful completion of that training, I will be assigned as a Peace Corps Volunteer and secondary school teacher in a Ghanaian school for approximately 22 months.
    On advice of the Peace Corps I plan to go overseas with my training group, with the understanding that the Peace Corps will return me to this country if it becomes necessary for selective service purposes. I request, therefore, that procedures be initiated to grant me permission to leave the

country on August 20th. My permanent overseas address, effective August 21, 1968, will be [a P.O. Box in Accra, Ghana].

My personal reasons for appealing my 1-A classification and requesting occupational deferment are as follows. I feel that the Peace Corps program is vital to the interests, security, and prestige of the United States. In helping the underdeveloped countries to help themselves, the Peace Corps is preventing situations that would be detrimental to the security of the United States. [. . .] It is on this basis that Peace Corps service has been held to be a deferrable occupation because it is in the national interest.

Furthermore, since I will be only 23 years of age upon completion of my Peace Corps service, I will still be subject to fulfillment of my military obligations.

[. . .]

Respectfully,
Jon E. Thiem

Countersigned:
Robert D. Cohen
Program Director
Ghana Education . . .

cc:     Legal Liaison Branch
        Office of Selection
        Peace Corps
        Washington, D.C. 20525

*Jon was entitled to a Peace Corps deferment, but his local draft board refused to grant it. 1-A classification meant that Jon was subject to immediate induction. There was a background of troubled relations between Jon and his southern Delaware draft board. In 1967, the board tried to end his student deferment when he enrolled at Dickinson College. Cap Thiem, Jon's father, appealed to the governor of Delaware, who intervened to stop Jon's induction.*

#  LETTERS FROM GHANA

*It is possible that the local board had learned of Jon's activities in the peace movement and sought to punish him. For other examples of draft boards using reclassification as a punitive measure against college protesters, see DeBenedetti 128 (in* Works Consulted, *below).*

*In August 1968, the situation is urgent. Peace Corps advises Jon to travel with his training group to Ghana, because once he is there, it is unlikely the board will recall him to the United States. The board, after receiving the above letter, refused to rescind the 1-A classification, so an appeal of the decision to the state's Selective Service Board was initiated. For further developments, see Jon's letters to his parents and sister below, Sept. 13, 1968, Oct. 16, 1968, and Feb. 4, 1969.*

*"I will still be subject to fulfillment of my military obligations." Jon knew that he might be subject to conscription, even after Peace Corps service, but he was nonetheless determined to avoid military service at all costs. His father Cap Thiem supported Jon in this, and offered to help him, if circumstances required, to go into exile in Canada.*

**August 22, 23, 24, 1968.** Thursday, Friday, Saturday. First entries in Jon's Ghana journal, written in Accra.

Met Kawahena and Kwame in Accra. He turned out to be from Kibi, studies Pol. Sci. at Legon. Accra is largely a great open air market with thousands of things for sale. Sandals are big. Food, fish, smells etc. Saw Homowo festival. Saw sea, kids bathing naked in treacherous waters. Fri. nite went to Lido Club, met Rose a fickle femme de joi, much like an American club. Sat. went to more traditional Tip Toe club. —All Ghanaian with soul band from Gambia + Ghana Navy band playing James Brown songs.
High table is English Chop, few places [to sit]. I prefer Nkatiankwan or ground nut soup. It's hot as hell but good. Comes with a big ball of rice. Ma bree me kɔ da. Da yiye.

*These are Jon's first entries in his Ghana journal. He arrived in Accra (by plane) on August 22. The University of Ghana is at Legon, near Accra. Kibi, about sixty miles north of Accra, is the town where Jon is to continue his Peace Corps training.*

*Ground nuts are peanuts.*

**August 25, 1968.** Ralph Slotten in Carlisle, Pennsylvania, to Jon Thiem, c/o Cap and Ginny Thiem, Wilmington, Delaware. Typed. Excerpts.

Dear Jon,

I do not know whether you are now in America or in Africa. I trust that all went well with "basic training." I understand that you have been studying Twi.

[. . .]

I got back from India in the morning on Friday last, day before yesterday. [. . .] I have studied India and Hinduism for years, but the shock of the presence of Hinduism is no less great for the preparation. I learned little new about India, academically speaking, but I learned much experientially! For one thing, no one can understand Hinduism who has not smelled it. The stench of Hinduism is a concoction of cow and human dung, jasmine and incense used for puja, and beans, curds, and rice. [. . .]

Many times on our trip I thought of you. You would have loved India and gotten much out of the experience. I especially wish you could have been with us in Benares on the sunrise boatride and at Sarnath, a few miles north of Benares, where we attended morning and evening services at the Buddhist monastery founded by Tibetan refugees. [. . .] [at a Hindu religious festival in Benares] the worshipers outside gathered around the temple orchestra, which accompanied a dwarf dancer with instrumental music and singing. The dance of the dwarf was pure ecstasy. After we watched for some time we turned to make our way through the street back to our car and I caught sight of an adolescent young man who was completely nude except for a home-made jock strap which did not quite do the job of covering the necessaries. Just before I got into the car he came over to me, looked at me benignly and kissed and touched my thighs, knees, and feet in a swift gesture that caught me by surprise. . . . apparently he was performing puja before me, that is, he was worshipping me, as wives are supposed to worship their masters and disciples are supposed to worship their teachers.

[. . .]

It would be pleasant to see you and talk to you if you are still in the country. You might not recognize me. I was quite ill in India and sank from 226 pounds at the beginning of summer to a mere 199 as of today! I am almost as cadaverous as you! I could talk endlessly about India, for example the erotic carvings of Konarak would interest you, I am sure!

I hope to hear from you sometime, sooner or later. [. . .] I would love to hear you discourse in and on Twi!

I trust that all will go well with you. [. . .] With all your talent and the charisma of your spirit you lack only one thing—direction; unless, of course, you really mean to be a life-long hipster. Don't. You have too much to offer. But even as a hipster you have distinct merits.

*Ralph Slotten was Jon's mentor at Dickinson College (Carlisle, Pennsylvania). A professor in the Religion and Philosophy faculty, Slotten had received a Ph.D. in History of Religions from the University of Chicago. He was also an ordained minister. Jon took advanced courses with Slotten in "Myth and Ritual," "Eastern and Western Mysticism," and "Judaism and Islam." Jon's fascination with West African worldviews, non-western religions, and comparative politics also owed a great deal to three other Dickinson professors: Fred Hartshorn (English and the history of ideas), Vytautis Kavolis (sociology of art) and K. R. Nilsson (the politics of modernization).*

*Twi (i.e. Akan) is one of the main languages spoken in Ghana.*

**August 25, 1968.** Sunday. Entry in Jon's Ghana journal. In the town of Kibi.

3 hour ride from Accra in (60 miles) packed lorry, people sleeping on each other's shoulders—tiny lorries, 8 people—1 cedi from Accra to Kibi. Road bad in low spots. Canteen near chiefs' palace filled with Ghanai[a]ns, girls dancing, men drinking beer. We met the Ohene [the king]. Not much ceremony, he was casual, almost American. "Have a

seat etc." Very proud of his position. Life size photo of him in younger days. He must be 60. Palace is huge w/ big court rooms etc. Talked to his sons who are in secondary school. One wants to be a doctor. They were impressed by my poor Twi and my spastically snapped handshake.

I am staying at the midwife's house. She lives near the clinic but her extended family lives here. A dozen children in [the] compound which is very nice and neat. Excellent soup w/ rice though a little hot [spicy]. About 4 or 5 middle aged women who are very nice. My room has a bureau (small) + mirror (remarkable), water basin, night table, and a good bed. Light is by lantern, ≠ electricity. There is a Presbyterian quasi spiritualist church (asɔre) behind [the] compound. My compound is Xtian. It is very close to the river. Played oware w/ children + talked. Children are beautiful. This week I'm supposed to go to a funeral (tomorrow) + Kibi's only spiritualist church, plus an nsafuo bar.

*As part of his in-country training, Jon stays for two weeks in the town of Kibi (Kyebi: roughly pronounced* chaybee). *This is called the "village live-in." Kibi has between one and two thousand inhabitants. The town is the seat of one of the most important kings in Ghana, the Okyenhene.*

*The* cedi *(i.e. new cedi) is a unit of Ghanaian currency, equivalent to a dollar. The "snapped handshake," popular in Ghana, creates a snapping sound. Jon, as a beginner, finds it hard to produce the snap.* Oware *is a popular "board" game played by both children and adults.*

*The Okyenhene, King of the Akyem Abuakwa, is Ofori Atta II. Jon estimates his age to be 60. He is actually around 69. The Okyenhene was "destooled" and banished to Accra in 1958 by the Nkrumah government. He opposed Nkrumah's policies and refused to obey court orders to give up the stool treasures of Akyem Abuakwa and vacate the royal palace. This episode led to a dramatic change in the balance of power between the government and traditional chieftaincy in Ghana. The harsh treatment of the Okyenhene intimidated the kings and chiefs of Ghana, breaking their traditional authority, and forcing them to tow the government line.*

*After the 1966 coup which deposed Nkrumah, the Okyenhene was reinstated and once again became an important figure in Ghana. In July 1969, Jon and the Okyenhene met again, when the latter was on a state visit to the Asantehene (the Asante King) in Kumasi. In the late 1960s, Jon knew very little about the pivotal part the Okyenhene played in recent Ghanaian history. Ofori Atta II died in 1973. For a detailed account of Ofori Atta II's opposition first to British rule, and then to Nkrumah's, and his role in the chieftaincy conflict, see Rathbone 38-47, 126f, 130-131, 161-62.*

Nsafuo *is palm wine, a white foamy alcoholic beverage made of the fermented sap of palm trees.*

**August 26, 1968.** Monday. In Kibi. Entry in Jon's Ghana journal.

Today was a very busy day and a good one. I arose at 8:30 A.M. Ghanaians arise ≈ 6:00 AM. They cooked me a high table breakfast. I am called MR. KOFI. This pleases me. In the morning Kwabena showed me the River Prim and a small cocoa garden, plus a "mercy ground" where the osofuo or preacher prays. Stones form a cross. Then I had Kubé and Kubé nsuo or cocoa nuts + cocoa nut milk. I taught some of the children handball. They were game. And hand wrestling (don't move your feet gi na ho!) etc. Played Oware + won. Noon went to Kibi's Men school w/ several of the kids. Played Frisbee w/ Bob Hav.'s Frisbee. Went over big.

Afternoon went to funeral. Service was Xtian but all in Twi. At grave I was asked to ritually dump earth w/ shovel in the grave. I was much lauded for doing this. Ghanaians are surprised [sic] + pleased if you speak a little Twi. They are amazingly friendly + gregarious. Language is the real key to being "in."

Tried Nsafuo (palm wine) for first time, it is good and strong like inexpensive American whiskies. I like it. It's not sold at night, people drink it in the day.

(Ohene [the king] didn't show at [the] funeral, by the way.) At funeral many people cried but were not despondent, excepting close relatives. During burial everyone pull[s] out hankerchief [sic] and waves goodbye to [the] deceased. Grave fillers (I was one) get palm wine at [the] deceased's home.

Boys lost [the] ball. I will buy them [a] new one tomorrow. Am supposed to see Zongo (Muslim section) also.

This evening we went to [the] canteen next to [the] palace. I drank beer, talked to Ghanaians. Met head of hospital lab (Kwaku). He couldn't get over [the] fact it took me 2 mos. to learn [the] Twi I had learned.

Before dinner I taught [the] kids how to broad jump. Standing broad jump. Also had them sign their names, give the English [version] and Twi names and birthdates. This went over big. Gave [the] little girl math problems (simple add.) which she eagerly did by finger counts etc. Tomorrow may have them draw pictures of things.

The kids, at least the boys have a hell of a lot of free time in the holidays. They do little study. They play many games or wander thru [the] city. They seem eager to do other things like learning. I think they like me.

Ghanaians love to joke and jest. When a stranger makes a jest or malapropism or pun it is even more hilarious.

The respect one gains from stumbling thru Twi could be useful in community development. Would recommend at least a month before begin[ning] things like that. Start w/ recreation, then go forward.

Importance of ①playing games ②snap handshaking ③eating w/ fingers ④dancing high life ⑤hand holding.

Dinner was good high table.

*Kwabena is Samuel Kwabena Bonti. He is seventeen and lives in the compound where Jon is staying.*

*By "high table," Jon means that he was served western-style food, and treated as an honored guest. "hand holding" refers to the custom of Akan men holding hands—the gesture is not considered homoerotic in Ghana.*

**August 27, 1968.** Tuesday. In Kibi. Entry in Jon's Ghana journal.

Take Malaria pill. Bought ball, 30 Pesewas—too much. Played ball w/ boys after cold water bucket bath. Juggled for boys (3 balls in air)[.] Three of us used 3 balls throwing simultaneously. Got [a] bang out of this.

The whole town seems to know me. "Maha Mister Kofi" etc. It is necessary to say a few words to everyone. Took over 1/2 hour to get to hospital. Many women were bringing their children there to get shots for Belharsia—a parasite caught from swimming in sweet water.

Had African grapefruit—"abranka," amazingly sweet.

Shoemaker nailed my shoes back together for nothing.

Matches from [the] U.S.S.R. Milk from U.S.A. "Donated by people of U.S.A." etc.

Breakfast, had porridge "koko." Have had

Abenkwan crabs + snails

Nkatiakwan nuts + meat

Kuntumorekwan—leaves + meat

foo foo—smashed yams

yam smashing operation

Smoke Gold Star non filter cigarettes.

They do my shirts etc.

Had nuts + bananas (plantain) for dinner, [the] latter like French fries.

Encountered curiosity concerning Caucasians physiological peculiarities.

Went to [the] "English Bar" and danced High Life. Apparently "Mister Kofi" is [the] most famous Peace Corps-ni here. Reiteration of fact that language + friendliness are keys. Bedtime for all is between 9 + 10 o'clock.

Did impersonations of alcoholic, gangster, hippy.

Many questions about Amer. Kennedy [assassination], conspiracy questions.

Image of America is bad: consternation about American racial prejudice.

Kids here are really bright. Know all of [the] facts about Macbeth etc.

Had some homemade wine; didn't relish it. An Apollonian culture, semi herbivorous, gentle, pacific.

Men do not seem to work a great deal. Not much togetherness at dinner table probably because communal all the time anyway.

Little privacy, as expected, but this not bothersome to me (yet).

Sko-fuo [school kids] do little reading during [the] holidays. Game playing is the big thing.

Ghanaians eat incessantly and perpetually. A well fed, friendly people.

*Thirty "pesewas" is about thirty cents at the official exchange rate. "Belharsia" is bilharzia (schistosomiasis). "Caucasians physiological peculiarities," i.e. circumcision.*

**August 28, 1968.** Jon in Kibi to his parents, Cap and Ginny Thiem, and his sister Judy, in Wilmington, Delaware. Included is a note from Kwabena Bonti to Judy. Excerpts.

Dear Father, Mother and Judy, (if you are there)

I thought I would drop you a letter giving you my whereabouts. I am on the "village live in" at Kibi about 60 miles out of Accra on the way to Kumasi.

[. . .]

. . . Everyone is very friendly. I live in a little compound near the river. It is an extended family of 12 people. I awoke at 6:30 this morning, took my usual cold water bucket bath. Had very good eggs and toast for breakfast. I have had a good deal of Ghanaian food; it is good and hot.

[. . .]

Kibi has about a thousand people. There are 6 other P.C.T.s [Peace Corps trainees] here with other families.

Judy: my friend Kwabena wants a penpal. He is 17 and an equivalent of a sophomore in High School. This is a distinction in Africa. He will write you a note in the space below:

Dear Mr. Mrs. Thiem and Judy, I think if you get this letter you will ask about me. Is through Mr. Jon Edgar Thiem that I got to know you. Am a boy of 17 year[s] and I attended the high school. In fact your son Mr. Jon is one of the most hamson [handsome] and kindness [kindest] man [men]

I have ever met. I will like to come and spend some holidays with you during summer holidays.
[. . .]
In fact I will be very glad if I had a letter from Judy. [. . .] Tell Judy to sent [send] me her photograph. I will be sending her African Native Sandals and rest. [. . .] Until I hear from you and Judy. Especially Judy!

*This is Jon's second letter from Ghana to his parents. His sister Judy, age nineteen, is a student at Miami University in Oxford, Ohio.*

**August 29, 1968.** Thursday. In Kibi. Entry in Jon's Ghana journal. Excerpts.

Last night after I "went to bed" the kids spent an hour parodying my use of the word "XPATAAAA."

The lack of aloneness and concentrated reflection while very healthy is disconcerting to a person who has adapted to alienation. Perhaps to be healthy is alienation to the modern man reared on Sartre + Kafka.

The kids in Secondary School retain mountainous amounts of school facts but these latter do not precipitate into [the] environment except as the sort of thing you say when a pedagogue is around. Am dubious about imaginative reconstruction receptivity. This will be a teaching challenge.
[. . .]
Kwabena's history of Kibi: Hunter in bush kills [a] monkey (adrincoto) and makes from its skin a black hat (ɛkye/bree) [bre is black], ergo "Kyebi" and finally Kibi. From black hatted hunter who live[d] here. Abeberemang is black country.
[. . .]
"Eh Brunee Bra ha" is constant refrain (eh white man come here)
[. . .]
I am enjoying the tactile aspect of interpersonal relationships; I was a little edgy at first.

# LETTERS FROM GHANA

Everyone thinks I am rich because I smoke 2 packs [of] cigarettes a day[,] have good clothes + have a couple of beers. For me these will be inevitable culture barriers.

*"the tactile aspect of interpersonal relationships" i.e. handholding.*

**August 30-31, 1968.** Friday and Saturday. In Kibi. Entries in Jon's journal. Excerpts.

Yesterday had avocados--delicious.
    Went to cocoa agricultural experimental station at Bonsu. Problems of yield + disease.
    Went to Zongo. Acromofo [Kramofo] or Moslems wear white robes + hats, speak Hausa + Twi, are the village traders. Zongo is unlike rest, much less affluent, adobe construction, more crowded, more animals (sheep + chickens), Mosques (2) very bare, small adobe buildings, mats + sheepskins, altar indent w/ hole + star of David around it. We were not allowed inside. People friendly. No bars in Zongo. But figural representations in homes + photos. An alligator in relief was sculpted into one adobe wall. Even so Zongo seems as much Twi [Asante] as it does Islamic.
[. . .]
    Subsistence farming is integral to Ghanaian village life. Nkrumah tried to institute exchange economy + destroy subsistence. But when cocoa dropped Farmers didn't suffer: the urban areas and bureaucracies suffered. Hia Nkyene [is the] name of villages where all you have to take w/ you is salt; everthing else is there to subsist on. Great abundance of equatorial areas, fruits + vegetables galore. Many different names and kinds of banana. Eating and growing are vital rites of these villages. (Spent whole evening discussing agriculture w/ Mr. Quansah.) Tomorrow I will go to [his] farm.
    Began reading Hugo's <u>Hunchback of Notre Dame</u>. Kwabena [is] reading abridged version of Verne's <u>Around [the] World in Eighty Days</u>.
[. . .]
    C.F. <u>Giles Goat Boy</u> to <u>Hunchback of Notre Dame</u>

# LETTERS FROM GHANA

*The "Zongo" is the part of town where "foreigners" live. Throughout his stay in Ghana Jon is fascinated with the many kinds of religion he encounters.*

*Hia Nkyene means "all you need is salt."* Giles Goat Boy *(1968) is a campus novel about the cultural and technological revolutions of the 1960s, written by John Barth. A computer is a major character. The influence of the communications theorist Marshall McLuhan on the novel absorbed Jon's attention. See also Ralph Slotten's poem about Jon: "Giles Goat Boy in Africa," note 25 to the Introduction.*

**September 2, 1968.** Jon in Kibi to his parents and sister in Wilmington, Delaware. Excerpts.

So far I really like Ghanaian village life and I am doing tolerably well assimilating it. I'll probably be sent to a "bush school," (my request) which means no electricity.
[. . .]
If I need anything I'll let you know. Right now I don't need anything + can't think of anything excepting books.
[. . .]
    See if you can get me the following in paperback: Histories of French, Spanish and English literatures in separate editions. Since mailing time is two months, mail to my Accra address. [. . .] Also mail me my editions at home of Steppenwolf, Sotweed Factor, + Tristram Shandy. What's new at home?

*In this letter, Jon, for the first time (and not the last) asks his parents to send him books he wants.* Steppenwolf *is a novel by Hermann Hesse. The Sotweed Factor is by the novelist John Barth and is partly set on the Delmarva peninsula, where Jon grew up.*

**September 2, 1968.** Monday. In Kibi. Entry in Jon's Ghana journal. Excerpts.

Got up early: met the Okenohene [Okyenhene] in all his pomp and mpaninfo. He and the elders were hearing legal cases: ① a man unable to pay [h]is seamstress ② a village desiring a chief to be stooled. Okenohene is very prominent, his palace is huge etc. The Akim symbol sits above his head (see inside front cover drawing by Kwabena).

Mpaninfo *are the elders. A new chief is "stooled"—that is, enthroned.*

*The Okyenhene during an adjudication, Kibi (Kyebi), September 1968.*

**September 3, 1968.** Tuesday. Entry in Jon's Ghana journal. In Kibi.

Akosua Bruni next door had money stolen (40 cedis)
Some people are affronted because I don't remember I met them. But I must have meant [met] a thousand people.
Everybody goes to bed ≈ 9:00-10:00
Girls lose intactness at ≈ 15
[. . .]
[an ink drawing by Amma, drawn into Jon's journal book] Amma's (8 years old) conception of an Eskimo's snow block house and an Eskimo. Drawing + subject suggested by herself.
butterfly = afafranto

Church of Lord Israel again tonite—talked to osofo [minister] + went to service. It is definitely spiritualist + widespread thruout Ghana. Prayer positions are the ultra kneel or prostration, funny little jumping exercize [sic] at end. All professions + churches blessed in service. All women [and] children + 2 men. Services are Wed. Fri. + Sun.

**September 4, 1968.** Wednesday. Entry in Jon's Ghana journal. In Kibi.

Up and off to Diamond mines of English Cast Ltd. at Akratia. 60 mile trip takes 4 hours each way. Lorrys [lorries] stop every five miles. Roads poor, holey, washed out. 3 classes of lorry. Minilorry, mammy wagon and V.W. type bus. Once at mines we were not allowed in for security reasons. Workers have nice homes. But British are aloof. At Club (where African senior officers attend) the Africans are snubbed by the British. The whole place had a very unfriendly unGhanaian ethos.

Reading Vergil's Aeneid in English translation.

Tomorrow I get assignment and go to a big city near it.

*Mammy wagons, or lorries, are the cheapest kind of transport. They are two to three ton trucks with planks for seats, open at the sides and with a canopy roof. They are meant to hold around fifteen people, but often carry twice that many—they're filled to the gills with men, women, children, infants, traders (market mammies), goats, chickens, baskets of produce. Potholes deliver strong jolts to the passenger's behind.*

*"Reading Vergil's Aeneid": this shows Jon's interest in epic, which will culminate in the Ashanti poetry project.*

*The "big city" is Kumasi, capital of the Ashanti region.*

**September 5, 1968.** Jon in Kumasi to his parents and sister in Wilmington. Excerpt.

Today I learned my posting was to be Acherensua, a small village and [secondary] school in the Brong Ahafo region. (You'd better get a map of Ghana.) I was rather lucky as this was the assignment I requested. It is bush + Twi speaking and in the rain forest zone. [. . .] There is another P.C.V. at my posting . . . .

*P.C.V. is Peace Corps Volunteer. Acherensua is three to four hours by lorry northwest of Kumasi.*

**September 6, 1968.** Friday. Entry in Jon's Ghana journal. In Acherensua.

Arrive Acherensua. Long route because of flooded roads. 8 hour trip for around 2½ hours [trip].

**November 1970.** "The Climate of the School." Article from the *The Achiscodian Times*. The Editor is Kwadwo Nkrumah-Boateng. Typed copy. Excerpt.

Acherensua Secondary School, considering its position, lies on the latitude 7° North of the Equator and longitude 2° 25′ West of the Greenwich Meridian. [. . .] It is a mile square, sharing boundaries with Acherensua township, farms and a stream.

The mean annual temperature is about 70° F., as it is within the tropics. Lying within the tropical belt, it is expected to have rain almost every month. Rainfall varies from month to month and the annual rainfall is about 56.24″.

In the wet season (especially July) a low pressure belt develops causing the S.W. Monsoon, moisture-laden winds, to meet the dry N.E. Trades, at the Inter Tropical Convergence Zone (I.T.C.Z.), which causes much rain amidst thunderstorms and lightning.

North East Trades, alias the Harmattan, in the dry season have very much influence on the school. It is very hot in the day with temperatures ranging from 70°-80° F. As the rate of evaporation is very rapid because of the lowness of the relative humidity, students' skins crack, especially the lips. In the morning the temperature is so cool that people feel reluctant to bathe . . . . However, the temperature encourages much sleep.

# LETTERS FROM GHANA

Antwi Nimako, fifth-form student

*The "mean annual temperature" is probably closer to 79° F. The actual daily temperature range during the Harmattan, the dry season, is from the mid-70s up into high 80s F.*

*Dave Fitzjarrald, in 2012, sent me a scan of the November 1970 issue of* The Achiscodian Times. *The newspaper was founded by Canadian volunteer Lawrie Altrows (1968-69), Jon's colleague at Acherensua Secondary School during his first year there.*

Achisco *is an abbreviation of Acherensua Secondary School.*

**September 7, 1968.** Saturday. In Acherensua. Entry in Jon's Ghana journal. Excerpt.

Acherensua is a small village but a fine secondary school. Vegetation is a little less thick + abundant here. We had [sic] a cook Mr. Opong who does cooking, laundry + sundry house chores. My fellow expatriates are John McClure, U. of Ill. physics, Irish Catholic from midwest, and Laurie [sic] Altrows, Magill B.A. chemistry, a Jewish French Canadian.

# LETTERS FROM GHANA

*View of the campus, Acherensua Secondary School, 1968-69.*

**September 9, 1968.** Monday. Entry in Jon's Ghana journal.

Spent nite in Kumasi. Had to ford flooded river in canoes. Risky and a cedi each. Stayed at Presidents hotel, went to dance club next door. Etc.

*This is the final entry in Jon's journal. Weekly letters to family and friends now take over from daily journal writing.*

**September 13, 1968.** Jon at the University of Ghana (at Legon, near Accra) to his parents and sister in Wilmington, Delaware. Excerpts.

... I will have my rooms in the administration bldg: a huge living room, a bedroom, private toilet and [cold] shower. [. . .] Though we have some comforts of home we are still very isolated.

I haven't heard any thing from the Draft board yet. I will be sworn in as a volunteer this afternoon. Peace Corps will notify my board to that effect.
[. . .]

I will not vote in the upcoming election. Neither candidate deserves a vote, at least my vote.

*Jon's draft board will reject his appeal of August 16, 1968 (see above) for Peace Corps deferment.*

*The "upcoming election" is the 1968 presidential contest between Hubert Humphrey, Democrat (who, as Vice President under President Lyndon Johnson, was seen as complicit in the administration's Vietnam policy) and Richard Nixon, Republican.*

**September 16, 1968.** [Monday]. Jon in Acherensua to his parents and sister in Wilmington, Delaware. Excerpts.

I have finally settled into my rooms which are very nice. Bugs are the only problem but the screens keep out the mosquitoes. I enjoyed getting your letters etc.
[. . .]
I use two [kerosene] lanterns after 10:00 when lights go out.
[. . .]
I would also like for my birthday subscriptions to Newsweek, Atlantic Monthly, and Encounter.
[. . .]
  I hope this film comes out. I told you [the] camera got super hot on this bus I rode on. Just pray. I'd like 2 copies made. You keep one + I'll keep [the] other. I'll go work on [the] tape now.
Love
Jon

P.S. tell me what's going on politically. What did you think of [the] Democratic convention + [the] police brutality. As I said I'm not voting!

*"I'll go work on [the] tape now." Jon is recording his first compact cassette tape to his parents and sister. He brought a portable cassette recorder to Ghana. His parents routinely send him cassette tapes and letters.*

*"Democratic convention." Police maced, tear-gassed, and beat protesters who refused to disperse at a rally near the Democratic National Convention in Chicago, August 28, 1968. Jon was already in Ghana at the time. Radical protesters taunted the police and threw rocks. Although Jon strongly objected to the police violence, he also disapproved of the radicals' provocations.*

**September 20, 1968 (date mailed).** Cassette tape transcription. From Jon in Acherensua to his parents in Wilmington, Delaware. Excerpt.

[Side One]:
Actually, everything is pretty nice here. [. . .] It's like the Garden of Eden. The food is plentiful and everybody waits on you and does everything for you.

*This excerpt is from the first of twelve extant compact cassette recordings that Jon sends his parents and sister.*

*In the tape Jon says Acherensua Secondary School is having trouble getting teachers because it is a "bush school." He asks his parents to send cassette recordings of T.V. commentaries on politics, which he plans to share with volunteers McClure and Altrows.*

**[September 20, 1968].** Friday. Jon in Acherensua to his parents and sister in Wilmington, Delaware. Excerpts.

Today McClure and I hitchhiked 2 miles into the bush to see Kofi EKURA, a village of less than 20 people. Thatched roofs, mud walls etc. If I am going to do any more hiking like this I'll need ① thick levies (not

sold here) ② heavy socks (to wear under leather boots I'm going to buy) ③ and a sheath knife, a heavy one to cut down bananas, kill boa constrictors etc.
[. . .]
(How are Judy's studies coming along) [. . .]

*Jon and McClure did not "hitchhike" to the village. They hiked there. The head of the village (or hamlet) is a fetish priest who specializes in exposing witches and counteracting witchcraft, etc. Jon is fascinated by the village and visits it several times. In the summer of 1969, he takes his father there. (See Cap Thiem to Ginny and Judy, July 26-31, 1969.)*

**September 24, 1968.** Tuesday. Jon in Acherensua to his parents in Wilmington. Excerpts.

Killed a Black Mamba snake (poisonous) in compound. (Send details later.)
[. . .]
How's Judy doing, etc. I have been working in library: stamping and classifying, etc. Everything is fine but anxious about draft.

*It was John McClure who killed the snake by throwing a large rock on it. The black mamba is the fastest snake in West Africa. It strikes at the head or face; the bite is usually fatal to humans. The snake in question came out from under the "Peace Corps" bungalow where John McClure and Lawrie Altrows had their rooms.*

*"anxious about draft": in a letter to his parents dated September 27, Jon continues to worry about his draft status. He writes, "Don't know what I'll do if they draft me. But I will refuse service, that is for sure."*

**Circa October 7, 1968 (date recorded).** Cassette tape transcription. Cap Thiem in Wilmington to Jon in Acherensua. Excerpts.

[Jon has re-recorded Side One (of the original recording) with Renaissance music and an oral reading of *The Canterbury Tales,* which is in the syllabus he is teaching.]
[Side Two]:
[TV newscasts. Walter Cronkite.]
[Much of Side Two Cap Thiem devotes to practical matters and logistics: the development of camera film, the sending of prints back to Acherensua, his plan to send Jon a knife and hiking boots, and so forth. In addition he asks a series of questions about Jon's perceptions of Ghanaian life]:

When you talk about African culture, what makes Africa look like Africa or different to you when you are over there?
[...]
Do you speak Twi when you are speaking with the natives, or do you speak English, or is it an option, and they like to talk in English? The language habits you use are very interesting to us.
[...]
Does the Peace Corps set-up that you have found yourself involved in differ from what you thought it would be? And does this difference improve or disprove [sic] your ability to function as you think a Peace Corps person should? Have you found fresh coconuts more delicious, or how do you find them?
[...]
How have you found the family life as you compare it against the United States? Have you run into polygamous families? What is the reaction? Are the men far superior? Do they overlord [sic] over the ladies? Where do the children fit into the family? How many meals do they [the people] eat a day?
[...]
I don't know if your mother is going to have time to say anything on this [tape] because I am definitely mailing it tomorrow morning.

# LETTERS FROM GHANA

*Side Two: This is the first tape Jon gets from his parents in Wilmington. Jon's mother does not speak on this recording. Jon will address most of Cap's questions in subsequent letters and tapes.*

**October 9, 1968 (date recorded).** Cassette tape transcription. Jon in Acherensua to his parents in Wilmington. Excerpts.

[Side One]:
Grandpa, if you're out in Wilmington now, I guess you won't get my letter until you go back to Cincinnati. But I hope you are doing well and everything, same with Don and Lu and all the kids, my cousins. Are they all married yet?

[Side Two]:
The Headmaster had trouble getting teachers this year. [. . .] School is supposed to have 30 teachers but we only have 22 or 23.

*"Grandpa" is Rudy Thiem. Don and Lula Thiem are Cap's younger brother and sister-in- law. The "kids" are Donna Lou, Hazel, Barbara, Tom, and Dave Thiem. Jon's question about his cousins getting married is facetious. Dave Thiem is six years old.*

**October 16, 1968.** "Letter A." Jon in Acherensua to his parents and sister in Wilmington.

Received your tape (#1) and thoroughly enjoyed listening to it. Received Judy's long letter + will respond to it soon. I've been very busy, too busy, and as a result, little time for writing. [. . .] Do send John Barth's Lost in the Funhouse (short stories, Doubleday Co. hardback) by airmail. I don't believe I'll have to pay duty on things.

Today received 2-D 2nd Dad letter about draft etc. I'm not worried. Split 3-1 decision is encouraging. Also received letter from Jim Kirk (P.C. Ghana director) informing me of cablegram from P.C. Washington about draft. I'll send letter to draft board this week using advice he gave me. [. . .] Peace Corps is giving me full support. I hope you are getting your shots for Africa etc., Dad.

Things have been hectic. Teaching is a really hard job. Really exhausting. The kids are really ill prepared for western techniques [of teaching]. Job in library (afternoon) is too much. Will probably have to drop it. The other 2 volunteers (McClure U.S. + Altrows Canadian) have pretty much decided to leave after 1 year here. I'm not that discouraged. I'll probably stick it out.

[. . .]

I'm going to mail a second letter with this

    See 2nd letter

*The Delaware state draft board rejects Jon's appeal for Peace Corps deferment, but because the decision is split, the case automatically moves up to a higher-level appeal board.*

*John Barth's* Lost in the Funhouse, *a collection of postmodern stories and fables, came out in 1968. Barth grew up on the Eastern Shore (the Delmarva peninsula) not far from Seaford, Delaware, Jon's hometown. An innovator in narrative technique, Barth is Jon's favorite American writer. His wit, irony, and sexual candor appealed to Jon.*

*"I hope you are getting your shots for Africa etc. . . . . .": Cap Thiem plans to visit Jon in the summer of 1969.*

*Jon decides to mail a second letter because the blue aerogram he is using doesn't have enough space.*

**October 16, 1968.** "Letter B." Jon in Acherensua to his parents and sister in Wilmington. Excerpts.

. . . I haven't been getting enough sleep. You need more in the tropics to avoid getting run down. I go to bed about 12:00 + get up at 6:00 A.M. Damn roosters don't let you sleep. The other two guys nap in the afternoon but my library job prevents that so I think I'll get rid of it. Besides I don't have much time to practice my Twi. Teaching is difficult. While the students are eager to learn, their notion of learning is memorization. [. . .] It's a real hassle getting them to argue about ideas etc. They're [their] English is poor + they don't feel comfortable over this. [. . .]

I really enjoyed the tape. The news was nice (not the sports, though). [. . .] Glad to hear Judy had a good weekend at Delaware. I enjoyed her letter from Oxford [Ohio].

**November 2 and 3, 1968 (dates recorded).** Cassette tape transcription. Jon in Acherensua to his parents in Wilmington. Excerpts.

[Side One, Nov. 2]:
We just heard today that Johnson stopped bombing North Vietnam, which sounds like a political move. Something may come of it, we hope. [. . .]
Everything is going well except for my triple catastrophe of sinus [infection], fall, and virus.

[Side Two, Nov. 3]:
[Answers to questions from his parents]:
You asked about Ghanaian music. Ghanaian music, well, you can't really say Ghanaian music because there are so many different tribes and every tribe has a different kind of music. There's Ewe music, Fante music, Ashanti music, Muslim music etc. Well, the music of the Ashantis and the Akan-speaking language groups tends to be High Life. This is the most characteristic kind of music and it's just like dance band music with its own peculiar beat. It is usually played by a dance band and is danced to. In many ways it doesn't seem to be very traditional.
[. . .]
About family life. Family life is very important. [. . .] Even though westernization has come in and begun to destroy it. Some facets of westernization even reinforce it, such as education. The family usually provides for the children to go to school, but once the son has gone to secondary school and begins teaching—this is usually a requirement, that he begin teaching—once he begins teaching, he is expected to give most of his salary back [to the family] . . . for the education of the small

children. Of course there have been many arguments if the system is good or not. (Some Ghanaians have broken off from the extended family.) And most people [teachers] think this [duty] is really burdensome on the teacher and that they should break away from the extended family. However, this would have serious consequences, because the family would lose its faith in education and come to think that the only thing education does for people is make them selfish. So you have even in the educational system reinforcement of the extended family. By extended family [I mean] . . . all the uncles, nephews, and nieces and everyone else. They often live in the same family compound . . . so the family gets to be quite large. [. . .] The mother does most of the work, just about everything. The father doesn't do that much. He doesn't do hardly anything except maybe work on the cocoa farm occasionally. [. . .]

There's quite a bit of polygamy here, but you usually only encounter it with wealthier people. This is because you cannot afford several wives if you are not wealthy. [. . .] Well, as an example, our Headmaster has two wives, one in Cape Coast and one here. As a matter of fact, he is in Cape Coast this weekend visiting his second wife. One wonders how this first wife feels about that.

[on students]:

They never seem to go off by themselves to read or do something like that. In a way this is very bad, because .. .. .. I think especially for the general development of the society, because it sort of stultifies personal ambition. Things are looked at in terms of the group rather than in terms of the individual. If the individual fails or is not a success, he can always rely on the tremendous security of his extended family and his circle of friends.

[. . .]

I like all the information you put in your letters, Mother. It's very interesting. I wish you'd write more often.

*Side One: "my triple catastrophe": Jon, McClure, and Altrows enjoyed sitting on the roof of the administration building and talking in the cool of the evening. At one point, Jon was climbing down from the roof. He slipped and fell hard onto the concrete terrace below, hurting his back. The virus referred to is probably a fever or a stomach infection. On this side of the tape, Jon acknowledges receipt of John Barth's* Lost in the Funhouse. *In addition, Jon thanks his parents for the "beautiful knife" they sent him (a Bowie knife with the name "Kofi Thiem" engraved on the blade). He carries it with him when he goes into "the bush" where it is useful for cutting open the pods growing on cocoa trees. The tart creamy gelatin surrounding the cocoa beans quenches the thirst.*

*Side Two: Here Jon answers questions Cap posed in his October 7th tape. Jon's responses reflect his experiences during the two months that he has lived in rural Ghana.*

*The popularity of High Life music was by no means restricted to Akan ethnic groups (as Jon implies here).*

*Two students and Jon examine a cocoa pod, near Acherensua, 1968.*

**November 9, 1968.** Jon in Acherensua to his parents and sister in Wilmington. Excerpts.

Sat afternoon I took off to Ada on [the] coast to visit Barry Caffee. [. . .] . . . we went swimming. It's a lot more treacherous there than in

Accra. A French Canadian girl almost drowned. That afternoon Barry + I decided to go to Akosombo, with the girls [Canadian and U.S. volunteers] to see the Volta River Dam and project[,] famous all over West Africa. It's a huge dam + will eventually supply power to all of Ghana + Togo and Dahomey [present-day Benin].
[. . .]
In your Xmas package I sent some Ghanaian brass (I think), art objects, and 3 yards of cloth (real African cloth that is the rage now in U.S.A.). It's enough to make 1 skirt and a blouse or shirt out of.

*This letter was written upon Jon's return to Acherensua, after short stays in Ada and Accra. A Peace Corps volunteer did in fact drown while swimming off the Ghanaian coast.*

**November 12, 17, 19, 1968 (dates recorded).** Cassette tape transcription. Jon's parents in Wilmington to Jon in Acherensua. Excerpts.

[Side Two]:
[Cap Thiem]: . . . I might say it seems like all I do in my spare time is make records, write letters, go to the post office, look for things for you or wrap packages. If you don't get home pretty soon, I'm going to be worn out.
[. . .]
[Cap Thiem, responding to Jon's discouragement with teaching]: You have the possibility of stimulating one or more minds to become educated and interested in their own country to the point where they could do some good.

*In other remarks on this tape, Cap expresses concern about Jon's back injury; explains that he has so far sent 19 small packages and boxes to Ghana (all but 6 of which have arrived at this point in time); wants to know more about a woman Peace Corps volunteer Jon visited in Kumasi; and urges Jon to send letters to his sister and Aunt Kaye.*

# LETTERS FROM GHANA

**Undated U.S. Parcel Post Customs Declaration.** List of items in a care package sent by Cap and Ginny Thiem to Jon in Acherensua. In Cap's handwriting.

| | |
|---|---|
| 14 Food tins | $9.08 |
| 2 Film | 2.50 |
| 1 Book | 2.45 |
| 1 Mag. | .25 |
| 1 Crackers | .25 |
| 1 [illegible] | 1.50 |
| Candy | .50 |

**November 21, 1968 (date recorded).** Cassette tape transcription. Jon in Acherensua to his parents in Wilmington. Excerpts.

[Side One]:
As I told you in my last letter, the Peace Corps bungalow, that's not my place but where McClure and Altrows live, was broken into and about 180 new cedis, or rather dollars, [worth] of goods were stolen including shirts, clothes and alarm clocks and watches, but most important McClure's radio was stolen, which is about our only real link with America during the week (and when we are not in Kumasi, or some place like that). And so we have not gotten very much news about what's going on, at all. And unfortunately the Ghanaian newspapers don't carry that much, so it is really exciting to get news [programs] from home . . . .
[. . .]
This is one of Ghana's problems: the fact that teachers spend all their time drinking palm wine rather than preparing lessons or improving themselves by reading or anything else. As a matter of fact, many of the teachers go to class only infrequently . . . .
[. . .]
Post office has been out of stamps and air letters for three days. This is a common occurrence. [. . .] We have to go to Tepa, which is forty minutes away [by lorry] to get our packages.
[. . .]

I just got Peace Corps to donate about a hundred books to the Acherensua library and I have been making up posters and things for the library. Right now, I don't know whether you know this or not, I am teaching first-year French, the equivalent of junior year English Language, and the equivalent of senior year English Literature which includes predominantly Shakespeare. Teaching is a rather frustrating thing. I am afraid that I am a little lacking in patience. [. . .] English language is a problem.

[. . .]

One of the surprising, fascinating and at the same time tragic things about this secondary school and about all secondary schools is the fact that most of the students here believe in this range of fantastic supernatural phenomena. They believe in ghosts, witches, demons, fetish priests, juju men. They believe in [invisible] dwarfs, in devils. [. . .] As a matter of fact, today in class, we had a class discussion of dwarfs, and it was just almost comic and absurd the way these naive people expressed their belief in this range of phenomena, which due to our scientific and secular consciousnesses, we tend to reject. Although, if one knows anything about the environment, it is very easy to see why these things are believed in. But I'm afraid that the fact that they still believe so strongly in this system makes them rather skeptical or almost uninterested in more secular explanations of the universe . . . or the social world or society. One gets the impression that they feel satisfied with the explanations they have. They feel satisfied to say that if they do badly it's because of a witch. Or they feel satisfied to say that people die because witches kill people. Etcetera. These are some of the interesting things that I have just lately begun getting into.

[. . .]

We're all kind of very excited about the moonshot, here. . . . one of the few things we can be proud of about America is the exploration of space.

[Side Two]:
McClure and myself have been doing quite a bit of practice in Twi. We're getting to be rather good, but it is still extremely difficult to understand the language at all. It's a language that is very much intoned,

or almost sung. And many of the words are just so easy to mispronounce, like *ankà*—you have to go up on the last syllable. That word means orange. Or like those birds we had last week to eat, *abromà,* you have to go up on the last syllable. Every phrase has its particular intonation . . . . Plus the verbs are more complex than we originally suspected because they change irregularly . . . even the simple present, simple future and simple past have weird variations on themselves.

[. . .]

[on the theft from the Peace Corps bungalow]:

We've offered a ten dollar reward to apprehend the criminal, and we're also planning some time this week to go to a fetish priest close to us and spread the word around that we're going to see a fetish priest, which may scare the person who did the crime. [. . .] Our houseboy Kofi was suspected. However, all three of us are fairly certain he didn't do it. He's only fourteen and unfortunately they put him in jail for a whole day and it was quite a traumatic experience for him. So we had to get him off that charge.

*Side One: There was no private radio at the school or in the village capable of accessing news programs from abroad.*

*"One of the surprising . . . and at the same time tragic things": Jon's dismay at students' belief in magic and witchcraft comes from the fact that those who attend secondary school belong to the educational elite of Ghana. Only a small portion of the Ghanaian population goes to secondary school, even fewer to university. Jon is disturbed that his students have these beliefs because he knows that many of them will go on to become teachers. He thinks teachers should be promoting a non-magical view of the world. A recent study by Gerrie ter Haar maintains that many Africans who are educated in Western science still believe in the spirit world and witchcraft (14). Haar makes the point that spiritual healing, which is inseparable from belief in a spirit world, is the core of African religion, whether traditional or Christian. At the same time, Haar examines the awful consequences of persecuting and killing alleged witches. His illuminating discussion focuses on the situation in Ghana (68-72). Particularly interesting is the fact that Ghanaian law, which is secular and tries to counteract the popular belief in witches,*

protects *those accused of being witches,* not *the supposed victims of witches. Other letters in which witchcraft is addressed: Jon to Mike, Jan. 11 and 28, 1969; McClure April 5, 1969; and Jon to Slotten, May 15, 1969.*

*The "dwarfs" or* mmoatia *of Asante mythology are mischievous beings who can make themselves invisible and who communicate with each other by whistling. Jon found them intriguing on several counts: belief in them was widespread, even among the school's faculty; the dwarfs are reminiscent of the fairies and elves in European folk tradition; and, finally, these imaginary beings may have been a mythologized Akan memory of a hunting-gathering people who inhabited the rain forest when the Akans first came into tropical West Africa. Jon later wrote a poem "The Ahafo Dwarf" incorporating some of the folk beliefs about these creatures. See Jon's letter to Slotten, April 30, 1970.*

*Side Two: "Kofi" is Kofi Ampofo. He eventually became the headmaster of a Junior Secondary School in Brong-Ahafo region. He and Jon still keep in touch. Although Jon is critical of Ghanaians' belief in magic and fetish priests, he himself is willing to exploit this belief to "scare" the thief who broke into the Peace Corps bungalow.*

**November 23, 1968.** Jon in Kumasi to his parents, sister and "guests" in Wilmington. Excerpt.

I'm standing in the big Kumasi Post Office writing this. I came here alone yesterday. McClure's at home and Altrows is on a Geography trip.

Kumasi is one of the best cities I've ever been in. It's big (≈180,000) but the people are extremely friendly and accom[m]odating. Last nite I stayed at the Midland "Hotel." Price 2 cedis. With a breakfast (cold egg sandwich + coffee) thrown in. It is less a hotel than a big family compound typical of towns and cities . . . . There is a bar attached. In the bar last nite I met a building engineer who spent 2 years in Russia under Nkrumah [i.e. during the period of Kwame Nkrumah's rule in Ghana] and then became disgusted. He was then put under Preventive Detention by Nkrumah. He was very pleased because I was teaching in Ghana and even spoke some TWI. So pleased in fact [that] he gave me 2 cedis which he wouldn't let me refuse. This morning I bought about $30 worth of canned food (the purpose of this trip). It's about 9 AM now. Next I'm going to the Kumasi Zoo and Kumasi Cultural Center. I'll leave tomorrow. I'll probably go to a dance tonite.

*The volunteers in Acherensua make periodic trips to Kumasi (a three to four-hour journey by "mammy wagon") to get provisions, mainly canned meat.*

**November 24, 1968.** Jon in Acherensua to Ralph and Martha Slotten in Carlisle, Pennsylvania. Excerpts.

Dear Dr. and Mrs. Slotten,
    Greetings from West Africa!
    Akwaaba!
    It was a great pleasure to receive your letter about India and your other amazing travels and travails. I have reread it many times since my arrival in Ghana. I have delayed writing to you so as to make sure of my impressions of Africa and to let myself reflect upon them. It is one of the more impossible things to try and recreate the range of my experiences here (and in training in N.Y.C.).
[. . .]
Living in Ghana has reinforced my preference for the tribal over the secular. I found the best part of the training program to be "language immersion." [. . .] When I arrived in Accra I took the F.S.I. language test and got a two rating. Only one other person in the group of 50 got this rating. Despite these successes I find it very difficult to speak and understand Twi. While the grammar and level of abstraction in the Akan languages (Ashanti Twi, Fante, and Akuapem Twi) are wondrously crude, the pronounciation [sic] is delicate, even fragile. Twi is a language to be intoned rather than spoken. There are for example nearly a dozen words spelled kɔkɔ (open o hard k) but each has a varied meaning depending on pitch and accent. Slowly I'm improving. Ghanaians find it difficult to believe that any non-Ghanaian can speak any Twi. So at least the effort is ego rewarding. [. . .]

My first and most profound taste of Akan culture began in Kibi . . . during what the Peace Corps calls a "village live in." For two weeks all I did was speak . . . Twi and participate in the semi-traditional life routines. [. . .] Life revolves around the family compound and [outdoor] kitchen. The men do little work (thank God) but do alot of eating and playing (traditional games like OWARE). Much time is spent visiting and being visited and repeating the Twi formulaes [sic] (greetings and goodbyes) that attend these occasions. The palm wine (nsafoɔ) bar is always an obligatory stop. The friendliness and sociability of the Akans is both breathtaking and tiresome. The rituals become formulas and the substance rarely diverges from the relatives or the weather. I find that being a student-celebrant of Ghanaian culture is more interesting than being either a pure student or a pure celebrant or participant. There is a great burden of para ritualistic social routine that the spectre of westernism will not be able to lift. There is unimaginable tedium —the doing of what has been done already and only that. The Ghanaian (Twi) word for history is ABAKOSEM or literally something like—the word that has been and comes back to us again. Or more chicly [sic]—the word that comes and goes.

So far, I have really enjoyed living in Ghana. At times my reaction tends to be dialectical. It is exasperating for an anti-hero or alienated westerner to live in such a healthy sociable society. There is not the intense fanatical individualism or aloneness or alienation. Alienation is loneliness but it is also privacy. And privacy is something lacking in these cultures. If I were to fulfill all of my Ghanaian social obligations I would have little time for anything else. Most Ghanaians have little time for anything else. Acherensua is a very bush town (no beer). I have to restrain myself socially to avoid what might be putting my iron into too many fires, here. One of the joys of travelling is being able to participate fully with those around you because you are in a strange village and will not need to become trapped in the social labyrinth.

Often times I've said to myself, "If only Slotten could be here." Ghanaian or Akan religion cannot be separated from the social life. It is in the everyday work and leisure contacts of the people that the traditionalism shows itself strongest. Even so no one or almost no one describes himself as being a pure traditonalist. Almost everyone is either Christian or Muslim. But Christianity, at least, is only relatively superficial. Still a Sunday affair. It is the ancestors, spirits and the witches (or sometimes dwarfs) that really make things happen. While ancestor worship is important the average Akan tends to view the forces around him as being witch inspired. Witchcraft is as much a fact of life in Ghana as electricity is in the west. Everyone believes. Even I'm afraid of Them. (My cook tells me that Ghanaian witches eat children and murder, but that the white man's witches make Benz buses and wireless radios.)

My attitude toward tribal culture is ambivalent. The boredom, disease and ignorance are difficult to ignore. My impatience with these problems is both ideological and personal. Yet I have been saved from being overcome by these problems by a fascination with their sources in religion. In Akan society alone we find: missionary Christianity, the prophetic or spiritualist churches, West African Islam, anti-witchcraft shrines, ancestor worship, and witchcraft. I've been reading everything I can get on Akan history and religion. [. . .]

There is a good deal of cultural tension between the para-Christian Ashantis and the Muslims (KRAMÓFO). The latter are segregated in ghettoes [sic] called Zongos and are sometimes called Zongofo (people). They wear neither traditional robes (eg. KENTE robes) nor western dress but use the smock and cap. Since they do not own cocoa or food farms they are given the most menial (i.e. degrading) tasks. They are snubbed, mocked[,] but are still tenacious of Allah. Few have the money to be Al Hajj. The "mosques" of their Zongos are pitiful and sufficient, housed in squalid mudbrick buildings[,] small and undecorated. The "prayer rugs" they use are sheep skins or a kind of straw mat with an image of the Ka'ba's mosque on it. You should be getting one of these West African straw prayer mats in the mail in the next month or two. It is by way of a Christmas present to you. The fact that this Christmas gift is a Muslim artifact places it in some sort of history-of-religions tradition, I hope. [. . .] These Muslims really fascinate me. They are an exotic form to a culture that is in my eyes exotic. Most Akans fear and recognize the Muslims as having occult powers. The anti witch shrines of the AKANS import all sorts of spurious "KRAMOFO" fetish spirits and charms (at great expense) from the more Islamic north. I wish I had more time to study some of these hierophanies and mock hierophanies in greater depth. [. . .]

[. . .]

Congratulations! on your new teaching position at U. of Penn. grad school! [. . .] I feel at a loss to predict my own academic plans. I'm tempted to go into an African Area Studies program. But even all of Africa seems like a limitation. I was given provisional acceptance at Columbia's Teachers' College where I could specialize in African studies. A lot of ex Peace Corps volunteers do that. But the education courses I'd have to take scare me. My return to academia is about two years away (a long time). After this stimulating experience in Africa I'm afraid I'll be bored more than ever with the tedious formalities of academic life. [. . .] In spite of this problem I'm certain I'll return to the academic whirl. I cannot conceive of any profession more exciting or rewarding. Your own study travels[,] accomplished and impending[,] to India, Athens, Jerusalem and I hope West Africa persuade me of this. [. . .]

Now I have to light my lanterns and prepare tomorrow's lessons (French I[,] English Language 4 and Shakespeare). I get the feeling that I am getting more out of Ghana than Ghana is getting out of me.

Until I hear from you again NYAME SHIRA WƆ or God bless you. NYA means get and AME satisfied. NYAME is the creator god who gives all that is needed for satisfaction. To Him no prayers are offered or sacrifices made. Even so He has given and He blesses.

*This is Jon's reply to Ralph Slotten's letter of August 25, 1968. The full-length reply is fourteen pages long. This letter reflects the romantic phase of Jon's engagement with Ghanaian society, and yet hints at a transition to the second stage, disillusionment. The letter is a summation of Jon's developing views, for which Slotten is an important sounding board.*

*"FSI" stands for Foreign Service Institute—the ratings of the FSI exam range from 0 to 5.*

*"It is exasperating for an anti-hero or alienated westerner to live in such a healthy sociable society." Jon thinks of himself as an "anti-hero,"*

*a figure representing in his mind the modern opposite of the traditional hero. For Jon the anti-hero embodies the adventurous side of the alienated individual. Jon's use of terms like* hero *and* anti-hero *when thinking about himself (and others) owes much to his undergraduate studies in literature and history of religions. He is keen on trying to apply the concepts he has learned in college to the complex conditions he observes in Ghana and to his reactions to them.*

*"My cook tells me . . . ." The cook (Mr. Opong) cooks for the three foreign volunteers in Acherensua. (About the cook—see the last part of the following letter written by John McClure on Dec. 10, 1968.) Beer was in fact obtainable in the town of Acherensua, though not perhaps when this letter was written.*

*Al Hajj is the designation of a Muslim who has made the pilgrimage to Mecca. "Aralen" is an anti-malaria drug.*

**December 10, 1968.** John McClure, Peace Corps volunteer in Acherensua, to relatives in Massachusetts. Excerpts.

I've just read about five books on history and customs of West Africa and become quite interested in historic Timbuktu. I would love to see that article you mentioned. Anyway, Jon and I planned to try to go there over Christmas but we just received word from PC [Peace Corps] not to [go] there because of the recent coup. We are so isolated that I hardly know anything about it.
[. . .]

I must have mentioned the Thanksgiving lamb feast that we had. By telling the chief [of Acherenesua], whose palm we greased with a Timex watch when we came, that Thanksgiving was a big holiday[,] we conned him into giving us a lamb. Delicious. We also feasted a couple days ago on another African delicacy—bat. We have a friend in Goaso, not far from here, where they periodically shoot elephant and we are expecting some nice juicy trunk or ear steaks from him.
[. . .]

We just had a set-to with our cook after finding that we are paying him an outrageous sum. We cut his salary and are saving the balance for secondary school fees for the cook's nephew who mainly does all the work around anyway. The boy is a very good, likeable guy and he wouldn't be able to start school without the money. I wish we hadn't got involved with a cook in the first place. It makes me feel like too much of a colonialist. At least we are supporting him and his family.

*The three volunteers would rather have prepared meals for themselves, but it was not possible to let the cook go without causing a local diplomatic crisis. The cook's nephew is Kofi Ampofo; he is the one who had been (falsely) suspected by the police of having stolen McClure's radio.*

**December 10, 1968.** Jon in Acherensua to his parents. Excerpt.

Last weekend we went (McClure and I) to Goaso to visit Tom (Peace Corps) and Sandy (post Ph.D. work—from Scotland) who live there. We went to a traditional Ghanaian funeral and wore robes. All this is in the [35 mm] film.
[...]
I have a sore throat. I may go to the Doctor [in Hwidiem] this afternoon. None of us seems to stay well very long. Altrows has the clap and McClure has a severe crotch rot.

Haven't got any mail in about a week except Xmas packages from Kaye (pre-recorded tape of Bobbie Gentry, very nice) and Judy (toys with which I can play Santa Claus).

*Goaso is an important town in the Brong-Ahafo region, about eighteen miles southwest of Acherensua. In Hwidiem, about seven miles down the road from Acherensua, there is a Roman Catholic hospital. Although the hospital building was rather basic, the physician and two nurses, all from the Netherlands, were first-rate. Private hospitals, such as the one at Hwidiem, were as a rule superior to the public hospitals.*

**December 17, 1968.** Jon in Acherensua to Mike Moynihan, c/o Mr. and Mrs. E. J. Moynihan, Nanticoke Circle, Seaford, Delaware. Written on a

Ghanaian Christmas notecard—on the front of which is a photo of the Okyenhene in full regalia.

Dear Mike,
I hope you haven't despaired yet of hearing from me.
[. . .]
Get Barth's Lost in the Funhouse. What are you doing next year. Why don't you come to Ghana? It's great here. Nyame schira woo. That's Twi for god bless you. Further correspondence is imminent. Love Jon

*This note is Jon's first mailing from Ghana to Mike Moynihan. They grew up across the street from each other. Mike is a student at Michigan State University.*

*Like Jon, Mike was an avid reader of John Barth, especially the early novels* The Floating Opera *(1956), and* The Sotweed Factor *(1960), both set on the Delmarva peninsula.*

**December 24, 1968.** Jon to his parents and sister in Wilmington. From Tamale, Northern Region, Ghana.

Christmas greetings! McClure and I arrived in Tamale late last evening. Look on your Ghanaian map and you'll see the road (thru Kintampo, Dawadawa, and Fufulsu). We had to wait in Kumasi Lorry park 4 hours. The essential trip took 7 hours. This was in a completely open lorry over wholly dirt roads. We breathed dust the whole way. This is the season of the Harmattan (the hot dry wind that blows off the Sahara, cold at night). Savanna terrain is quite different, sandy, real bushes, no jungle, scattered trees. Everywhere one sees the fires of the farmers. It's a cut and burn agriculture whereby the farmer burns the bush [brush] + plows it under thereby replenishing the savanna's soils. You see a lot of cattle and corn. This is Ghana's equivalent of the midwest. Indeed, some of it looks like prairie. The wide open spaces are really refreshing after the tightness of the jungle. In the jungle Twi is the Lingua Franca but here due to so many tribes English or Hausa is more common. Most of the people are Muslims. There is a Catholic Church here, so we'll probably go there since McClure is an ex-Roman Catholic. The service is in English.

Last nite we crossed the Black Volta (see map) where we had delicious fresh fish and fried yams. This morning we went out to Tamale Secondary School and met a Canadian + his family + had rum + coke. He is a teacher + set up quite nicely here. Then we went to the market and priced shirts (Muslim shirts etc). I also went to a photographer to get some visa photos for an Ivory Coast visa.

Since tonite is Xmas eve I don't know what we'll do. It's just not like Xmas here. Two Xmases ago I was in Russia and now in the heart of West Africa. Strange, eh? If I spend another year here, that'll be 3 out of 4 Christmases away from home.

Tomorrow after Church we may go out to a savanna village to get some pictures. I imagine I'll be going thru at least 2 or 3 rolls of colored film. I've also loaned McClure 2 rolls which he'll get his parents to replenish for me. So far we've been having a pretty good time. McClure + I often talk about our respective families + Xmas and all that. We'll be thinking about you in the savanna bush as you sit around the old Xmas tree. You'll probably get this after New Year's so happy New Year,
Love Jon
P.S. send me alot of pictures and articles + scientific stuff on the moon shot!

*Foiled in their plan to go to Timbuktu (in Mali) by political events, Jon and McClure have undertaken an extended trip during their Christmas break via lorry and train, through northern Ghana, Upper Volta (now Burkina Faso), and Ivory Coast (Côte d'Ivoire).*

*The "moon shot" is the Apollo 8 mission, launched on December 21st. The astronauts orbited the moon, but did not land on it.*

# LETTERS FROM GHANA

*Two Muslim boys, Tamale, Northern Region, Ghana, December 1968.*

**December 31, 1968.** Jon in the city of Ouagadougou, Upper Volta, to his parents, Judy, and Aunt Cora in Wilmington.

Happy New Years from Ougadougou [Ouagadougou]. French [speaking] Africa is quite different from such former British colonies as Ghana. I've been practising my French a lot. The food here is delicious and cheap, especially meat (1/2 chicken, a sizable shishkabab, a huge salad, bread and 1/2 bottle of wine for $.80)! There is also French coffee. And French pastries. In a way it resembles Paris. Day after tomorrow we leave for Ivory Coast, then after six days → Accra. McClure and I are still miraculously healthy and in good spirits. (We just got our Ivory Coast visas and changed some travellers cheques, unfortunately this trip is costly, the train from Ougadougou [sic] to Abidjan is about $25.) Don't know what we'll do for New Year's eve tonite. I guess eat alot.

*Five months' spent living in a rainforest village have reshaped Jon's perceptions to such an extent that he can now compare Ouagadougou to Paris (a city he visited as a student in Europe, 1966-67).*

# LETTERS FROM GHANA

**January 11, 1969.** Jon in Acherensua to his parents, his Aunt Cora, and Judy in Wilmington. Excerpts.

I've been getting Newsweek and for the first time Atlantic Monthley [sic] so please continue them. I also got your privately mailed Newsweeks.
[. . .]
Mother, I hope you cut out all of the propaganda about how wonderful it is that I joined the Peace Corps. I'm getting more out of Africa than I can give it. I got a nice little note from Mrs. Moynihan. Wrote Mike a 16-page letter (enjoyed his tape stammerings) but don't have his address. [. . .] Trying to persuade him to join the Peace Corps. You all sound like you have set up a second home for him there. That's good. I miss Mike.
[. . .]
I'll be anxious to hear about your African history course, Judy.
[. . .]
I'm still as excited about climbing Kilimanjaro as ever.
[. . .]
How was your party at the Sours. What's the full deal on Mr. Moynihan? Are they moving? It was nice to hear about Kim's adventures. Sometime I'll get around to writing him. I got Kaye's tape + enjoy[ed] it alot. Also sent Kaye + Marv. a New Year's card.

Before Xmas I got [a] nice card and note from McLaughlins. Tell them thanks + . . . would like to write but little time. Also thank Marge Smith etc for her thoughtful card + note, and tell Margaret and Johnny I think of them often and was just telling a friend about Kennett + [the] nice people there. Time To Prepare Lessons,

*This letter contains the kind of material that has been edited out of most of the other letters included in this collection: i.e. reports on notes and news from friends and relatives.*

*"Kilimanjaro": Jon and his father Cap have discussed the possibility of climbing Africa's highest mountain, during their upcoming trip to East Africa in the "summer" of 1969.*

# LETTERS FROM GHANA

*"Kim" is Jon's cousin Kim Markert; he is in the Navy. Kaye and Marv are his parents.*

**January 11 and January 28, 1969.** Jon in Acherensua to Mike Moynihan, 108 Fee Hall, Michigan State University, East Lansing, Michigan. The main letter, sixteen pages long, is dated January 11, 1969. A one-page "Preface" is dated January 28, when the letter was evidently sent. Enclosed in the letter is a snapshot of Jon sitting in front of a fire he built at night while waiting for a ferry to take him and McClure from Ivory Coast into Ghana. Excerpts.

Preface
[. . .]
I've been messin [sic] around trying to sing folk songs, McClure and Altrows (the other two expatriots [sic] here) are both learning the guitar; neither can sing. My imperfect singing complements their primitive pickings. Anyway they've got these songbooks with such old favorites as "It's hard ain't it hard," "Hard Travellin," "Richard McCorley" (goes to die etc), "Drill ye Tarriers," "Midnight Special," "St. James Infirmary." Needless to say the virgin folk[s]iness of my renditions are contaminated with a Limeliterish gusto.
Jon

Dear Michael,

Ramadan the month of the Muslims' fast ended a couple of weeks ago with a feast. Harmattan, the hot dry wind the [that] comes across the Sahara and dessicates the rain forest has just begun. Now [that] the new year is in, the vacation is over. Tomorrow I go back to teaching. I've decided I don't like teaching. [. . .] I'm up at 7, teach intermittently til one in the afternoon and have [the] afternoon and evening thundershowers to myself.
[. . .]
Out here in the bush in the rainforest things are still witchy. [. . .] We don't get much meat to eat. But lots of fruit and yams, sometimes wild

birds and bats. [. . .] My room here is better than any college pad or dorm I ever ruined.

I was hotshit in P.C. training but after the fire and the anger, came finally apathy + adjustment. I guess I'm a shitty volunteer. Lazy, ineffectual, over intellectual. I just sort of get on and am not unhappy. While I despise the educational system + incompetence etc. I like many of the ways and ideas of African culture. Reading is what I like most to do . . . and I have time, thank god for that, to burn. A lot of low keyed drinking and fucking makes existence well nigh paradisicall [sic]. That and self pity and nostalgia. By god after next year I'll have spent 3 out of the last 4 years out of the U.S. and I really don't mind. When I do return I'll go back to the university, which is the only place adequate to my genre of laziness and literariness.

Three things [that] I have somehow gotten out of the habit of doing are being such a sexploitationist, a pot head, and a political thinker. [. . .]

For the glorious privilege of voting the first time, I didn't. I could no longer pretend to be a a radical after I joined the Peace Corps. Kennedy's death, McCarthy's defeat and apostasy, Humphrey's shittiness and Nixon's election combined to screw any idealism and radicalism I once had. Politics is only boring now. It's even worse in Africa (political digression: there is no hope for African development, contrary to what anybody says and most intelligent Africans know this).

The disappearance of these excesses, I guess, puts me closer to Moynihanism, whatever that is. By the way, on my Xmas jaunt I met this Irish contract teacher (Ghana) who is from Dublin and who teaches English. [. . .] Kiss my ass in Gaelic is "Pog Mo Thon" [sic] pronounced Pōg Mō Hŏn. I've also picked up a lot of the local language TWI. [. . .]

You said in the tape you might want to join the Peace Corps. It's a good, almost absurdly easy, option to the draft. You can quit after a year or actually any time you want. Teaching is an annoyance but it's only 4 hours a day, rest is free time. Studying the local culture is interesting. Traveling is great: I spent 3 weeks [vacation] Xmas, get 3 weeks Easter, and a coupla months in the summer. The only problems are heat + food. I don't mind the heat and I've gotten used to the food.

# LETTERS FROM GHANA

[. . .]
Anyway I am glad I joined. I found out I don't like secondary school teaching, at least. Even though Peace Corps isn't doing much to help Africa, it does a lot to educate Americans about this weird place.
[. . .]

I really hate writing. Too much effort. All activity is worthless. Some day I won't write you a decent letter. I hate to say it but nobody's ever going to collect our correspondence except maybe ourselves. I've decided definitely not to get married, so even now I won't have no kids [sic] to read these letters or yours or wash the pretty African stamps off for a collection. Shit, I think my I.Q. has really dropped since I've been here. You meet other guys who've been here a year and they can bearly [barely] speak English. A lot of us just sort of deliquisce [deliquesce] (where did I get that word? an occasional dike in the flood [of] stupidity).

Letter writing is so inferior just to sitting around having a beer or going for a ride in the [Austin] Healy. How's it doing by the way? Me + the other two guys here . . . . We get along pretty well. [. . .] McClure is an ex Roman Catholic Irish guy, B.S. physics, who worked for I.B.M. for 2 years (he even has a patent). He really hated it, even though he raked in the money. He's going back for graduate work. [. . .] Altrows is a Jewish Canadian, went to Magill in Chemistry (BSc) but [is] going to go thru undergraduate [school] again in sociology. Luckily we are all pretty brainy and are becoming imbeciles at about the same rate. McClure is 25, Altrows 21. We're like 3 humans on the moon—Afronauts.

That moon thing is really cool. [. . .] One kid in class said he was afraid if we landed on [the] moon it would be too heavy and fall on Acherensua.

It is kind of lonely. We Three out here. An incredible view of America.
[. . .]

News from America is late, slow, sometimes never. Our only good radio was stolen. If you join, you'd better forget about sports.

One guy out here, Peace Corp[s], two hours down [the] road has gone insane. He's gone into [the] bush. He went mad . . . . Like Conrad's <u>Heart of Darkness</u>. He's gone into the bush to torture himself and to become a "palm wine drinkard."

The cities aren't bad. There are a lot of other whites. Movies, night clubs, western food, educated Ghanaians.
[. . .]
People talk about culture shock. There's a hell of a lot when you're stationed in the bush.
I came hoping to groove to the traditional and tribal things. Utter romanticism.[. . .] But the people are friendly.
[. . .]
Recently a Ghana[a]ian teacher was found out by his wife to be fuckin a girl in town. Solution? Headmaster adjudicates. Awards wife equivalent of $5.00. Ever[y]body goes away happy.
[. . .]
The senior house master (#3 administrator) told me if I went to Nzima on [the] coast I could give a child a penny and it would fly. They all believe in this nonsense. Who cares if somebody goes to the moon. Africa is the moon. Witches, dwarfs, tree devils, magic, ghosts, gods, God, possessed children. ([The] Gym teacher says Indians are [the] best athletes because they use magic in track and field events). In the north of Ghana parents mutilate their kids' faces by scarring. Here the[y] only give them 2 1/2 scars on the cheeks. They compare it to vaccination.
[. . .]
If this damn draft situation would clear up I might quit [Peace Corps] after a year. Both McClure and Altrows are doing that. Altrows who is a Canadian and McClure who is 1Y have no draft problems. Are you graduating in English Lit?
[. . .]
I'm damned afraid that once I get back to America I'm going to get the itch to wander off again. Jesus, I have no direction. My parents are going to be pissed when I never get married and when I end up being just a kind of literati bum. All these fucking people keep blabbering about all these honors + shit and never give me a moment's peace in pleasurable mediocrity. God almighty, the pressure they put on you. Like Peace Corps, and now I'm a complete failure as far as I am concerned.
. . . I was thinking you and me ought to buy a jeep once this draft, peace corps, university shit ends and take off on our planned, ever delayed trip

across the U.S. Sling a boat on top (aluminum 14 ft. with 25 H.P. motor). I've been to Russia, Africa, Europe and Mexico but never to California, Montana or Western Canada. One thing I've decided I like better than anything is just moving and travelling, seeing strange cities.
[...]
Pog Mo Thon
Yours
Jon

*The tone of this letter registers the onset of Jon's disillusionment with his work and with Asante culture. This is phase two of the four successive mindsets that characterize his evolving experience of life in Ghana: romanticism, disillusionment, reconnection, and fatigue. See the Introduction "Splendors and Miseries."*

*Especially in the letters to Mike Moynihan (the arch-skeptic and nay-sayer), Jon flaunts a mordant view of the world—a view that owes a good deal to his favorite writers, especially John Barth and Vladimir Nabokov. The letters to his parents and Slotten, on the other hand, are less cynical and sometimes quite cheerful.*

*Preface (January 28):*

*The "old favorites" that Jon lists are songs he and Mike listened to on LPs—songs performed by the Limeliters, the Clancy Brothers and other groups.*

*Main body of the letter (January 11):*

*"Kennedy's death" refers to the assassination of Senator Robert Kennedy on June 6, 1968. Kennedy was poised to win the Democratic presidential nomination. He had come to oppose the Vietnam War.*

*"He's gone into the bush to torture himself and to become a 'palm wine drinkard.'" "palm wine drinkard" alludes to the title of a Nigerian novel Jon greatly admired:* The Palm Wine Drinkard *written by Amos Tutuola and published in 1952.*

*McClure and Altrows, who are frustrated by tropical heat, the teaching situation, and the school administration, have decided to leave Ghana at the end of their first year. Jon intends to continue.*

# LETTERS FROM GHANA

**January 22, 1969.** Jon in Acherensua to his parents in Wilmington, and to his sister Judy.

I have greatly enjoyed reading all of the letters I've gotten from the family recently. [. . .] I'm sorry I haven't written more lately but with the heat and everything I just keep putting it off. My tape recorder has also quit recording on me. That is, it doesn't erase already-recorded-tapes.

We are all depressed now that we are back in old Acherensua with the heat, the boredom and the monotonous diet. This semester I like teaching a little better but I've run into some other problems. First of all, Peace Corp[s] found out about McClure + I absenting ourselves over Xmas . . . . [. . .] So they sent up an official . . . to reprimand us for not telling them we were out of the country. They didn't particularly care that we left, only that we didn't tell them.

Then all 3 (Altrows, McClure and myself) . . . missed the term's first staff meeting by 3 hours, because we got in too late. Par consequence the headmaster blew his stack.

Just recently he blew his stack at me alone because I refused to teach 4th form Shakespeare without any books. Whereupon I rather frankly told him I thought it absurd to teach without books. We got in a big argument. I'm supposed to get a letter from him soon. He may have fired me. Temperamental Africans!

Anyway it's been rough going this last week for all of us and we sort of wonder what we are doing here, in the first place. I guess we can weather it out unless we all get kicked out for our gay and adventuresome spirits. But I at least am not worried and will accept whatever happens. McClure and Altrows are both leaving after this year which would leave me here alone, friendless. Actually, it is surprising how well we get along together. Same interests etc. We've all started eating our lunches in the student cafeteria since the food there is better than the food our cook makes. Altrows and I have been studying French in our spare time (and me a little Latin), and reading lots of other things to while away the hours.

*Lawrie Altrows, Canadian volunteer, with the staff of* The Achiscodian Times, *1968-69'; Courtesy of Lawrence Altrows.*

[. . .]

<u>2nd story</u> Then on the way back to the dorm I heard a commotion of students. Near the compound barrier I met a couple of masters. Their story was this: while in town the school typist heard someone was seducing his wife. He informed the above mentioned masters who promptly staked out the unfortunate typist's house to apprehend the culprit. Mr. O.P. peaked [sic] thru a window and witnessed the alleged act whereupon the culprit sensing a witness fled the house in the direction of the school. All of the students were let out of the dorms to facilitate the evil seducer's capture. Finally, Mr. B tackled the fellow and gave him a good drubbing. There will be a public trial soon, wherein the lecher will pay the affronted husband 2 cedis. After that all the parties will go away pleased.

This is somewhat representative of Ghana's plights and delights.

We were all amused.

I've got so many letters to write. Please send Mike's address so I can send him his letter. I've got another package at Tepa (where we have to pick up our packages). I think it's food. By the way the food was very good, especially the steaks and anchovies. We all shared it. I think the cost [of sending it] is too much. I can buy more or less the same thing in Kumasi but I am just too stingy. [. . .]

By the way, I got an interesting letter from Kim about his travels etc. [. . .]

I'm looking forward to your coming over, Dad. Everything seems pretty definite as it stands, unless I get fired. But then you could come over a little early. Old Mt. Kilimanjaro doesn't know what it is in for.

So far I don't need too much from you all except mail. Maybe next letter I'll send some titles of some more books, since my library is getting exhausted as far as novelty goes.

Say hi to my fan club back in the States and tell em I'm glad I'm here or else I don't know what they'd talk about. [. . .]

". . . I refused to teach 4th form Shakespeare without any books." *Many faculty members in the school were convinced that the Headmaster had pocketed the funds earmarked for the purchase of textbooks in several courses.*

". . . *my library is getting exhausted*": *Peace Corps supplied each volunteer a big box of paperbacks—high quality fiction and non-fiction. Besides receiving books from his parents and from his former professor Fred Hartshorn, Jon also bought books at the University of Ghana bookstore in Legon.*

**Early February 1969 (recorded).** Cassette tape transcription. Jon in Acherensua to his parents, who are in the process of moving from Wilmington, Delaware, to Chattanooga, Tennessee, where Cap Thiem has been transferred. Excerpts.

[Side One]:
[sounds of traditional drumming and music]:
That music you hear in the background is the music of a funeral which we just attended. I borrowed a tape from Lawrie Altrows, a brand new tape which doesn't have anything on it, and I decided to record it. Right now I am walking through the town . . . . On the second side [of the cassette] you'll hear a lot of music, drum music, music of this kind of

metal object which sounds like bells, and then stick music and dancing and singing.
[. . .]
[Jon records a conversation in Asante Twi he has with someone he meets in the street and tells the man to speak into the cassette recorder: "ka, ka" "speak, speak." McClure and Altrows who are with him also speak at this point.]
[. . .]
I feel like a news reporter walking through the city talking into this microphone. [. . .] All around me people are looking at me talking into this mike, standing in the middle of this street. They must think I'm really insane—of course I probably am. [. . .] Here come two teachers right now. I'll greet them. They are in [traditional] robes and I think they went to the funeral. [Jon speaks with them at some length in Asante].
[. . .]
Now I'm walking down the main street of the town. There's not much here, there are fires and smoke going up in the air, and cooking pots. To our right is the market. [. . .] There are a few women selling smoked fish out in the market. [. . .] To my right is a little stand next to the market. There are several Muslims there selling cloth. They don't do much but sit there all day, all night. They don't drink, they don't smoke, they don't go dancing.
[. . .]
Here is some good music. We'll record some of this right now. This is at a local akpeteshie bar. [Jon now tapes some of the recorded music playing in the bar.] [. . .] That's Miriam Makeba. [. . .] [Jon and Lawrie speak some French with a man from the neighboring country of Togo. Then more conversation in Asante] O.K. There was an interesting phenomenon. There was a French speaking man from Togo, and Lawrie and I were just talking to him, plus another Ashanti came up and said rather belligerently that he was going to visit me at my house tomorrow, and I rather diplomatically said, OK, you can come to visit me. I don't think he will, but he may. I hope he doesn't.
[. . .]

We are now entering the beer bar which is on the opposite side of town. I hope you have your tape recorder fixed by the time you get this, so you can listen to it and enjoy it. [Lawrie says]: Why don't you ask them to send me the tape after . . . they're finished with it. [. . .][Jon]: Lawrie likes this tape so much . . . that he wants you to send it back here. [Lawrie]: No, no, to my parents in Montreal.
[. . .]
Now we're getting into the beer bar here. And as you see, the noise increases. [. . .] [Ghanaian man's voice]: Hello Jon. [Jon]: Hey, how you doing. [. . .] Wo hoi ye. [Jon converses with the man in Asante.] [Jon tapes the recorded music playing in the beer bar.] This is typical Ghanaian music, known as High Life . . . . [. . .] The bar tender just told me we . . . got the last two beers in the beer bar.
[. . .]
[Jon to a woman]: Ka [speak], ka [speak]. [Woman's voice exclaims]: Eieeee. [She converses with Jon in Asante. He explains to her she is speaking into a tape recorder. She cries out again]: Aaaahh, Kofi! [laughter and more conversation in Asante, and several women chant a song, and more conversation, and Jon flirts with the first woman.] [. . .] O.K. I was just talking to some of the local girls in the bar here. And we were just talking to them and just making small talk. And I was asking them to try and sing something, but they didn't feel like singing. I told one of them I loved her and she was kind of shocked at that, so then I just told her that I kind of liked her, and she liked that better. She happens to be one of the girl friends of one of the teachers here in the college [secondary school]. [. . .] I just took a picture with a Ghanaian girl. Rather McClure took a picture of me with the microphone and the tape recorder going. I had my arm around her. She is the friend, the girl friend, of this teacher, the Bible master in the secondary school, who is also married by the way. We call that, we call her his *alomo*, his girl friend.
[. . .]

*On this tape Jon begins to experiment with recording Ghanaians and the sounds of events in the village.*

# LETTERS FROM GHANA

*Side One: "akpeteshie" is a strong liquor distilled from palm wine or sugar cane. The market does not have a lot going on because most of the people are at the funeral.*
*The Bible master referred to here is "Ohene," Mr. Owoahene.*

**February 4, 1969.** Jon in Acherensua to his parents and sister, still addressed to Wilmington, Delaware, even though his parents are in the process of moving to Chattanooga. Excerpts.

I enjoyed your long and informative letter, Mom, about the happenings at home. You seem happy to be going to Tinaseeee [sic]. At least the climate's milder . . . . I hope Judy has survived her concussions, colds, empty rooms and boy friends. I've been lucky here as regards health. Good news from my draft board: the Presidential Appeal Board voted 3/0 to give me a IIA deferment until Jan. 5th, 1970. At that time I guess I'll have to go through the rigamarole again.
[. . .]
I read Mrs. Moynihan's letter. Tell her I often think of the good old days when I spent 1/2 my time over at there [their] house. (I sent Mike's letter too, by the way)
[. . .]
I'm enjoying teaching much more this term. We have a 5 day midterm break on Feb. 20. [. . .] These last few weeks it's been hotter than it's ever been before. You can slice the heat. It's dry, no rain in months. McClure went to Kumasi today to buy meat. I'm really exhausted since I taught 5 hours today, 4 in a row. Talking and explaining even 3 hours is . . . too much. Easter begins April 2 or so. That'll last 2 weeks and then 3rd term til about mid-July when, Dad, you fly over to Africa. Then one more year etc.

I hope they send someone else out here after McClure and Altrows leave. We see other white people maybe only on[c]e a month. This place is really isolated.

*To his parents, Jon gives a more upbeat view of his teaching than he does to Mike in the letter of Jan. 11 and 28, 1969.*

# LETTERS FROM GHANA

**February 10, 1969.** Mike Moynihan in East Lansing to Jon in Acherensua. Fourteen pages. Excerpts.

Dear Jon,

Received your letter today, to my wonder and astonishment, read same, was duly impressed, and decided to send my entry for your posterity file. I agree completely that no one is going to care one bit about our correspondence, now or any time. It all reeks of insanity, disillusion, meandering and nothingness. If we two are the great minds of an age, I'm sure no one wants us immortalized by publication for future generations to savor. [. . .] Our sporadic correspondence is really ridiculous, you know it.

Anyway, thanks for not boring me with long narrative digressions on the people, their customs, living conditions, or with descriptions of your trysts (even though I described one of mine last letter). I've really not got much to say in the way of stories or information or anecdotes or puns. I shall now probably proceed to contradict myself for the next dozen pages or so. I'm writing at night now but probably will continue over several days before I finish + mail this. [. . .] I can never decide whether my undisturbed ramblings at night are real and valid or whether they are simply Bull Shit. Anyway, that's one of my greatest pleasures, just to sit alone quietly with a cigarette or two, and think. Sometimes I remince [reminisce], sometimes I create worlds + situations of my own, sometimes I argue with myself about whatever questions come to mind at the time. It's truely [sic] a fascinating + rewarding experience to just sit and think. To follow your mind wherever it leads, just set it going and let it take you away from everything for a while. Its escape, and its better than drink or drugs or travel. Reading novels is the only thing that approaches it. This summer I used to take a long walk every night after dark around the campus. [. . .] Remember how we used to walk around the annex in the summer evenings + just talk. This is a carryover from that, I guess, only the only person I can really talk to now that understands me is myself. [. . .] Everyone around here is worked up about student politics + student power, which is a joke, but the biggest joke is SDS. People actually believe in these things + are trying to become active in forging their own destiny. Christ you can't tell anyone how stupid they are and how useless such campaigns are. So you argue for no student protests on rational grounds, but to no avail. What a crock of shit this place is. My whole education has been a useless failure + I'm really sorry I had my parents sacrifice for it. I even feel guilty about it. I've grown up a lot and grown older a lot, but not because of this school. [. . .] Having to face all those damn lectures really irritates + infuriates me. I know I've set school records right + left for most classes skipped by a student who eventually graduated with a 3.00 average. That's what bothers me, Jon. There's no relationship between classwork + tests that I can see. I never take notes on anything in class when I'm there. My notebooks last me year in + year out, each term requiring about 2 pages a class.

I ain't changed my status yet as vestal Mike. I've had ample opportunity, I suppose, but I haven't chosen to use it yet. I still never go out except on very rare occasions. I've discovered something frightening, though. I always supposed that everyone was as perceptive + suspicious as I am about other people's intentions, but I find that quite the contrary is true. Girls are quite gullible as a species. They have boy-girl relationships all outlined in there [their] minds as they honestly believe they exist in real life, because of all the stupid stories they've read in McCalls and Seventeen, and the movies they've seen. [. . .] I've searched and searched and have found two well-adjusted, unneurotic girls around this campus. One is negro.
[. . .]
By the way our trip across the U.S. sounds good, but like most other ventures it will probably die as an idea, a vague wish that will be defeated by all sorts of little practicalities and day to day obligations. We'll never do it. I don't think.
[. . .]
I have some sort of youthful attachment for Seaford, but any real feeling for it is caught up in memories + the past, not present realities. Really it's an all right place to grow up in, but not such a hot-shit place to live in if you are between age 18 and 40. I like Kennett Square a lot more for some reason. Seaford depresses me. Not because of home, but just the town.
[. . .]

I'm glad to hear you've finally lost all sense of personal direction, though I don't believe it for a minute. I know my Jon Thiem better than that. You're destined for something, and I hope you hurry up and accomplish it, so when you're famous I can tell everyone that I was a personal friend of your's. Sort of status by association.

[. . .]

I am thinking of joining the Peace Corps, but your advice about applying was not useful. I wrote the bit about why I wanted to join the Peace Corps, and I made it cynical and non- idealistic as possible. I didn't lie at all. Which is bad, I guess, but someone told me not to be too gung-ho and not to be all pro U.S. and idealistic, because it's people like that who go crazy from the Cultural Shock. Maybe there is some truth to this approach too.

[. . .]

Nothing bothers me except personal discomfort. I'm not the least bit worried about Viet Nam or the draft. I just sort of go along with this blind faith in providence, knowing that I'll get out of it somehow.

[. . .]

If I'm accepted by the Peace Corps and come to Africa, I'll be down to see you, I guess. I don't know if I have the will power to drive myself to the necessary effort to get through. God, God, God, God, God how ridiculous I am. Paramount talent and no guiding force to use it. I wonder if I could pick up some at [the] drug store? These confessional letters are really relaxing and what a bunch of Bullshit they are.

[. . .]

I've just been reading about Nkruma[h] and the Ashantis and all kinds of African history. I'd like to say it's fascinating, but I think tolerable is the only suitable word. I've got a course in African His. [History] which is pretty good. The lecturer in this case is excellent. [. . .] Expert on Ethiopia.

[. . .]

A beer sure would be good right now. Cold Budweiser, with droplets of water running down the side of the can. Remember going out towards Lenape and going off in some field in your '56 Chevy and cooling some beer in a bag of ice. It was a warm summer afternoon and we just sat there + polished off a six-pack in perfect calm, tranquility.

# LETTERS FROM GHANA

*SDS: Students for a Democratic Society. "I ain't changed my status yet as vestal Mike." In other words, he is still a virgin. "Kennett Square" (in southeastern Pennsylvania) is where Mike's bachelor uncles and maiden aunt lived, siblings of Mike's father. "Lenape," near Kennett Square, was an amusement park where Mike worked one summer.*

**February 20, 1969.** Jon in Acherensua to his parents in Cincinnati, where they are visiting Kaye (Ginny's sister) and Marvin Markert. Excerpts.

Dear Mom and Dad,

Midterm vacation has finally struck and I'm in the first day of it. McClure and Altrows have taken off for Takoradi. I was going to go but at the last minute bowed out. It will be more of a vacation if I just stay here and rest up for the rest of the term. Over Easter I'll probably go somewhere. Teaching is going well but it is exhausting. I'm also trying to save up some money for the East Africa trip. And then I have about 90 pages to correct.

Glad you received the tape O.K. and enjoyed it. I enjoyed your long letter (9 pages) Mother and also your latest [letter] from Chattanooga, Tenn. Like Dad I guess I'm not much of a letter-writer.
[. . .]
Most of my spare time I've been sort of preparing for grad. school since I don't want to get rusty and since competition may be greater once I get back to the States. I've also been studying French, at least an hour every day; it's really difficult. So many words to learn! Lately I've been reading a lot of Shakespeare.
[. . .]
I guess the south is quite a bit different from the east. You'll have to write me about how the people are different, the customs, race relations. Is Vanderbilt U. in Tennessee? I hope you are careful with all my books and art books, don't throw anything away.

Speaking of books[,] I need some for my studies[,] especially: [there follows a long list of titles, mainly literary history and criticism] [. . .]

I think I'll go blind from so much study. It's depressing too because the more you study, you realize the stupider you are. I've got to do my French lesson, now.

**March 6, 1969.** Jon in Acherensua to his parents and sister. Addressed to 237 Masters Rd., Chattanooga, Tenn. Excerpts.

Today's Independence Day in Ghana so we have off. Several days ago McClure and I went to the Post Office in Tepa to pick up packages. Lo and behold we both got about 2 tons of food. I'm really glad you sent the food, it's a fine treat and Xmas present. [. . .] It's funny because McClure + I got some of the same things i.e.: popcorn, hard sauce, spam type meat etc. He got compressed can cheese which we used on my crackers. We've had a good time feasting the last couple of days. We also both got date nut rolls. Also glad you sent <u>Steppenwolf</u> and <u>Playboy</u>.
[. . .]
 Fortunately I'm not really unhappy here, so I'll probably stay two years. Especially since I'm just getting used to teaching etc.
 I'm looking forward to going to East Africa this summer. I'm not sure about Egypt or Israel. I don't think you realize how hot and dangerous this Middle East crisis is. [. . .]
[. . .]
 By the way, I got your two tapes. The 2nd tape (where Dad talked about E. Africa) was good but the first tape was opened for inspection + ruined. I raised hell but to no avail.

**March 13, 1969.** Jon in Acherensua to his parents and sister, addressed to their Chattanooga residence. Excerpts.

Not much news here. I enjoyed though hearing all about your moving adventures from Wilm. to Norfolk to Chatta. Kim sounds like he is doing well in the Navy, etc. Is his ship a destroyer or aircraft carrier? Dad, I hope you are getting into good physical shape. Only about 4 more months to go.

[. . .]
McClure and Altrows are anxious to leave. They're both going to Europe for several months.

*Jon's cousin Kim Markert is assigned to an aircraft carrier, the USS Boxer.*

**March 26, 1969.** Ralph Slotten in Carlisle, Pennsylvania, to Jon in Acherensua. Typed. Excerpts.

Dear Jon,

The Muslim prayer rug arrived Monday while I was in Philadelphia doing a bit of worthless scholarship for the Encyclopedia Americana (I am doing some Indian religious terms for the G's and H's)! [. . .]

Thank you very much. I shall use the prayer rug to perform a rak'a before my Religion 112 class in a couple of weeks.
[. . .]

Herb Sullivan at Duke finally responded to my letter of inquiry into the possibility of your getting into the study of the History of Religions at Duke. He says, Come, if you wish. I am not sure that this is the best course for you to take, but there is plenty of time to consider your future.
[. . .]

We have been having a campus revolution, as you may have heard. Ralph Sandler initiated it by announcing that he was going to give all A's to 150 students—in advance! We had a moritorium on classes soon thereafter in which students raised their voices against the System — mostly with good effect, I think. [. . .]

I see your friends Bill . . . , Jeanie . . . , and Mark . . . occasionally. Bill has just flunked out of Dickinson for the second time. He usually avoids me but he confided recently that he had just gotten excited about Norman O. Brown; it seems that he has met a Neo-Freudian mystic of some kind while visiting at Princeton. [. . .] Mark took off for the open road this past summer and fall; he had a religious conversion to Krishnamurti, Gurdieff, Ouspensky, and Company and is a changed person. He lost his student deferment and is up to be drafted any day. He refuses to talk about it or deal with it rationally; he just walks around in a glassy-eyed daze, passing out flowers and, on Valentine's Day, valentines in the Student Union.

[. . .]

I preached a sermon in chapel in January on "The Divine-Human Comedy" in which I developed and incorporated aspects of our discussion (and your little paper) on Trickster and His Transformation. I even had my congregation laughing. I treated Jacob and Peter as revalorized Trickster-types.

[. . .]

It is very good to receive word of and from you; . . . . You did a great deal to redeem the wasteland 1967-1968 here at Dickinson. I miss your bright and tricky spirit. Thank you for the Christmas card from Ouagadougou.

*Norman O. Brown was the author of* Life Against Death: The Psychoanalytic Meaning of History *(1959). Widely read at the time, this book had an influence on Jon's conception of history and also confirmed his pessimistic view of humanity.*

**April 4, 1969 (recorded).** Cassette tape transcription. Jon in Acherensua to his parents and sister in Chattanooga. Excerpts.

[Side One]:
Hi there, folks. Today is Good Friday and I thought I'd take the tape recorder out today just for a stroll downtown. [. . .] At the moment I am walking into town . . . . I have the microphone in my pocket so I don't have to hold it and carry it. Quite convenient in town because that way people can't tell you are taping them. Just a little flick of the switch and you are just standing naturally there with your tape recorder over you [over the shoulder]. It's even difficult to tell the tape recorder is running because it's a cassette tape recorder. I hope this turns out well. [Jon shouts]: "Oh Mr. Badu Nkwansah!" There's our Assistant Headmaster who is also delegate to the Constituent Assembly. And he just called me

over. He's decked out in his ceremonial robes, probably for the Easter vacation.

Jon to Mr. B.N.: What?

[Inaudible word of Mr. B.N.]

Jon: No, no, I'm just taping. Tape recorder, yes.

B.N.: _____ music _____

Jon: Ah, yea, I want to get some church music. Why don't you say hello to my parents?

B.N.: [laughs]

Jon: It's on, it's going.

B.N.: [laughs] Is it going?

Jon: Dad and Mom and Judy, this is our Assistant Headmaster. Mr. Badu Nkwansah.

B.N.: Let, let .. .. .. I want to hear it.

Jon: Oh, you want to hear it.

[. . .]

Jon: Here comes John Casper McClure, [laughs] who just got his mustache and sideburns shaved off.

B.N.: Oh where have you been, Mr. McClure?

Jon: Hey, what are you doing carrying a beer on Good Friday? Peto! [Jon to his parents]: Peto is a local corn liquor.

McClure: _____ I see you still have your mustache [to B.N.]

B.N.: Yes, and yours is not _____

McClure: Yes, I shaved it _____. Let's go over and _____. Want to come over? I'd love to talk to you and pump you for information.

B.N. I want to go and wash before I come. Wash my hair. I used a dye on it.

Jon: You used a dye on it? Why?

B.N.: Well, because you get some gray hair. I want to cover it you see.

McClure: What an interesting sign of modernization, you know. A few years ago I bet people would have cultivated their gray hair. That's interesting.

B.N.: But this time we don't want gray hairs, we want black hairs.

Jon: Opanyin Badu Nkwansah. [i.e. Badu Nkwansah the Elder]

B.N.: Oh, but have you started it [the recorder]? Oh! Why?

[All laugh]

Jon: I want to get you on tape. I want you to make some political statements....

McClure: What do you think about Mr. Nkrumah. [laughs]

Jon [continues]: .. .. for your electorate in America. [laughter]

B.N.: [laughs] O.K. I shall come in a moment to give you any sort of ideas you want. [laughter] I will come and we shall talk about all political problems around the world.

McClure: Not just to talk about them, solve them. [laughter]

Jon: Did you go see the chief [of Acherensua] by the way?

McClure: No, you know the chief has been sacked, in town.

B.N.: Oh yes, he is.

Jon: When was he sacked?

McClure: Oh, a week ago.

Jon: Why?

B.N.: Is it a week ago?

McClure: Not very long ago.

B.N.: About three days ago.

McClure: Oh, three days ago, is that all?

B.N.: When they slaughter a sheep, [it is] a sign of destoolment.

Jon: Why did they sack him? What was the .. .. .. ?

B.N.: Well, well, I know only about two of the charges, so far. First, that he doesn't come to the chief's house .. ..

McClure: Yea, his palace is in town, remember, where he received us.

B.N.: And second, that .. .. .. according to what he does, it doesn't seem that he is interested in the people themselves. His own elders are on him.

Jon: Uh huh.

B.N.: He doesn't consult them whenever he is taking a decision.

Jon: So he's been destooled then.

McClure: Well, also, according to Opong, some men were fishing in some river and they put some DDT in the river to kill the fish, so they'd get some fish. And somehow the chief found out about this and this is a crime. You can't poison the water supply. And instead of taking them to the police, he accepted a hundred dollar .. ..

B.N.: Ah, yes, yes.

McClure [continuing]: bribe/fine. [laughter]

# LETTERS FROM GHANA

B.N.: This is the most important charge. This is the most important

[. . .]

B.N.: No, no, a new chief has not been _____ [enstooled?]

McClure: Apparently, it has to be adjudicated in Kumasi.

Jon: The Asantehene.

B.N.: Well there is no question of any adjudication which might end in reversal. [. . .] So normally you just settle the matter. If you can't and you destool him, you slaughter a sheep and then send a part of the sheep to Asantehene.

McClure: Uh huh.

B.N.: You show it to him [the Asantehene] you have performed all customary _____

McClure: Isn't there something about making his feet touch the ground? His feet or something, isn't that part of it too?

B.N.: Oh, yes, that is another way of destooling him. If he is stubborn, he wouldn't like to be destooled. And you still want him to be destooled, all you do is probably use force. And if you force him _____

Jon: to touch the ground

B.N.: his feet and his feet touch the ground .. .. .. [background sounds of children and a cock crowing] then it means he has been destooled

Jon: automatically

[. . .]

Lawrie and I are walking downtown now. I just went back and fried myself a couple of eggs and some noodles and beef. I decided I am really good at frying eggs and now we are going to walk downtown again. [To Lawrie]: Better talk a little louder or it probably won't come onto the tape.

[. . .]

Lawrie: As a matter of fact, I was just saying I feel rather ill after eating your eggs.

[. . .]

Jon, while walking, says to his parents: You may have read in the newspapers: General Ankrah, the head of the National Liberation Council, that is the [military] government, has been sacked, or deposed, and as a result of this Colonel Afrifa, now Brigadier General Afrifa, will

be the head of the National Liberation Council. Ankrah was sacked for corruption and accepting money from firms. I think he accepted 6,000 New Cedis. This was considered very bad.
Lawrie: 30,000.
Jon: Oh, 30,000 New Cedis.
[. . .]
[Jon and Lawrie continue walking; they run into the Okyeame; Jon converses with him in Asante; they encounter the Sports Master; then Jon and Lawrie go to a house compound to drink akpeteshie with other masters]
Here comes our Sports Master who is riding his bicycle with his ceremonial cloth on. [. . .]
Jon to the Sports Master: Did you go to church today?
Sports Master: Yea.
Jon: You did. Did you sing?
Sports Master: The other friend came.
Lawrie: Who?
Sports Master: McClure.
Altrows: Mr. McClure. Yea, well I'm going to church too, you see.
Sports Master: _____
Altrows: I am going, now.
Sports Master: You're going now?
Altrows: Yea.
Sports Master: Where?
Altrows: To church.
Jon: To church.
Sports Master: Catholic?
Altrows: Yea, I think so.
Jon: He's a Jewish Catholic.
Altrows to the Sports Master: Is there a synagogue?
Sports Master: What is it?
Altrows: A synagogue.
Sports Master: Synagogue?
Altrows: Yea, synagogue, for Jewish people.
Jon: He's Jewish.

Sports Master: No, I don't think so [in answer to Altrows' question].

Altrows: I guess I'll have to go to church.

[...]

The Sports Master, after asking what the tape recorder is and about the rope holding it, says: We have no idea about tape recording.

Jon: Why not? Are you afraid of it?

Sports Master: No, not that we are afraid of it, but, then, the only thing is that we are not capable of inventing such a thing. [

Altrows mumbles: _____

Sports Master: It's working, I can see.

[...]

[Jon and Altrows arrive at the akpeteshie bar, in the compound of a house]

Jon: In Ghana the drinking doesn't stop on Good Friday. [Laughs] Holy Communion.

A Ghanaian master: It doesn't stop on Good Friday, it intensifies. [all laugh]

[...]

A Ghanaian master: Jon, you got pouring some libation? [sic].

[...]

Jon: In Twi or in English?

Other masters: In Twi.

Jon: I'll do it in both, hey. [...] [Jon gives the libation in Twi]: "Onyankapon [God] ...."

Ghanaian masters: Continue in English!

Jon: O.K. "Christ bless us all gathered here! Mother Earth bless us all gathered here! Let nothing be evil! [yes, yes, cry the masters] Let our ancestors live! [yes, yes, cry the masters] [...]

[Jon repeats a suggestion by another master]: Don't let us be impotent! [laughter and approval] [and Jon continues]: Don't let our penises die! Let all women bring forth! Let there be fertility in the land!

A master: Good! [...]

Jon: Let all the masters whack every night! [pandemonium]

[...]

[Jon on McClure's having gone to a Catholic church service]: I think he's a bit religious still.

[Side Two]:
[The Ghanaian masters at the akpeteshie bar begin to sing/chant traditional songs.]
A Ghanaian master explains to Jon: [In Ghana] the teacher is thought of as a god somehow.
[Jon, Altrows, and McClure sing "John Brown's Body"; the Ghanaian masters join in.]
[Jon records part of a Roman Catholic street service in Asante Twi.]
[Jon and Lawrie walk to the beer bar with Mr. John Odro, a Ghanaian who served with the Americans in the Second World War. He speaks English. They run into Ohene, the Bible master, at the beer bar. He speaks Asante into the recorder. Jon then goes to a house compound to eat a meal arranged by a Ghanaian master.]
[The last part of Side Two is dedicated to Jon's sister Judy, in honor of her upcoming twentieth birthday. "The Acherensua Irregular Band" and the "The Judy Thiem Fan Club," i.e. Jon, McClure and Altrows, sing to her their version of "The Midnight Special."]

[This tape concludes with Altrows and Jon singing a farewell to General Ankrah, the former Head of State. Altrows wrote the lyrics, to be sung to the tune of "Goodnight Irene." McClure plays the guitar]:

"Ankrah, Good Night. Ankrah, Good Night. Good Night Ankrah, Good Night Ankrah, I'll see you in my dreams. Times you live in the country. Times you live in the town. Sometimes you take a great notion to jump in the river and drown. We love Ankrah, God knows we do, we'll love her till the palm wine runs dry. And if Ankrah turns his back on us, I'd take morphine and die. Good Night Ankrah, Good Night Ankrah, we hate to see you go."

*Side One: The "Constituent Assembly" is the national delegate body charged with drawing up a constitution for the Second Republic,* which is to replace the current military regime after national elections to form a National Assembly (Parliament) have taken place. Concerning Mr. Badu Nkwansah's dyeing his hair, McClure says: "What an interesting sign of modernization, you know. A few years ago I bet people would have cultivated their gray hair." In traditional Akan society, it is good to look old. The older one is, the greater the respect. Jon jokingly calls the Assistant Headmaster "Opanyin Badu Nkwansah." 'Opanyin' is an important term and ideal in Akan culture. It refers not only to being advanced in years, which in and of itself commands respect, but also to having a reputation for leadership, generosity, well- spokenness, and tact. Jon's wordplay on 'opanyin' is based on the fact that Mr. Badu Nkwansah, though still young, has become opanyin in the second sense. For a subtle analysis of the term and its cultural significance, see Miescher "Becoming an Ɔpanyin" 253-269.

That both the chief of the village and the Ghanaian head of state have recently been deposed because of corruption and accepting bribes is a telling coincidence.

Akwasi A. Afrifa (1936-1979) was one of the conspirators who overthrew Nkrumah, and is a leading member of the military government. After yet another return to civilian rule in 1979, Afrifa was elected to a seat in the new National Assembly. Two weeks later he was arrested and executed by a new military junta.

The eclectic libations (in the compound where akpeteshie is served) epitomize the ebullient blend of Christianity, indigenous religion, ancestor worship, and Akan drinking ritual celebrated by the Ghanaian masters of Acherensua.

**April 5, 1969.** John McClure in Acherensua to relatives in Massachusetts. Excerpts.

This is our spring break and I'm planning to stay here in Acherensua exploring the local traditions as much as I can. Today we went with a couple of students who live in town and called on one of the town elders and asked him to tell us about the history of Acherensua. I have written down the story which we were apparently lucky to hear in detail since we are told that Ashantis are very reluctant to reveal all their secrets even to their children. The boys said that their being educated has excluded them from a lot of folklore. Until about 10 years ago virtually no Ashantis sent their children to school so there is quite a bit of distrust of education. Young educated Ashantis have a difficult problem of reconciling old and new ways. Of course the same has been true for many other groups, but you see it right before you here. For example, should you will your possessions to your children or your sister's children, like tradition dictates. Anyway, if things go well we'll be able to see a river idol which has among . . . other things cured the Asantehene's sister (100 years ago) of infertility.

I've been delving more into the superstitions here which I find have a much deeper effect on the people's daily lives than I had suspected. I get so disappointed and angry with our cook's son who is the smartest boy in his class, reads voluminously, and believes in all the superstitions including, surprisingly enough, Christianity. For example, they have a very interesting idea of complete equality of intelligence. So the smart students are thot [sic] to be wizards who can snatch knowledge from other boys during tests. This boy has been accused of being a witch and boys won't sit near him when studying. Despite this he still believes that some other bright boys are witches.

Don't be too concerned about [my] terminating early in the P.C. About . . . 1/3 of volunteers do and there is no particular opprobium attached to it.

[. . .]

Mother sent a copy of George's letter and it is priceless. Ghanaians have a real silver tongue when speaking and writing English.

*"For example, should you will your possessions to your children or your sister's children, like tradition dictates": Traditional Akan society is matrilineal, so, typically, a man leaves his possessions to his sister's children, not to his own. His own children will inherit from their mother's brother. Often the relation of a child to its maternal uncle is closer than it is to its father.*

# LETTERS FROM GHANA

*"George's letter": George is a Ghanaian who wrote to McClure's relatives.*

**April 18, 1969.** John McClure in Acherensua to relatives in Massachussetts. Excerpts.

In the <u>Center</u> [magazine] there was a letter about PC [Peace Corps] which was quite interesting. They presented the argument that PC is really just another facet of the U.S. foreign policy. You might say that this [is] a good part of a generally rotten U.S. foreign policy and should be supported. But the fact that the U.S. would never tolerate an internationalized (say under the U.N.) PC shows that it springs not from humanitarian motives but rather [from] a desire to convince people that our [foreign] policy really isn't as obnoxious as it is. This [letter] does seem quite reasonable and from what I've heard, Peace Corps in Accra has had to take a lot of crap from the government which it wouldn't take if it wasn't under a lot of pressure from the State Dept. to remain here regardless of the desires and needs of Ghana. What do you think of this? [...]

I'm looking forward to receiving that box of goodies, Ruth. I think I miss food more than anything else.

We had an interesting talk, through an interpreter, with a 96 year old man here in town. It is hard to believe but Africa really has changed in 100 years. He even fought the British in their last war in 1903.

*The last Ashanti-British war was in 1900-1901. It is called the Yaa Asantewaa War, after the Queen Mother, who was the principal leader against the British. The British defeated the Ashanti nation and turned it into a Crown colony.*

**April 1969 (sent circa April 28).** Jon in Acherensua to Mike in East Lansing (Fee Hall, Michigan State University). Twenty-three pages. Excerpts.

Dear Michael,

I just finished digging thru stacks of letters (mainly from parents since I don't write) looking for your address. I started to reread it (your letter) but the penmanship and bulk got me down. I hope your address hasn't changed yet, since you said it would by the end of spring, whenever that is. Things must be greening out and warming up in Michigan by now. Here the monsoon is just starting and I'm glad of it. The black clouds and lightening [sic] give the sky an attractiveness it lacks in the dull dry Harmattan. Your long walks and novel reading express a marvelous alienation. The heat forbids the first activity here but I do plenty of reading. Being stuck out in the jungle has made me realize how indifferent I am to human companionship. [. . .] The white people in Africa are easy to hate. I don't know which race is worse. Probably the whites. They expect all sorts of behavior from you. The blacks however treat you as an alien and so you have more license—which for me is staying in my room of books and pictures. Somehow I've developed a very irrational, quite syphilitic rage towards my fellow humans. This is apart from a well reasoned hate which is in me also. Strange to say this very rage sustains me. I think this rage and a bit of mirth are the only emotions I've got now. The rest are only lusts or sentiments which are less felt than manipulated and enjoyed.

This business of learning other cultures is a pretense for getting the hell out of your own. It's a good escape. Naturally you get crotch rot (I find the scratching one of the highest of tactile pleasures) . . . . [. . .] I have little love for African culture but it's pretty interesting to know about. Most white people here don't like this kind of talk as they are "cultural relativists." All values are relative and equal. And stupid and worthless (I say). But these tribal ways are interesting. [. . .]

The electricity just pissed itself out so I just lit up my lanterns. They make the place quite cosy and often I dream [of] monks or Abe Lincoln.

The Beautyful ones are not yet born is an African novel by a Ghanaian that is very good. I think it's the only bit of African literature I would recommend to anybody. Someone told me it's even popular in America now.

[. . .]

One of my latest and most funfilled [sic] things has been reading Mark Twain. Now he's interesting. [. . .] What maintains my interest in Twain is his vast and American vanity of spirit. In short his knack for serious loathing and serious laughing. For a time at least this temperament repeats my own.

Most of the other tons of stuff I've been reading I don't really identify with. I've been reading medieval epics, McLuhan, African fables, contemporary French literature, Latin satirical "novels," Shakespeare, James Baldwin's essays (not bad), science fiction, and late 19th century American realists. Most of this stuff you can't identify with but some of it you can enjoy. The reason for these labors (apart from my need to be omniscient) is an obsession I've developed about what the hell literature is if anything more than "something that is not life but that in certain glorious ways resembles it." There are [a] few things you can say about Man when you analyze some of the types of literature he likes either as an individual, a society, or a race. A good deal of this literature has been didactic and only incidentally entertaining. Most of it is the stupidest stuff imaginable. Yet somehow the simplist, directist story I'd rather read than do anything else (like play tennis or talk to people, who are lousy storytellers, or do good deeds). Granted a lot of this in my case comes from a pure love or passion for analysis. One possibility is that when we read or hear a tale we know somebody has made it up or interestingly modified it. There is the illusion of organized creation. The only tales told by idiots (i.e. unorganized) are life itself and the Sound + the Fury and recent novels of that ilk which are a lot less idiotic than their titles let on. Anyway, when you read a tale you exercize [sic] a kind of control that lets you be briefly controlled (by the teller). This is all very divine and unchaotic. And if you miss chaos you just slap the book shut. But most men are creative, if defectively. They, I, you slap shut the story and begin telling little tales in their own mind. Little worthless dreams (day or night dreams) of the past or future. Here is invention, organization + control. But some of these ordinary guys (they, I, or you) are better at this invention business (of dreaming away chaos) and a fraction of these even record these things + get published. Hence people who read novels are merely acknowledging the superiority of some one else's defense mechanisms over their own. Now all this is obvious I guess . . . . But it took me a long time to think it. I reckon (to disembarass [sic] myself) it takes a lot more savvy to tackle the obvious than it does .. .. .. .. etc. I'm tired. I think I'll wait a day or two before I let you in on my next disembowelment.

(wait 1 solar day before you read the next section)

I skipped a whole day before continuing. Easter vacation is over tomorrow. I just wound my clock so as to arise at 6:00 A.M. Teaching days I have to do that, on vacations I don't, because I sleep til 8:30 then. Actually I always wake up before the alarm but I find if I don't wind it the nite before, I sleep til 8:30. I love mornings because when I wake up its still black out but as I walk over to the Peace Corps bungalow the dawn starts to come in. I go into the bungalow (McClure + Altrows are sleeping since they have late classes) which is still very dark in the early dawn and I light up the gas stove for coffee. Soon as that's made I light up my first cigarette (Embassy filters) and sit around for 40 minutes, day or dawn dreaming til my first class at 7:00. This is the most solemn and perfect time of day. It approaches coolness and it's usually damp. Sometimes in the dampness I can hallucinate winters, which are a dear thing in the perpetual summer.

I'm not looking forward to tomorrow morning since we ran out of coffee. Everything's hard to get here and once you get it you run out of it quickly. So I'll probably be forced to drink Nestea which I don't like, though I like real tea, some of which Judy sent me for Xmas but which has run out, too.

You might as well visit my parents. A free stop is a good excuse for a trip to New Orleans (avoid Fla. if possible). I think they miss me and whenever you go see them they think of me since we were so inseparable for so long. They like you now much more than they did when we were in our "youth." They think you are a stabilizer or something for me. Of course Dad really likes you because he can talk freely with you, perhaps more freely than with me since he always moralizes when I'm there and of course then I have to anti-moralize.

[. . .]

I've been reading a lot of epics lately and a lot about them. They are so completely alien to me and everything else today [that] I took pity on one and got interested. All this shit about the glories of war and heroism. But when you read them and get suspended in them you start to wish you were Aeneus or Roland or the great Cid or one of them. The comfort of sacrificing yourself to something completely. They appeal to potential suicides, people who want to scuttle themselves whilsts [sic] straining for the noble shore (electricity just went out). The S.D.S. is in that tradition and I admire their folly. [. . .]

We've had some things here. Poisoned watersupply [sic], attempts to burn down the school, successful sabotage of the power plant. The students don't have any political . . . motives. There have been inconveniences but they have been worth it. I thrill at chaos. You may be beginning to think I'm an anarchist. God no. I told you I renounced politics.

[. . .]

April 26

I guess a couple more days have passed. [. . .] Now I know what I want to write but I'm too lazy so I'll stick to description and analysis. The room is hot and stinks of Shelltox bug spray. I'm on the second floor of an administration bldg. in an adequate room with a patio. This was where I was standing and pondering a few minutes ago. There, I shortly decided, was not the place for favorite reveries. The deformed moon and big stars diminished the mind's grandeur. So I remembered my undone letter to you and rather eagerly realized that writing about moon attended patios is much more pleasing than standing on them. Poetry has so misused the heavens that they are difficult to contemplate without real confusion and nausea. All those damn myth names, extravagant adjectives and now space jargon. Print has buggered the visible world to the extent that you can't see it straight without a lot of faulty allusions intervening.

I've taken to drinking soft drinks or "minerals" as they are called here. It's too hot to drink alot of beer in this climate and it's not worth it to walk downtown for just one beer. I put away 3 Fantas (trade name) at a sitting. They're sweet and orange tasting. (Shit! the lights just went out.) In the cities I drink lots of gins and tonics because of the ice and the 1/2 bottle of tonic that's left over and tastes good enough straight. It's no lie that gin is the best tropical booze.

One guy of the two I'm "stationed" with is very chatty. He was an I.B.M. physics guy who's got a patent and had a 12,000 dollar income. I don't know how he got in the Peace Corps. (I think we make 2,000 a year). He's leaving this July.

[...]

I just swigged out of my water bottle. The water is yellow, yet boiled. It tastes like most water but not like the water of a big city, mor[e] like Seaford water. Every night I carry a bottle up here; this evening's bottle was exceptional because it was a Johnny Walker whisky bottle. Whenever the Peace Corps staff visits us, they give us a bottle of booze in way of apology for putting us here. It's a relic of that. It has disadvantages as a water bottle though. Since the glass is clear the yellowness of the water shows through which makes it difficult for a sensitive person to drink. My usual water bottle is a green-glassed, 1 quart beer bottle. The opacity of the glass pretty much suppresses the yellowness. Unfortunately I put my kerosene in this same kind of beer bottle, so more than once I've had to spit out a mouthful of that. My shift from beer to sodas has been already mentioned. This is definitely related to the critical problem of the water bottles. It so happens that my passion for orange Fantas is sometimes betrayed by an occasional Sprite. These Sprites have the shape of a soda bottle, so they cannot be easily confused with my lager kerosene containers. Their colour is a dependable green that perfectly hides the scandalous yellow of the water. But, alas, these trusty sprites don't hold enough water, not nearly the quart I drink every night. This means I'll have to carry two bottles every night, and two bottles will be awkward along with a satchel full of books. I'm at a complete loss as to what to do. Now that I've made the Great Beverage Shift there is no going back to beer. If you have any suggestions, I'll consider them, but don't build your hopes up that I'll accept them; this crisis is much more complex than a cursory glance would indicate. It has already spoilt an otherwise utopian setting, so I'm sure you can at least sympathize with my anxieties.

I get so upset when I think of water bottles that I don't think I can write much more without lapsing into complete madness. [. . .]
I am
Distressingly yours,
Jon (E. A. Thiem)
P.S. In case you haven't heard, the "A." stands for Africanus.

I just lit up my pipe to meditate upon the false bottom that was the "last page" of this letter. It has become a tradition already that I [begin to] write just before the electricity goes away. I'm in a happy mood (one whose frequency increases the longer I'm here) probably from playing a recording of Shakespeare's Twelfth Night and especially hearing the Elizabethan song at the end of the play sung in a truly exuberant Elizabethan way, "For the rain it raineth every day." You must thank or curse Shakespeare for the continuation of this letter. I was going to send it off to get it to you before the end of spring. Hesitant to break this tradition of writing away the minutes before the electricity wanes, I was thinking of writing one more time. I received a favorable sign from Shakespeare tonight hearing the line "But as a madman's epistles are no gospels, so it skills not much when they are delivered." Of course Feste, the clown, delivered that.

In case you are wondering, this Shakespeare recording is a kind of evening supplement to the day's lectures. I've come to love teaching, even para-literate Africans. Perhaps it's the vanity I feel in being forced to present something in a related, clear and dramatic manner. I've learned Shakespeare only insofar as I've taught him. At times the bizarre responses of African students enter into the enjoyment. You can't conceive how remote anything written is to them. Marshall McLuhan is about the only writer who gives an honest analysis of the difference between the oral-tribal and the literate industrial modes. Most of his information is probably untrue but as a real artist of ideas, these fictions [of his] give you an authentic feeling for an underlying truth. My admiration for him is not a little conditioned by the fact of his influence on the later Barth.

I may kill an elephant before I leave Africa. In the full Harmattan they come down from the savannas in search of the food of the Ahafo forests. Maybe if I can't get you a tusk, I'll get you a molar. Tom Marum (alias Osei Kwame) (a farm boy turned peace corps co-op worker) killed an elephant last fall about 30 miles from here. [. . .] Think of me: scholar, lover, misanthrope, a killer of wild elephants—a madman who writes letters to Mike Moynihan. Next I shall begin to fear death. Finally an American who adds an "s" to toward. This is my mood of joy. (The goddamned lights just went out.) Is this a presage of blacker moods? [. . .] (I don't understand any of <u>this</u> ↑ either but it flows does it not?) If it flows let it flow. (I just stopped flowing). Is this a passage of lighter moods? Parentheses are the finest (I mean to say handiest) of literary crutches.

All this business about flowing is probably subconscious nostalgia for running water. (As the stoppages are for solid feces.)

The running water stopped two days ago and my bowels began to flow about the same time. Now water is dear. It is a curious thing that when the water stops running and becomes rarer, and you start using impure water, that soon you get a flowing in the bowels, your ass gets to be a fountain and as a result your body crys [sic] for more and more water to replenish that which it has so irresponsibly flushed out. I had Kofi boil ten bottles of river water. (Unfortunately boiling doesn't rid the water of the D.D.T. that the local fishermen use to catch fish). I told him that tomorrow night he'd have to boil 20 bottles (he giggled) and that the next night a 100 bottles (he giggled-giggled) and the next night a 1,000 (same response only moreso) and finally a 1,000,000, 1,000,000 bottles. He giggled and giggled . . . . (While I was dashing to the toilet).

Other wisdoms I get out of this miserable place concern the sad state of a toilet that lacks running water.

An unflushed toilet fills up to the brim in 2.2 days (given the healthy or unhealthy craps and wipings of 3 men). Luckily it doesn't smell as bad as you might think since every hour it has to be sprayed with SHELLTOX to keep the 1,000,000, 1,000,000 flies out of it. If we didn't do that these flies after a nice shitbath would alight on our food for their breakfast. We would then suffer amoebic dysentery instead of simple diarrhea. It is no coincidence that this week the headmaster and several favored teachers are going to Accra on "business." (Did I tell you I was nearly fired for refusing to teach Shakespeare without books?)

This letter (vanity would have me reread it each night but laziness permits much less) is I see quite a mosaic. Not the sort to be put in a stained glass window. Windows. All windows in Africa are of the louver type. Each storm blows them open causing no end of terror and wetness. There is nothing like a tropical thunderstorm at night (given louvers) to put the fear of God into man. God. There is a new myth here that God once lived on earth but that with the introduction of louver windows he became annoyed and fled to heaven.

My desire for water is so great that at this minute (11:42 P.M. April 28, 1969 A.D.) I would welcome a storm (that puts the fear of god into man) in order to get a full rain barrel. I didn't tell you about our rain barrels. Forgive me. These rain barrels could be very useful and make my life wholly pleasant excepting that without rain they are just like any other filthy old barrel. It takes at least 3 storms to wash out all the rhinoceros beetles and lizard tails (and ghosts that are reputed to copulate in them during the dry season). Ghosts in Rain barrel: an interesting human analogy to this is the practice McClure and I have developed of going swimming in the water tower when there is a full moon. In fact we got on to this when the night watchman conned us into climbing up there to see if the local witches might not be using it as a urinal. (Don't laugh. There must be some explanation for the yellowness of the water.) Actually I'm supposed to discourage these sorts of notions. But sometimes when the students get out of hand it's good to put the fear of juju into them.

[. . .]

I see this letter has become long enough to demand some sort of dedication. So I, hereby, dedicate this letter to: Tristram Shandy.

[. . .]

Jon Edgar Africanus Thiem

*The Beautiful Ones Are Not Yet Born (1968) is a novel by Ayi Kwei Armah (b. 1939). A major theme is bribery and government corruption in West Africa. The novel ironically proposes that resistance to corruption is impossible and perhaps unethical in a society where there is enormous* moral *pressure to give and receive bribes—for the sake of one's family, colleagues, and petitioners. Jon does not mention here three other West African writers he especially admired: the Ghanaian Ama Ata Aidoo, the Guinean Camara Laye and the Nigerian Chinua Achebe whose great novel* Things Fall Apart *he taught in Acherensua, and again later as a university professor in the States.*

*Marshall McLuhan, a communications theorist, wrote* Understanding Media *(1964), a key book for Jon. McLuhan believed that the emergence of electronic, aural media would transform the world into a "global village." He famously proposed that "the medium is the message."*

*"I've been reading a lot of epics lately and a lot about them." Jon's familiarity with epic had been limited to Homer and Virgil, along with two or three works in British literature. Now his extensive reading in the genre makes him wonder if there exists an oral epic tradition in Ghana, especially among the Ashantis.*

*In Shakespeare's* Twelfth Night *the extravagant wit and dark humor of the clown Feste appealed to Jon.*

*"I may kill an elephant . . . .": Jon the poseur, again.*

*"Kofi" is Kofi Ampofo, Opong's assistant.*

*The "new myth" about God and the louver windows is Jon's invention.*

*Tristram Shandy is the narrator of Laurence Sterne's highly digressive novel* Tristram Shandy *(1768).*

**April 29, 1969.** John McClure in Acherensua to his aunts Ruth and Dinie in Massachussetts. Excerpts.

One of the articles you sent said that African men frequently walk hand in hand. Very true and I've gotten quite used to it. You don't realize how absurd our sexual hangups are until you see a comparison. For example, you are frequently riding like sardines on a packed lorry and to make room put your arm on the back of the seat next to you, resting against some stranger's back. If a man ever did this in the states he'd be shot.
[. . .]

# LETTERS FROM GHANA

The political situation here is quite interesting. Right now district representatives are writing a new constitution in Accra in preparation to the return to civilian rule and elections next Sept. I'm afraid I'm a one party socialist when it comes to developing countries like Ghana. Democracy with 20% literacy (as it often is with 100% literacy) is a sham. Ghana has enough problems without interparty squabbling and patronage. People are hoping that the same violence as [in the] last elections in '57 [does not occur]. [. . .] I don't expect the same violence this time and in any case would not be affected by it.
[. . .]

Isn't Nixon a perfect ass. <u>Newsweek</u> said that his most significant "new direction" is a his and hers cabinet meeting with the wives. I wonder if somebody will have wit enough to stop our spy flights over North Korea now.

*The Assistant Headmaster, Mr. Badu Nkwansah, was the district representative to the Constituent Assembly, charged with creating a new constitution.*

**May 2, 1969.** Jon in Acherensua to his father in Chattanooga. Excerpts.

I thought it would be good to write another letter about our trip, since time is so short, especially considering how long it takes letters to go back and forth.

I will be going to Accra around May 30th and that would be a good time for me to get my visas. I am planning to get them for Kenya, Tanzania and Ethiopia. Technically it is illegal for Peace Corps to leave Africa on vacations (this is not much of a consideration). [. . .] I don't think Peace Corps people are allowed in South Africa (we tend to be too racially liberal). In both Ethiopia and Tanzania you get the flavor of a real Arab influence, plus the latter is English speaking. [. . .] It is in Ghana that you will see and feel how Africans really live. In East Africa we won't have the time or cultural knowledge to get a real African immersion. East Africa is a dramatic place because of the wild animals but West Africa is the place to see real jungle and real tribalism. Plus we have a guide: me, and I have a lot of contacts here. So let me know if this sounds reasonable.

Other preparations: we should try to look into what we should take. I don't know if the Kilimanjaro Club supplies clothes etc. Since it's chilly in East Africa I will have to get a few warm clothes for just plain sight seeing.

[. . .]

[Jon asks his father to bring a better tape recorder with him]: A unidirectional . . . microphone would be very useful, too, since my summer project (after you leave) will involve collecting oral traditions.

[. . .]

I would advise you to put at least $200 into American dollars CASH since the black market rate for Ghanaian currency creates a 40% profit. I haven't yet decided on the ethics of black marketing (I've already turned down offers) but this sort of operation is safe and there is no sense in being ill prepared.

[. . .]

Don't bring a lot of medicine. I have the best pills made (and they work!) for diahrea [sic] and dysentery, salves for crotch rot, Aralen for malaria, dexedrine for staying awake, bandages etc.

[. . .]

Books. We should read some ① cultural books and ② travel guides for Kenya and Ethiopia or Tanzania so we don't go into these places cold cocked. Customs vary and sometimes you can endanger your life if you don't do the correct thing. This is more true of East Africa than West Africa since white men are less loved there and since the Arab influence is much greater.

[. . .]

I guess you've had most of your shots by now. I'm counting the days for this trip and am looking forward to seeing you.

[. . .]

(You might try and learn a little Swahili since it's spoken in both Kenya and Tanzania.)

Don't work too hard or do too many pushups.

# LETTERS FROM GHANA

*The planned arrival of Jon's father in Ghana is towards the end of July 1969.*

*". . . my summer project (after you leave) will involve collecting oral traditions." The first reference to oral poetry project in the correspondence.*

**May 2, 1969.** Jon in Acherensua to his parents and sister in Chattanooga. Excerpts.

This term's shorter, therefore the work will be harder. Already I have several hundred papers to grade due to the 5th form mock G.C.E. exams, plus the normal load. I succeeded in getting <u>Macbeth</u> and <u>Twelfth Night</u> recordings for my classes to hear as a supplement to the lectures.
[. . .]
[Answers to questions about photos sent to his parents]:
My window curtains are funeral cloth. The bottle was a beer bottle which we use as water bottles (I hardly drink anything anymore except when I travel and then only gin + tonics.) The tropics are too hot for drinking beer, it makes you feel hot and nauseated. The "village girls in orange and red" are part of a Christian religious sect.
[. . .]
. . . I'm beginning to like it here. Besides, I have to steer my 4th form students thru 5th form next year and their big final exams.
[. . .]
[Jon on plans for his father's trip to Ghana, and their trip together to East Africa.]: I want to spend at least 6 days in Ghana to give you a real taste of African living. Live in a compound, eat foo foo and wild bird etc.

*"4th form students": the equivalent of high school juniors. 5th form students are seniors. Acherensua Secondary School had no 6th form, which is a special grade for students intent on going to university.*

**May 8, 1969.** Jon in Acherensua to his parents and sister in Chattanooga. Excerpt.

It's nice to get such newsy, scandalous letters like your last one, Mom, since life is so slow and unvaried here. [. . .]

In two more months Dad, you'll be taking off for Ghana. [. . .] I'm going to start running in the mornings. I haven't had any luck w/ giving up cigarettes. It seems it's the only pleasure we have here, what with no parties, no girls, not much drinking and crappy food.

[. . .]

Well it's time for dinner. Altrows + I are playing a practical joke on McClure. Instead of having creamed eggs we are replacing the cream mix with custard that is of the same color. I told McClure he plays the guitar too slow.

**May 10, 1969.** John McClure in Acherensua to his aunts Ruth and Dinie in Massachussetts. Excerpts.

Last week I went into another school in Kumasi and borrowed a telescope for my 1st form class. One night I got Juppiter [sic] but lost it before the students could see it.

[. . .]

[John writes that the clouds of the rainy season hinder seeing planets and stars through the telescope]

Speaking of clouds I noticed an interesting reverse image in a Twi folk song that I read. It said something about—the skies are cloudy, I know my lover will come back. A footnote explained that cloudy skies here are a happy, hopeful image because they mean cool weather. Just the opposite of our poetry.

We have been invaded by a charming variety of giant tropical ant that can't be squashed or even sprayed with repellent or it emits a horrible B.O. skunk oder [odor].

*McClure teaches physics. The interest in astronomy among volunteers and students was whetted by the upcoming Apollo 11 mission to land human beings on the moon.*

# LETTERS FROM GHANA

**May 15, 1969.** Jon in Acherensua to Ralph Slotten in Carlisle, PA. Excerpts.

I fooled around with the idea of sending you a tape. Letters lack resonance. A poem would be more adequate to what I want to say. [...]

Mainly . . . I've been reading, teaching, and playing with my tape recorder. An annotated reading list is in order. <u>Oral Tradition: A Study in Historical Methodology</u>: Jan Vansina. This is sort of definitive and dry but I've been doing a little "collecting" and it has helped a lot. It's mostly a manual. This is where my tape recorder comes in (I call it Mac for McLuhan), I am really wild about the oral. Incredibly most of what I can confirm about McLuhan's ideas here prove him true. He is really hip to the body, the senses, and he has made a great new thing. I've [ran]sacked the library going through Twi folk songs, the folk blues of the American Negro, The Beggar's Opera (precursor of the minstrel show), Shakespeare's airs (which I'm learning how to sing with Mac's help.) I feel like a disciple to a new prophet, though I feel my own inevitable heresy. Much of my Barth Mailer study is devoted to their response to McLuhan. Barth is obsessed with the artist as minstrel and Mailer with the tribal sensorium. <u>Sundiata: An Epic of Old Mali</u> by a griot [a bard], translated into French by D. T. Niane (Longmans: London). This is an oral epic passed on from generation to generation by royal scops (griots). It's magnificent. The griot even polemicizes against the printed word. "What paltry learning," he chants, "is that which is congealed in dumb books" or letters. "Learning should be a secret" i.e. trapped in the labyrinthine memories of griots. Those who use print, he says, "do not feel the past anymore, for writing lacks the warmth of the human voice."

The Pheul say that "writers are no better than magicians."

The Twi speaker attacks literacy when he says, "We write our books in our calabashes." The tale, like a palm wine libation, is poured out and disappears into God, not into "dumb books."

<u>The Radiance of the King</u>, Camara Laye. The best African fiction I've read and one of the best from any continent. Obvious comparison to

Kafka's Castle but notably richer. It makes beautiful tricks and puzzles out of the ways in which a westerner misapprehends the tribal. I've read a lot of African literature but can't in good conscience recommend much of it. Most of it is novelistic, socio-economic stuff, dumb books. Strange that African writers don't let more oral influences warm their forms.
[. . .]

Three books which have become my bibles are: McLuhan's Understanding Media, Northrop Frye's Anatomy of Criticism (archetypal, mythical anatomy of literature) and Eliade's Patterns in Comparative Religion.
[. . .]

Borges's Other Inquisitions (essays) is the only book I read from religiously, day by day before going to sleep. It is a symbol of all symbols, a labyrinth made of other labyrinths, an insolent interrogation of the other. How will my mind ever rid itself of Borges?
[. . .]

I think the letter is at the nadir of literary forms. You can convey the spectacle of your own mind but you cannot communicate because there is no [immediate] reply. Letters are no less dumb than books. If only there was some way we could replicate the style of our past conversations!

I'm very grateful for your endeavors in getting me into History of Religions. I am beginning to feel, however, that my true interests are in literature. The way literature and literary studies tend to use other disciplines make me feel less claustrophobic.
[. . .]

I miss the Slotten cosmos more than [I miss] America, Dickinson, or even my friends of the fragile Fringe.

I find I like being in Ghana so much I may even stay for a third year. Teaching is more demanding and interesting than I had anticipated. [. . .] It's such an odd hybrid of fun, sadness, and drudgery. I'm not really in love with Akan culture as I find it today.
[. . .]

Witchcraft [the belief in it] I despise. Fortunately the Ghanaians lack [as persecutors] the zeal of our own Puritans. Witches and Wizards in Ghana are [considered] totally and arbitrarily evil. Any student or villager who is unusual in ability, age or physical appearance risks the accusation of witchery. The Akans have forgotten their tradition of admiring outstanding people [such] as shamans. [. . .] A noticeable result in the schools is incredible mistrust and paranoia even among friends. John McClure, a Peace Corps physics teacher here, has been accused of Juju for being able to do complex equations in his head. I'm a little peeved that I've been spared similar charges.

*This letter reflects in several ways Jon's growing fascination with oral literature and the theories of Marshall McLuhan. At the same time, however, he writes in detail about West African writers, which he does not do in his letters to Mike.*

*Throughout this letter, Jon uses the adjective "dumb" in the sense of "non-speaking"— that is, the absence of voice, of sound.*

*"We write our books in our calabashes." The calabash is a hollowed-out, dry gourd, the traditional drinking vessel for palm wine. The sense of the proverb is "our books are the words we speak around the palm wine pot."*

*". . . my friends of the fragile Fringe": also known as The Lunatic Fringe. This consisted of a loose grouping of around 25 students. The lifestyle of Fringe people was distinctly bohemian. They smoked pot. They defied bourgeois sexual taboos. Many of them actively protested the war.*

*"I find I like being in Ghana so much I may even stay for a third year." Has Jon had a change of heart?*

LETTERS FROM GHANA
# A GHANAIAN PORTRAIT GALLERY

*Barber and client, Kumasi, September 1968.*

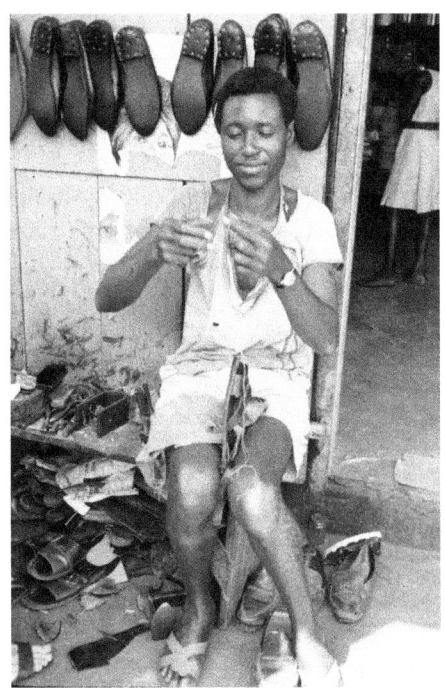

*Shoemaker, Kumasi, September 1968.*

*Stool carver, Kumasi, November 1968.*

*Motorcyclist next to a lorry, northern Ghana, December 1968.*

*Fetish vendor, Kumasi, no date.*

*Children at play, Kokofu or Sebedie, June 1969.*

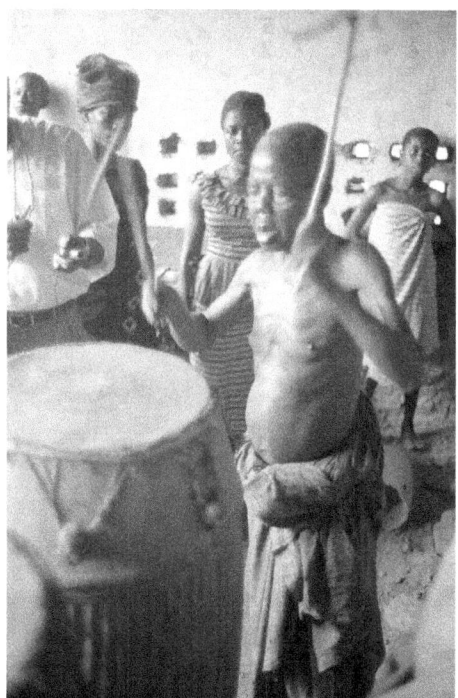
*Drummer, Sebedie, June 1969.*

*A princess of Kokofu (standing next to a traditional Asante stool), August 1969.*

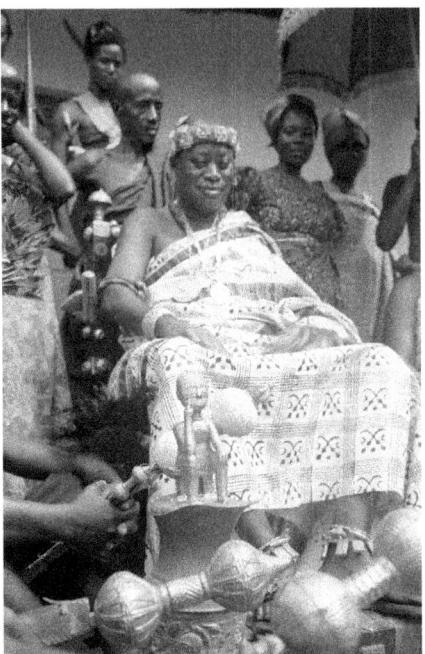
*The Kokofuhene with members of his court, Kokofu, August 1969.*

*Farm woman bringing plantains and yams to Acherensua, September 1969.*

*Cocoa farmer near Asiwa, December 1969.*

*Women at a funeral, December 1969.*

*Woman, Kokofu, 1970.*

**May 15, 1969.** Jon in Acherensua to his parents and sister in Chattanooga. Excerpts.

This weekend I'll probably go to Sunyani with the Debating Society (whose patron I am) for a debate on the Biafran war.

Lawrie Altrows (Canadian) + I have been getting up about 5:30 every morning and running 1/2 mile. It is too hot to do this at any other time. Our muscles were really aching at first (we were in such bad shape) but now we're getting stronger.
[. . .]

The weekend after this (24th May) McClure and I are going to Kokoefu [sic] near Kumasi to visit the chief there who is a relative of one of the masters here.

*Sunyani, the capital of the Brong-Ahafo region, is (by road) around fifty miles north of Acherensua.*

*"Biafran war": the secession of several prosperous southeastern provinces in Nigeria set off a civil war. The conflict is of great interest to Ghanaians because Nigeria, like Ghana (and other West African nations), is an agglomeration of ethnic and religious groups that were arbitrarily thrown together as a political/administrative unit by the British during the colonial period. If the secession succeeds, it might become a precedent and model for other secessions in West Africa and lead to the balkanization of the continent.*

*". . . one of the masters here": that is, Mr. Owoahene, nicknamed "Ohene." The nickname is appropriate in that he is related to the Asante royals. The surname Owoahene literally means "he who bears kings."*

*The Kokofuhene, chief of Kokofu, to whom Ohene is related, has close ties to the Asantehene and the royal court in Kumasi.*

*The trip to Kokofu on May 24th is finally postponed because Ohene learns that the Kokofuhene is unavailable at that time. Instead, the three friends go in mid-June. (See the transcript dated June 13 and 14, 1969.) The main goal of this trip is to collect oral poetry. Ohene and Jon have become close friends and are now collaborators in an effort to preserve Asante traditions.*

**[Sent after May 15, 1969].** Mike in East Lansing to Jon in Acherensua. Mike wrote at the top of the letter "April 19, 1968"; the year is clearly an error. A sixteen-page letter. Excerpts.

Dear Jon,

I sit here to write, not knowing exactly what to say or why I'm even bothering to write to you. I've gotten myself into a couple [of] mixed up situations over the last three weeks, and have been sitting around thinking, dreaming, mulling things over in my mind more than I usually do. My friend Harkness, knowing something of the situations + seeing me in something akin to melancholy stupor, humorously said "I can see a letter to Thiem coming up sometime in the near future." I laughed, but we both understood what was meant + implied in that statement. [. . .] Realizing that I don't usually write to you about the weather or my latest party on campus, but tend to talk about different kinds of stuff (what a word "stuff" is), he [Harkness] recognized in me the emotional state conducive to confessional letter writing—thus his perceptive + well timed observation that a letter to Thiem was in order.

[. . .]

I applied for Peace Corps last week. I don't think I'm going to graduate from college. My credits are too messed up. I don't think I care. Not bitter or anything, I'm just kind of indifferent, like it doesn't really matter anymore, if it ever did.

My roommate is playing some weird record by John Coltrane called "OM." Makes it hard to think. But I'll try anyhow, however feeble the effort + the result.

When you wrote me last time you mentioned in some derogatory way, my status as "vestal Michael." I commented extensively on the truth of that statement, and hinted at it as a doomed virtue. I don't remember exactly what I said, which is probably just as well, but it was something about the opportunity had been there but I'd chosen not to take advantage of it for ethical reasons. I get ethical nausea very easily these day[s] + my stomach can't take the beating. Neither can I.

[There follows an account of how Mike ceased to be "vestal."]

I sent in my application for Peace Corps + took the test which I did well on. I'll be in Africa if I make it, but right now I don't know where I'm headed. If I get drafted I'm thinking about two years in jail. That would be good for me. I could sit around and read all day. Or sleep. If I should get to Africa, I'll stop by + see if I can look you up. My God, that would be weird if we spent time screwing around in Africa. I probably won't make the Peace Corps, though. Raymond's supposed to be applying for the Navy, but he took all his entrance tests and passed them with flying colors, had his choice of any job he wanted, and then went into Phil. yesterday to sign up finally. When he got to Chestnut + 12th St.

he decided he wasn't going to sign and he didn't. They just turned around and came back. He's out of his mind. No ambition in our family. All lazy, except Franky + he isn't too ambitious. Fortunately, laziness is a luxury I have been able to afford throughout my life for one reason or another.

[. . .]

It's funny how you, living in Ghana, write 24 page letters to me commenting on such topics as Barth, Mark Twain, Shakespeare, English lit, S.D.S., student revolt + all the things related to the U.S. Nothing on Ghana + voodoo rites or human sacrifices. But that's actually good, since I don't care that much about a travelogue. Must be a sort of imaginative wishing for that good ole manicured lawn, roast beef, coca-cola, hot dogs, ice cream, and cool weather, all left behind when you went African. But you'll stick out your two years in that God-forsaken place (except when the louvres [louvers] are open), just to prove you can take it. A hero for his country he fought to the very end, until his last drop of sweat was spilled on the soil, regretting that he had but one two-year stint to give for his country, never aban[d]oning his ever greater quest for freedom, hope, human understanding, and the well being of the world. [. . .]

[. . .]

I'm preparing to do a paper for P[h]ilosophy which will be a Barthian (maybe) satire on something. I've already got the title written + it is 1/2 page long. I tried to get Lost in the Funhouse, but it's not out in paperback so I'll wait until it is. Or maybe go to the library. I took my army physical last Monday + will probably be drafted because I'm not a full time student. But no matter. I don't think I'm going. I hope I can go to Africa. I wish they had Peace Corps trainees working in Ireland. I wouldn't mind going there. Anyhow keep up the good work. I'll try + write again this summer or give my address to your Dad, or something. What the Hell!

God Bless You

*"Raymond" is Mike's younger brother.*

# LETTERS FROM GHANA

**June 1, 1969.** John McClure in Acherensua to "Everyone" in Massachussetts. Excerpts.

I hear Mailer just got a national book award for Siege of Chicago. It is good to read some of the hate and derision that was piled on Johnson. I don't know why the same sort of campaign isn't mounted on Nixon. I am very irritated over the campus disorders. Of all segments of society the universities are least guilty of the racism and militarism that are wasting the U.S. The Pentagon should be occupied before the nearest administration building is.

[. . .]

I believe [I] wrote you a few months ago about why PC is doing no good here. What Ghana needs is someone to (ruthlessly if necessary) root out their outmoded and backward ideas toward tribalism, superstition, corruption, subsistence agriculture, old age, etc. This is exactly what PC cannot do because it would offend vested interests and give Ghana an excuse (which it and many other W. African countries including Nigeria and Liberia according to [the] New York Times and my own observations [are looking for]) to kick out PC. This would be a tragedy for the U.S. since it is the U.S. which really gains from PC because we fool people into thinking all Americans are such friendly tolerant people.

*"Johnson": former President Lyndon Johnson.*

*Norman Mailer's* Miami and the Siege of Chicago *reported on the Democratic (Chicago) and Republican (Miami) conventions of 1968, but it was Mailer's* Armies of the Night *(an eyewitness account of the 1967 march on the Pentagon) that received a National Book Award, not the former book.*

**June 4, 1969.** A handwritten letter to Jon (in Acherensua) from a Ghanaian woman.

Dear Lover,

It is the aim of your goodness that I am writing you this my humble words.

I came to your bungalow but I was very sad that I couldn't meet you there, and I heard that you all went to Accra, I plan to send a nice gift to you but as you were not there I sent it back.

Morning star, only fish in the sea, Mirror, King of Kings Handsom of Handsoms. I feel I am with you to give me sweet smiles nice romance and kiss me joyfully.

There are thousands of men moving in the streets but you only I called as my lover, Mr. Thiem.

How handsom you are to me only the Almighty God can tell my feelings towards you.

Since you take me at first I have not take any man in town you only I love, so we may stay in love without concieve.

Prepare to meet me at your room on Sunday from 12 o'clock in the afternoon, or Tell Kofi to tell me what time that I should meet you at your room not at Mr. McClure's bungalow.

If you need something from me, you have to tell me if only I can help you or I have that thing you need, don't feel shy.

Also if I come to you, you have to lead me for some yards not to say Good bye, Then I go my way.

Untill we meet, I wish you good luck.
Your Lover
Miss . . .


**June 5, 1969.** Jon in Acherensua to his parents and sister in Chattanooga. Excerpts.


I've been cooking my own lunches (potatoes french fried, flat fried + boiled and hot dogs mainly). Sometimes omelettes. Since there are few ingredients it's monotonous.
[. . .]
(By the way[,] if you can airmail a few more packets of that Sloppy Joe powder mix that would be good. We really enjoyed that. We usually bypass the local meat because it is so bad but this sauce makes it good.
[. . .]

(I weighed myself at [the] Peace Corps office [in Accra] and I'm down to 125 lbs. but that's due to exercizing [sic], otherwise I'm the picture of health. A lot of people have lost 30 or 40 lbs., though all the girls who were fat to start with, have gotten fatter.)
[. . .]
Bedtime (10:00 P.M.) If the [tape] recorder doesn't go caput I'll try to finish the tape I'm working on.

*"the local meat" from the open market usually tasted slightly spoiled due to lack of refrigeration.*

**Early June 1969.** Cassette tape transcription. The recording is before June 14th, the date on which Jon travels with Ohene (Mr. Owoahene) and McClure to Kokofu. Jon in Acherensua to his parents, sister, and Aunt Cora in Chattanooga. Excerpts.

[Side One]:
*[Lawrie and Jon sing Festus's last song from Shakespeare's Twelfth Night.] [Jon is in his room in the administration building with the Senior Prefect of Students, Augustine Gyamfi, and the Assistant Senior Prefect of Students, Cosmo Acquah, both in the fourth form. So that they can experience how the cassette recorder works, Jon invites them to sing a song in Asante Twi, which Jon records.]*
I might as well introduce you to these people, Mom, Dad, Aunt Cora, Judy. First off, I introduce you to Augustine Gyamfi. [. . .]
Augustine: Anyway, I am pleased to meet you but I do not see you. However, I see Mr. Thiem. Therefore I am pleased to meet you. [laughter]
[Now Augustine and Cosmo recite in unison a prayer in Latin.]
[. . .]
Jon: Is that Roman Catholic?
Augustine and Cosmo: Yes.
Jon: You are both Roman Catholics.
Augustine and Cosmo: Yes.
Jon: Uh huh. You go to Mass every Sunday?

Augustine and Cosmo: Yes.
Jon (ironically): Uh huh.
[laughter]
Jon: You never miss?
Augustine and Cosmo: Tooooooo [Asante].
Jon: Because if you miss what will happen to you?
Augustine or Cosmo: _____ God will punish you.
Jon: Do you believe that?
Augustine or Cosmo: That is what we believe.
Augustine: And I do believe in dwarfs, too. Dwarfs.
Jon: Dwarfs. You believe in dwarfs. What about juju?
Augustine: Eh, I certainly believe in juju.
Jon: And what about witches?
Augustine: Certainly. [laughs] And I will take you to my town and show you my Uncle's juju.
Jon: Where, in Tepa? When will you take me to Tepa?
Augustine: During vacation.
Jon: You want to meet my father?
Augustine: Will he come?
Jon: Yes, yes. He will be coming to Acherensua.
Augustine: Fine.
Cosmo: So, when is he coming?
Jon: About July 20th.
[. . .]
Augustine: I will give palm wine to your father.
Jon: Oh, I am sure he will like it.
Cosmo: You [Americans] know how to drink it?
Jon: He likes to drink a lot.
Cosmo: There is no palm wine in America?
Jon: No, no. No palm wine. No akpeteshie. No peto.
Augustine: Only beer.
Jon: Beer, whiskey. Gin.
Cosmo: And schnapps?
Jon: Schnapps.
Augustine: And Afro Americans.

Jon: And Afro Americans, yea.

Augustine: We like them very much.

[...]

Cosmo: ... Judy, we have seen your picture and we will be very glad when you come to Ghana here as a Peace Corps. We shall receive you warm-heartedly in Acherensua Secondary School. Next year our school is going to be a coeducational [school] and I wish you [to] come here to be a tutor or our guest.

[...]

Jon: How old do you think she is? [from the photo]

Augustine: She is about 22.

Jon: 22. Well, I'm only 22.

Augustine: Are you 22?

Jon: Yes.

Augustine: Then many of our boys [students] are older than you are.

Jon: I know, many of my students are older than I am.

[laughter]

Augustine: How, how do you teach us if you are younger than ourselves?

Jon: I don't know. I have been asking that question myself. Maybe I shouldn't be teaching here.

Augustine: We can teach *you*, because we are older than you are.

Jon: O.K. [laughter]

[...]

[Cosmo asks about the upcoming school debate competition. Jon is patron of the debating society.]

Jon: What are we debating, the first debate? What topic? Whether or not .. .. ..

Cosmo: _____ girls, women should be accorded the same rights with men.

Jon: Right, in Ghana. And the second topic?

Cosmo: The second is birth control.

Jon: Whether or not women should have birth control. What do you think about that? Is our team going to take the proposition?

Cosmo, Augustine: Yes.

# LETTERS FROM GHANA

[inaudible . . .]
Jon: What arguments are you going to use?
[inaudible . . .]
[discussion of whether Jon can make it to the first meeting]:
Cosmo: I think your presence will grace the meeting.
[. . .]
[Jon, with his parents and sister in mind, asks Augustine to explain the role of the student Prefect]:
Augustine: To be a Prefect is no joke. Before I was appointed Prefect, I did not know this work was as tedious as that. But you don't sleep at night. You have been thinking about how the school might be ruled. _____ children are running about. We have to subdue them. Go here, come here, then do many other things. Especially when you are appointed, you thought you were coming to enjoy. But now you are suffer[ing]. _____ but _____ it's no joke.
[Cosmo interrupts; he asks Jon's mother to give him one of her daughters.]
Jon: Well, I support what Augustine says because I know before he became Prefect he was a very wild boy, but now that he has become Prefect he has become very much subdued I think. And I think he feels his responsibilities are too much of a burden. So I think we must give him back his great freedom.
Augustine: No, no, no. Not that.
Jon: You like being .. .. ..
Augustine: Yes, I like being a Prefect.
Jon: What do you want to do when you leave Acherensua?
Augustine: _____ if I qualify, I shall go to sixth form [pre-university courses]. And if not, I'll go and find a _____ job.
Cosmo: And if the Peace Corps shall help us, then we shall go to America.

*See also Augustine Gyamfi's letter to Jon, dated June 1, 1971.*

**Circa June 7, 1969 (date recorded).** Cassette tape transcription. This is an excerpt from Side One. Excerpts from Side Two of this tape are below, under June 13 and 14, 1969. Jon in Acherensua to his parents in Chattanooga.

[Side One, circa June 7]:
Your letters sound very strange, Mother, because, you know, everything sounds so peaceful and nice in your letters, but yet I keep reading *Newsweek* magazine and all I hear about is students being shot to death by police, riots, and student protests and things like that. The complaints about the Vietnam War, new draft systems and all this. Which is quite a contrast from your letters. It doesn't sound as if the Good Old South has reached the state of change where these things are occurring. Which may be good, or not so good, I'm not so sure. I hope you read the article I sent you about student radicals, etc. Good old student radicals. Which was kind of interesting because of .. .. .. it wrote [sic] more or less from the perspective of parents.

*Side One: Jon (like other volunteers) cannot fully comprehend the disturbing events taking place in the United States. See Ginny's reply to Jon on this matter in her cassette tape to him, October 15 and 16, 1969.*

**June 7, 1969.** Jon in Acherensua to Mike in East Lansing. The letter was sent to Fee Hall, Michigan State, and then forwarded by the Post Office to 415 Albert St. Excerpts.

This isn't too prompt I guess. Because I ran out of my accustomed stationary [sic]. I didn't get around to writing. [. . .]
[. . .]
    Song (from As You Like It—2nd stanza)
    Who doth ambition shun,
    And loves to live i' the sun,
    Seeking the food he eats,
    And pleased with what he gets,
Come hither, come hither, come hither:
    Here shall he see
    No enemy

But heat and tropic weather.

[. . .] Pastoral is a dead convention mainly because most cowboys are illiterate and the Eskimos all are tubecular [tubercular]. But someday some Peace Corps volunteer is going to write African Eclogues .. .. ..
[. . .]
These songs somehow sum up my feelings: misanthropy, joy, the idea that nature is no lark but it's sure as hell better than man. Africa is probably worse than most places, excepting possibly India, but it's a good place to be an expatriot [sic] in. It is not difficult to cultivate a superb aloneness, which philistines denounce as alienation.
[. . .]

The one annoyance is having to be a hero. Necessarily a teacher has to be a hero and here a white is a hero. I wouldn't mind the ticker tape parades, they're short. The next issue of Time sports someone else's face on the cover. Relief. But here the adulation is constant. Hundreds of them imitate every fetish of my dress and gesture. [. . .] The demands are enormous and many times bureaucratic. I sit at my desk swamped with papers, requests for my shirts, or my autograph or my person. Letters have to be written to refuse speaking engagements (I'm not joking, dammit). The superlative ungrammatical feelings of female-admirers must be assuaged. [. . .] Will never this end [sic]? How I envy Achilles his heel, Adam his fall!! O Moynihan (and Harkness if you're harking) how superior is the anonymity of the tribesman to the loneliness of the Hero.
[. . .]

One crowning bit of wisdom more. Don't fool around being an Anti-Hero. This is a very grave, very modern, very tempting disease. Worse even than modesty is this repulsive business of admitting your own faults, glorifying them. These people who admit they are not good at anything (and worse yet they are not). This is an insidious form of humanism (for what is humanity but a medley of faults and flaws.) (Twain precursed me in this insight.) Cultural relativism and agnosticism are variants of anti-heroism.
[. . .]

# LETTERS FROM GHANA

Lately my most important critical judgments have at once been vindicated and annihilated. As you know several of my cultural heros [sic] are: Jorge Luis Borges, John Barth, Vladimir Nabokov and you. (Twain = a folk hero). All of these have in common certain styles of excellence and also relative obscurity. Suddenly this spring <u>Time</u> and <u>Encounter</u> were graced with cover portraits of Nabokov and Borges respectively. You see the dilemma. My joy derived from the idea that these people were great <u>and</u> that this greatness was my secret.

[. . .]

[Jon's proposal to write Mike's biography]:

This biography is going to be one hell of a thing. Even though for 11 years we daily palled around like brothers we certainly didn't anticipate you getting fucked. There is no way to convince anybody, let alone scholars, that all those years were to consummate you in the role of a Lothario-cum-novelist. You had better write something autobiographical about that period or else I'm going to be forced to invent something. In this case alone I feel my invention would prove inferior to the truth that's <u>still so mysterious</u>.

[. . .]

Through me you reached Barth's <u>Floating Opera</u> and unbeknownst to me you studied Todd Andrews' saint period, you were struck by the puns on penetration. (In trying to penetrate my mystery, says Todd, they in turn got penetrated).

[. . .]

I refuse to write your biography and if you are wise you will renounce your life work—the <u>Delawariad</u>. Somehow we must even pledge not to publish one another's letters or ever mention such a ridiculous idea again.

Suddenly I just received an overpowering, majestic inspiration: that art which is greatest and requires the most skill is the suppression of art, is silence.

*"Delawariad": that is, an epic about the State of Delaware—the humor here being the paradox of treating—with the grand sweep of epic—such a diminutive state.*

# LETTERS FROM GHANA

**June 8, 1969.** John McClure in Acherensua to "Dinie, Ruth, Grandmother and Granda" in Massachusetts. Excerpt.

[McClure on a visit to Accra]:
One nite there I met a PC friend whom I hadn't seen since last Sept. and he suggested we eat dinner at this Ghanaian place nearby. I went there and had a good meal in nice clean surroundings. When I was finished I remembered that I had been in here my 2nd day in Ghana but was grossed out by the awful smell and food and dirt. Such have my standards dropped.

**June 13 and 14, 1969 (dates recorded).** Cassette tape transcription. Jon in Acherensua (June 13). Then, Jon, with McClure and Mr. Owoahene, riding in a lorry to Kumasi (June 14). To his parents in Chattanooga. Excerpts.

[Side Two: June 13]:

This weekend, or rather that is tomorrow morning, John McClure and I are going to Kokofu, south of Kumasi. [. . .] We are going there to see the Kokofuhene, who is the uncle of the king of all the Ashantis, the uncle of the Asantehene. I plan to do some taping there and talk to him and we'll be there for the weekend. [. . .] We are going with Mr. Owoahene [i.e. Ohene], who is one of the teachers here. He teaches Bible knowledge and he is a direct relation to the Kokofuhene. Hence our ability to go and see him.

[Next day, June 14]:
We're in a lorry now on our way to Kumasi. [throaty roar of the lorry's engine] [. . .] That's John McClure and Mr. Owoahene. Say hello to my parents. [. . .] [Owoahene]: Hello to the parents of Mr. Thiem _____, [we are] now travelling to Kokofu to visit the king. [. . .] [Jon]: I plan to tape some poetry there . . . .
[. . .]

We were just passed by another lorry which says "Oh God Help Me" on the back. [. . .] We almost had an accident. The lorry in front of us, the one called "Oh God Help Me" was flying down the road and another car in front of us decided to slow up and decided to stop, to be exact, . . . . If it wasn't for the "Oh God Help Me" it would have been a sad scene. [. . .] [McClure]: What's our lorry's name? [. . .] What's S U M K W A mean? [. . .] [Owoahene]: It's "a cry for long life."
[. . .]
[Owoahene explains some of the Asante festivals, for example, the *Akwasidee*]
[They arrive in the lorry park of Kumasi—a barrage of sound come through on the tape.]
Jon: The traffic is heavy here and there are a lot of people in the streets. The difference between Kumasi and Acherensua is almost infinite. [Ohene laughs]. Isn't that right Mr. Owoahene?
Owoahene: Yea, it's right, it's true. _____ boisterous.
Jon: Boisterous, that's the word.

*Side Two: Jon, McClure and Owoahene had planned a trip to Kokofu on May 24, but it had to be postponed because the Kokofuhene was not available. Kokofu, a village south of Kumasi, was a member of the original Ashanti Confederacy. Ohene's "hometown," Asiwa, is not far from Kokofu. His parents and many relatives live there.*

**June 17, 1969.** Jon in Acherensua to his parents, sister and Aunt Cora in Chattanooga. Excerpts.

Last weekend McClure and I went to Kokofu. [. . .] The Kokofuohene (chief) was not there as he said he would be, but had gone to Kumasi. He did come the next day but as we had to leave we were rushed in seeing him. After all this waste of time I did, however, record a Twi poem from a fetish priest whose father was an executioner (abrafo) for the Asantehene.

# LETTERS FROM GHANA

*Ohene introduced Jon to the fetish priest and reciter of apaeɛ, Kwasi Dum, who is from the village of Sebedie, very close to Kokofu. Kwasi Dum, like his father, recited apaeɛ at the Asantehene's court in Kumasi. This trip inaugurates the apaeɛ project.*

*The apaeɛ recited by Kwasi Dum are oral praise poems (in Asante Twi). For more details on the project and some sample apaeɛ, see the section of the Introduction entitled* The Oral Poetry Project, *and also the excerpts from Thiem and Owoahene's manuscript* Apaeɛ,, *under the date "Early December 1969."*

*Jon, McClure, Kwasi Dum, and Ohene, in Sebedie, June 1969.*

**June 24, 1969.** Mike in East Lansing (415 Albert St.) to Jon in Acherensua. Excerpts.

Dear Jon,

I'm going to summer school here at State, living off campus, and having a fairly decent time of it. Lots of reading, but lots of leisure to lie idling with a book in one's lap. [. . .] I went home [to Seaford] for a week about two weeks ago, where all was warmth and beauty. Paid nostalgic visits to several of our haunts, saw no one of common acquaintance, visited my draft board + came back. The [Austin] Healy did the job again. I'm always amazed when it survives the trip.

Your letter arrived the day after I got back. It had been forwarded from my dorm address and was a pleasant (at least until I read it) surprise. I didn't expect such an immediate response to my last missive and/or quite the personal reaction that resulted. Certainly in this very personal quality it is the most puzzling and yet most intriguing of our communications.

[. . .]

I finally got hold of a copy of Barth's "Lost in the Funhouse" in the Graduate library and read some of it. While I don't attack Barth's work like a chemist gleefully seeking the components of a complex compound, breaking it down into all its constituent parts, I do enjoy his form of ridiculousness on an intuitive level. My friend Harkness (sounds like the title of a movie) knows a writer quite in vogue now named Kurt Vonnegutt [sic]. I'm not sure but I think you had a book of his in high school called "Cat's Cradle." Harkness makes big stuff out of him and independantly [sic] puts down Barth. Vonnegutt's allright [sic], but he's certainly not a great writer or even a great modern writer. He's too compact and explicit, with more concern in achieving clever situations, dialogue, and nice punch lines without a broad conception of the ambiguities of his themes. Barth manages to percieve [sic] the ambiguity as a theme, as personified in Henry Burlingame's discourses, and then approaches this theme quite ambiguously.

[. . .]

Its times like graduation that make one aware of moving through time, of growing older and leaving parts of yourself + your life behind, irretrievably gone except for occasional forays into memory. Even that dilutes and dims the possession of the past to such an extent that it becomes formless and unreal, a mass of [illegible word] names, places, events, ideas all jumbled together and tossed into some dusty, cobwebbed corner of the mind where they lie slowly rotting, classified with some catch-all phrase such as "THE PAST," or "CHILDHOOD," or "THEN" (as opposed to now).

[. . .]

Back to your letter. Again I've forgotten exactly what I wrote to you, so I find myself digging to try + remember what you are talking about in some of your references. [. . .] Truth as far as that letter goes was implicitly + simply the truth that I did not know the truth. Truth, I am partially convinced, is only a euphemism for the consensus opinions of some majority, able to exert its will through sheer numbers, + [truth is] not [a] grasp of any fundamental law or laws of existence (if any such exist). Everyone I hear is seeking truth, is looking for some sign of the word.

I did not, as I recall, accuse you of heroism. That crap was just a humerous [sic] diatribe not meant to be taken seriously. I didn't think you would look upon it as an accusation.

[. . .]

My role as a Lothario-cum-novelist is ridiculous; my autobiography would be boring, my past that is <u>still so mysterious</u> is hardly unfathomable, much less mysterious. All in all I rejoice in your desire to do my critical biography but I can't see the merit of the deed. [. . .] No, there is no mystery—there is not change, no emergent flowering (or deflowering) of youth come of age. Just series of chance events of no particular overall significance. Perhaps, though, my very denials are evidence of the mystery that even I cannot penetrate with all my additional resources and knowledge of my own thoughts + actions. Who knows?

[. . .]

Suppression of Art? That's no great Art. Anyone can do that. Silence is not talent, although it may be a greater virtue than the search for truth through Art. But do we wish to embrace virtue? Hell No! We must embrace art and perpetuate the histories + stories or else we end up being true to ourselves, which is unthinkable. The great thing about the modern writer is that he renounces the truth that silence represents, the truth of no truth existing. He sets out with a sly grin to convince the world he is seeking + finding what he does not even believe, + then toys with the world in his work in such a manner as to create an artistic practical joke. His is not a virtuous silence but an ignoble voice in the darkness searching for the candle in the corner when he knows there is no candle in the corner. He tries to convince everyone else in the blackened room that there is, though, and leads them on a merry chase seeking the <u>wicked</u> light that will keep hope alive in the hearts of his followers.

Are you, Jon, going to be the humanist who reveals the candle as myth, or will you choose to shirk virtue + duty and follow the misanthropic lead of previous artists by maintaining the ruse. It is times like this that the powers of darkness must stand and be heard, else their silence will end Art and end life itself. The ending of hope for life—how humanitarian can you be. Perpetuate Art + you perpetuate life, cruelly + endlessly forever. What better Misanthropy than to give men reasons to live.

So much for that.

[. . .]

The wonderful aloneness of the past three weeks has been balm for my anomie, bathing it in sweet anonymity and priceless seclusion.

[. . .]

[He gets fired from his job in a pool hall]:

I can't believe the amount of time I allot to total isolation from everyone around me, how complete + total psychical self-immersion can be. And how useless. But it sure screwed my job. I didn't realize that it was that obvious to people who watch me. Must be.

[. . .]

I'm trying to track down my Peace Corps application + find out what happened to the damn thing.

[. . .] Ah Damn You Thiem, your letter reawaken[s] a profound and deep sense of underlying disdain + superiority which is not real or justified. I have to go to great lengths to suppress + control these urges to make biting comments.

[. . .]

[Postscript]:

Movies + books prod the fancy and lead me to dream all sorts of ridiculous fantasies and situations, plots for real life adventures + tragedies. It's unfortunate that such a love for the unreal leaves me so unprepared to deal with the real. I feel that my fate will be sealed + stamped upon me by this penchant for dreaming, for living in another part of life. It will probably kill me. It's strange when you see people around you who can put such little stock in anything but their own lives and personal problems. They dismiss the grandeur of a novel or a movie as mere entertainment which involves them no more than a good meal or any other pastime. And I, I put more faith in grandiose, fantastical, imaginary beings than I do in my own life and my own purposes. It's not just literature or movies that can have that effect. History can, too. Reading about Abe Lincoln, the rail splitter, and mulling over the problems he faced, and wondering what kind of man he was and what it was like for him to order thousands of men to their deaths.

[. . .]

Sometimes I think I ought to go to Vietnam just so I can experience horror + blood + pain, poverty + savagery, anything to escape the inane narrowness of my own world + being as a middle class college student who knows nothing, sees nothing + does nothing. [. . .] I'm a coward, fortunately, so I'm not likely to really sign up for V.N., but I'll still give primary emphasis to the unreal + continue to lounge around in trance-like stupors, suspended between my roommates' conversations and the foggy world beyond my senses + sense.

"*a writer quite in vogue now named Kurt Vonnegutt . . .*": Kurt Vonnegut has a large readership today, whereas Barth's popularity has waned. Vonnegut's Slaughter-House Five *(1969) is one of the most important novels of the later 20th century, and probably had a greater impact on public awareness than any novel Barth has written. Nevertheless, Barth was instrumental as fiction writer and essayist in introducing Americans to Latin American writers such as Borges and Garcia Marquez, and also in disseminating to a larger public an understanding of the idea of what it means to be postmodern.*

"*Are you, Jon, going to be the humanist who reveals the candle as myth, or will you choose to shirk virtue + duty and follow the misanthropic lead of previous artists by maintaining the ruse*"? *By this time, Jon has opted for literary scholarship (revealing the candle as myth) rather than creative writing (maintaining the ruse).*

**July 7, 1969.** Jon in Acherensua to his parents and sister in Chattanooga. Excerpts.

I'm in bed now trying to get rid of a cold I've had for a week. I've been drinking gallons of water and took 2 terramycin [sic] pills (penicillin). The fever has gone down.

McClure left Acherensua today for the last time! Altrows left the day before.

[. . .]

July 5th we had speech day. It was hell: sitting for 4 solid hours. The Dutch ambassador was the speaker. He brought his son, Flor Vaerekamp [sp?] and daughter. McClure and I invited Flor + Peeps (daughter) over for some beer + we talked til 2 in the morning. [. . .]

The headmaster behaved pretty poorly towards Altrows + McClure before they left. He hasn't been kind to me either. If he gives me any trouble I shall resign. [. . .] When I get the chance I'll tell you some pretty tales of corruption.

P.S. I hope to see the moon shot on [the] 16th but I'm afraid the live T.V. doesn't extend to Africa.

**July 26, 1969.** 10:15 A.M. Cap Thiem in Accra to Ginny and Judy Thiem. Written on Hotel Continental stationery.

This is just a note to signify safe arrival, all systems A-OK, glad I came, Jon looks fine + how the hours will fly past. Have met a nice young peace corps couple (they enjoyed some of the cookies) + McClure (he enjoyed some of the cookies); went to some typical (+ I mean typical) Ghanaian bars + outside night food markets + generally roamed the unlit + fairly deserted streets (very safe).

Trip went fine—no holds at any airports + [we] were in the air to Africa by 5:05 P.M. HOWEVER the front landing gear wouldn't go up so we had to jettison fuel to turn back + land. Finally fixed landing gear, re-fueled + was in the air at 8:15 P.M. On second take off our pilot Capt.

Manchester said "Let's take another crack at it" + off we went. We subsequently were 3 hrs. late in arrival + Jon was getting worried. Had words on airplane on my extra weight but I won out + paid no extra. Went thru customs in a few seconds (had a little help from one of the officials who's saving up for a Mercedes Benz.) (Jon + I enjoyed some of the cookies.) This is the best Hotel in Accra + although Jon + I are satisfied I'm afraid many would not be. Jon had his first pork chops + hot shower since arriving [in Ghana]. McClure ate with us last night. The eggs this morning tasted terrible but I ate them (can't waste the pesewas—pennies). I had a hair cut; Jon's getting his now. Just got back + they butchered his hair. Jon is up to 130 # + we'll pack a few more # on soon. We are leaving for Kumasi on the 1:00 P.M. State Transport Bus. This is the big bus. Trip takes 5 hrs—(1 stop).

Jon was pleased with all the goodies + I believe we have fixed him up OK. We will try to make a [cassette] tape before leaving Acherensua (We will have the recorder there)

I thought of you on the road Thurs. + Fri. Hope the trip was uneventful + everything was OK.

<u>The beach is fine</u>
<u>But Africa sublime.</u>

Will try to write as often as possible but don't hold your breath. Jon says hello + thanks for all the stuff.

We say hello to you + neighbors + friends who may drop in.

Hope the Rogers are over at the beach with you.

Love

Cap +

Jon

*Cap Thiem arrived in Accra on Friday, July 25; Jon met him at the airport.*

*McClure, after leaving Acherensua, decided to spend several weeks in Accra before going on to Europe.*

*The State Transport bus trip from Accra to Kumasi is the first leg of Jon and Cap's journey to Acherensua, with a stop in Kumasi. They will stay in Acherensua two days before returning to Accra, with another stop in Kumasi. In Acherensua Cap meets, among others, Jon's friend Ohene and the Headmaster, to whom he presents a bottle of expensive whiskey.*

*"I thought of you on the road Thurs. + Fri.":* Ginny and Judy have driven up to Rehoboth Beach, Delaware. *For more detail on Cap's trip to Ghana and East Africa, see: "Cap Thiem's memories of the trip to East Africa in August 1969" (recorded in 2003); Ohene's letter to Cap, Sept. 1, 1969; and Cap and Ginny's cassette tape to Jon, Sept. 29, 1969.*

**July 26-31, 1969 (dates recorded).** Cassette tape transcription. Cap Thiem in Ghana to Ginny and Judy. Excerpts.

[Side One]:
[Cap and Jon on the bus from Accra to Kumasi, July 26. Cap on his first experiences in Accra]: The men here dance with men. I was asked by McClure if I wanted to dance, but I refrained. [laughs] I figured it was no place for me to take up the local custom. [. . .] So far I've had no water. Their beer, the Star beer, that beer box that Jon sent his gifts back in, that is a very, I think, fairly good beer. None of it's very cold. [. . .] When you go to one of these little cafés they're playing what they call High Life, High Life music, but when you go, then they start playing American records. We tell them to shut it off.

[Cap and Jon spend two nights in Kumasi and then hire a car and driver to take them to Acherensua. On July 28, in the Peace Corps bungalow, where Cap is staying, two Ghanaian masters formally present him with a ceremonial sword in honor of his visit.]:
Mr. Baidan (the music master): Jon, here is a token for your father in appreciation of his visit to us and from Mr. Owoahene and his family and everybody in the room here. It is in remembrance of this visit. We had expected him to have stayed a little longer than he has done. However, we shan't like to disrupt the program he has already made. So wherever he will be, this reminds him of his visit to Acherensua. Thanks for his visit.

*Presentation of ceremonial sword to Cap Thiem in Acherensua.*
*L. to R.: Ohene's wife, Mr. Baiden (Music Master), Ohene,*
*Cap, Gene Katona, and Mrs. Boakye, July 28, 1969.*

Cap Thiem: Thank you Mr. Baidan. Now I am going to have Jon introduce each of the people in the room and they'll say hello or whatever they wish.

Jon: This is Mrs. Owoahene.

[Mrs. Owoahene addresses Cap Thiem in Asante Twi. Then Mrs. Boakye.]

Jon: This is Mr. Owoahene, who wants to speak even before he is introduced. [laughter] Go ahead, speak.

Mr. Owoahene: I thought Sir John [Cap Thiem] would stay longer, but because of pressure of time, he says he is leaving. Well, we present this sword to him, that he may remember us when he goes back to the States. And we do this in appreciation, with my wife and others . . . . And we hope that Sir John will show this to Judy and Mrs. Thiem and also share our gifts. Thank you very much and we hope you will always remember us.

[. . .]

[Cap Thiem on dinner at the Headmaster's]: In the meantime we met the Headmaster who invited us to dinner. We were very glad to accept. [. . .] Around 7:30 we kind of splashed a little water on our face and went over for dinner. The school master [i.e. the Headmaster] is a great beer drinker and the Ghanaian custom is that as soon as he sees a little out of your glass he pours it up. I called my glass the magical glass, which would never empty. [. . .] Then we went to dinner. His wife did not eat with us. She prepared the meal. It was a big serving of rice on top of which I had the leg of a chicken . . . . It was really very very good. And we were hungry. [. . .] We did give . . . the Pinch bottle of Scotch that I brought over . . . to the Headmaster, which I think was a good idea.

[Next day, July 29. Cap reports on the day's events. He, Jon, and Gene Katona, a tourist from New York, are riding in a hired car taking them back to Kumasi]:

After breakfast Owoahene, Jon and Gene and I went over to the fetish [priest's] village. First we went to Owoahene's farm, took pictures of okra and garden eggs, cassava, a picture of a wawa tree, odum tree, a picture of a silk cotton tree, which is really a kapok tree, and I took typical pictures of the garden so you can see how they casually cultivate. They really do a good job. The cassava is a root that they make foo foo out of and it matures in about a year. You pull it out (I have some pictures of that) and then you just cut off sticks and put it back in the ground and it grows. [. . .] And they also have . . . coco yam.

*Ohene and Jon harvest a cassava on Ohene's farm plot, near Acherensua, July 29, 1969.*

# LETTERS FROM GHANA

As we are driving here we are passing many many logging trucks. The logs are so large that only one goes on a truck. [. . .] The visit to the fetish priest at the village was very good. Of course you have to buy your way in. I gave him a half pack of cigarettes. Jon gave him a cedi. [. . .] Then he gave a fetish dance, one of the tribal dances. We took pictures of these. [. . .] When we came back Opong [the Peace Corps cook] brought from his home foo foo, palm nut oil soup, and some fried plantain. Well, that was quite an experience. You take the foo foo and drop it into the soup and then you take your fingers, you get a little soup on the foo foo or it's too sticky, and you take a small amount and put it in your mouth. And the funny thing about it is you don't chew, you swallow it. Well, actually the food, this foo foo was made out of cassava and plantain. You can also use coco yam in it. [. . .] I thought the taste was fine. A little salt would have been helpful. But you're not supposed to chew it and to swallow it is almost .. .. .. , well it's quite opposite to the way we are used to eating food. But enough was enough. I liked the fried plantain very much. But we did have a typical Ghanaian dinner there.

[Side Two]:

[Cap reports on the visit to Kumasi—taped on the State Transportation Bus to Accra, July 31.]: We saw the Asantehene who is head of all of these people, and the Okyenhene. Now both of those are kind of equal top chiefs over everyone, but the Okyenhene is the one who has less power. But he's the one that Jon has all these pictures of when he was at his "live-in" [at Kibi] . . . . Jon walked up to him and sure enough, he recognized him, so they talked and Jon introduced me and he also introduced Gene. I asked him if he liked American cigars and I gave him a couple of American cigars. We had a very good time talking there, just shortly. Then he got into his Rolls Royce and took off. Then about fifteen minutes later the Asantehene came out . . . and actually he waved to us. He's a rather old man. And he's one of the most powerful figures in Ghana.

*Side One: In Acherensua, Cap is treated with great honor and respect, partly because he made the long trip from America to visit a Ghanaian village, and partly because of his respectable age (47 years old).*

*Jon's relations with the Headmaster are still strained. Cap's friendliness, along with the bottle of Scotch he brings, creates a harmonious atmosphere at the Headmaster's dinner. The Headmaster explains to Cap that the school badly needs a telescope. Due to the successful landing on the moon on July 20th, space exploration has achieved a high profile. Acherensua students are becoming interested in astronomy. (See November 1970, "Achisco Module 2 in Space," from the student newspaper.) Cap says he will do what he can to get a telescope for the school.*

*Gene Katona is a social scientist from Rensselaer Institute in upstate New York. He is traveling through Ghana alone when Jon and Cap make his acquaintance in Kumasi. They invite him to go with them to Acherensua for a closer look at rural life.*

*Cap says in the tape: "As we are driving here we are passing many many logging trucks. The logs are so large that only one goes on a truck." The size of an Odum tree is reminiscent of redwoods or sequoias. The extensive forests of the Brong-Ahafo region were a major source of timber for western logging companies. These firms made a lot of money. Ghana made very little. The extensive logging contributed to widespread destruction of the forest canopy. Peace Corps and Canadian volunteers in the region were appalled by the greed and thoughtlessness of these operations. It is doubtful that the great forest canopy will ever recover. Today, in a time of rising levels of atmospheric carbon dioxide, it is sad to think of the loss of these rich, $CO_2$-absorbing forests. See Corbin and also Birmingham 111.*

*On the visit to Ohene's farm plot. Cap and another Dupont colleague bought a farm near Seaford, Delaware. They worked it themselves—hence Cap's interest in growing vegetables and methods of cultivation.. When Jon returned to the States, he brought Cap a pair of cassava sticks he had cut in Ghana. One of the sticks took root and grew into a bush. Only later did Jon learn that cassava was the same as manioc, an indigenous plant of America that had later been naturalized in West Africa.*

# LETTERS FROM GHANA

*The "village" of the fetish priest was in fact a very small settlement; it had about ten to twenty inhabitants. Jon, Ohene, Cap, and Gene walked to the hamlet, which was several miles from the school and in the depths of the forest. In the hamlet there stood the fetish of a god, about two feet high, molded out of earth, slightly anthropomorphic. The fetish is the physical abode of a powerful spirit. The spirit enters the fetish, when it is invoked by the priest, usually by means of a dance. This fetish priest was the same one to whom McClure and Jon turned when McClure's radio was stolen. (See the cassette tape transcript dated Nov. 21, 1968.)*

*The day after this recording, on August 1st, Cap and Jon fly from Accra (via Lagos, Nigeria and Entebbe, Uganda) to Nairobi, Kenya. This is the beginning of their long-planned trip to East Africa.*

**Cap Thiem's memories of the trip to East Africa in August 1969.** Transcription of a cassette tape, made September 20, 2003, in Wilmington, Delaware. Transcribed by Jon Thiem, January 9, 2012. Excerpts.

[Tape 1: Side One]
[C: Cap Thiem
J: Jon Thiem]

[First Night at Ngorongoro Crater, Tanzania]:
J: You've got down here [on a list of things to talk about] "wildebeest." I know we saw wildebeest. There's [also] the "muddy climb to the crater" [i.e. up to the ridge of Ngorongoro Crater].
C: Yea, that's where the oxen were in the road and of course
J: Water buffalo [African Buffalo]
C: Water buffalo, which are very very dangerous and we were up to our hubcaps in mud in that little car that we had rented—Eve [?], the driver and the owner—and I think the [same] day, a week before, a bus had gone off that road and killed a bunch of nuns and we, it was dark, and the water buffalo scared the devil out of me, I don't know how high we were and then,
J: It was pretty high, I remember,
C: Well, I don't know which part we were on, and we were .. .. .. there was a sheer drop off on our left, we were going up, straight up, and on our left

was a drop off and of course as you drive these little cars the back end was swerving back and forth and if we had gone off .. .. .. that's where the nurses, or the nuns, had gone off, and I was quite upset and you were kind of leaning back in the car and you said, "Dad, are you worrying?" and I said "Yea" and you said "Well, then I won't have to." And you just kind of relaxed till we got to the top. That was a long night because when we got up there everything was black. I mean you couldn't see any light, and we saw a place that we thought was a restaurant,

J: From the top of the ridge, we went down into the crater and,

C: Well, that was the next day. But this is at night, and we saw this place, and we said, gee, maybe it's open. We were hungry! And here it was a great restaurant, like a palace up there, like a .. .. .. you don't call them palaces .. .. .. well I don't know,

J: Yes.

C: And we went in there and it was fantastic and we took our driver in, and they were .. .. .. each evening they would have meat [from wild animals] that had been killed [in the crater area] . . . and there was wildebeest that evening, and so we ate wildebeest. It wasn't very good. Well, you know, at least I knew it wasn't rat. And I remember the driver we had. I said, "This is the first time I've ever had dinner with an African and he said this is the first time I've ever had dinner with .. .. .." whatever he called us. You know everybody was on holiday over there.

J: Yea. I guess it must have been an unusual thing for him, probably most of the tourists that he knew [were],

C: Very separative,

J: Would have been separative. He was a very nice fellow, the driver, I remember.

*Ngorongoro crater is the largest intact volcanic caldera in the world, 2,000 feet deep and 12 miles in diameter. It is the habitat of a wide variety of wildlife, including rare black rhinoceroses (see Peter C. Alden et al 131). It is now a World Heritage Site. At Ngorongoro and at Nairobi National Park in Kenya, Cap and Jon observed and photographed over two dozen kinds of birds and mammals, including a black rhinoceros (at Ngorongoro) that began to charge their Land Rover, and then changed its mind.*

*Black Rhinoceros and Oxpecker Bird, Ngorongoro Crater, August 1969. Photograph by Jon Thiem.*

The "water" buffalo to which Cap refers is the African or Cape buffalo: it is not domesticated but wild. A herd of these animals loomed out of the night, shambling very close to the small car Cap and Jon were in. The bulls weigh up to 2,000 lbs., each horn around 3 feet long (measured along the outer curve). Usually benign, the Cape buffalo is one of the most dangerous of animals when angry or injured. They kill lions.

The wildebeest, or gnu, is a hump-backed antelope, with horns like a cow, a black mane and tail like a horse, and a white beard. The front of the body has dark vertical stripes.

The above information is drawn from the entries on the African Buffalo (509-10) and the Wildebeest (496-97) in Peter C. Alden et al, and the entries on the African Buffalo (27-31), and Wildebeest (53-55) in Astley Maberly.

[On Mount Kilimanjaro]:

J: Well I remember when we were on Kilimanjaro I had you for both, a bed companion and a hot water bottle.
C: I was lying on top of you to keep you warm. You were shaking.

J: Right. I remember pretty much what happened there, but what's your memory of it—as we were, you know, going up to that hut [Kibo hut]. I remember I more or less collapsed.

C: Well, you were way ahead of us. It was like a plain [the saddle between the peaks].

J: It was about 13 to 14 thousand feet, wasn't it?

C: No, no. We were 15 thousand, 16. No, see, it's 19,230 feet. And we were almost at, we were well over 18 and 1/2 thousand feet. And you had been eating quite a bit and there was a kind of a plain, and you walked ahead of us, cause we saw the hut [Kibo hut]. And when I got up there, you were relieving yourself [at] both ends. I was trying to help you.

J: This was before the hut as I recall.

C: Before the hut, yea. And so we finally got you to bed, and I packed covers on you, and I gave you my sleeping bag, and Fatali came over. He was our head guide. And he looked at you seriously and put his hand on his chest, and said, "He'll live," and I said, "you['re] god damn [right] he better live." [all laugh] I can remember him telling me that. He didn't speak English. He just knew "yes" or "no," "up slow" and "down fast." But I laid on top of you for a long time. You were just shivering.

*Cap Thiem and Kilimanjaro, August 1969.*

J: I was shaking I remember. I felt sick and was shaking.

C: You were sick. You were vomiting and you had a .. .. .. I mean, you were a mess. If I'd a had a hose up there I'd a hosed you down. [all laugh]

J: But I remember Dad just crawled in with me [in] the sleeping bag to warm me up. I would have died of the shakes if you hadn't done that.

C: Well the sleeping bags were too small anyway. I could hardly get in mine. Mrs. Brewer, remember Mrs. Brewer?

J: Yes

[. . .]

J: Well, the next day [after the descent of the mountain] I felt bad because Dad was in great shape, you know. He didn't get this altitude sickness, but it was because of me .. .. .. we were within a thousand feet, I think, of the summit of Kilimanjaro, and he would have made it up easily, you know, the next day. You had to get up fairly early in the morning when the scree was frozen, so you could walk the scree up to the top.

*Cap and Jon's memories of altitudes on Kilimanjaro are not accurate. Because of the attack of altitude sickness suffered by Jon, he and his father were unable to proceed higher than Kibo hut, which is at 15,420 feet. The real summit of the mountain is 19,340 feet (at the crater)— the highest point on the African continent. Most trekkers do not go beyond Gillman's Point (18,640), which is 3,400 feet above Kibo hut (not 1,000 feet as Jon said). Gillman's Point is reached by climbing over a slope of scree. The "plain" to which Cap refers is the high saddle between the Kibo crater, the highest point of the mountain, and Mawenzi peak. This saddle is between 14,000 and 14,500 feet in elevation. Kibo hut is between the saddle and the scree slope. When the scree is frozen (by the frigid night air), it is less unstable than when it thaws and loosens up during the middle of the day. For these and other statistics, see Ian C. Reid's* Guide Book to Mount Kenya and Kilimanjaro *152-154, 160-62.*

**August 30, 1969.** Jon in Asiwa, Ghana, to his parents and sister in Chattanooga.

As you know I was going to Kokofu with Mr. Owohene [Mr. Owoahene] to collect some [oral] poetry. We stayed there two days and then went from there to Asiwa, a very small, poor village about 20 miles away. Unfortunately the lorry broke down so we had to walk w/ our luggage for about 12 miles over a series of hills about 1500 ft. high. It felt like Kilimanjaro again.

Mr. Owoahene's parents live here. I've met nearly every one of the ≈ 500 people here. The people are very friendly and I am treated like an important diplomat. The life is somewhat monotonous: meeting people and drinking palm wine from 8:00 AM to 8:00 PM (bedtime).

There's neither electricity or [running] water[,] and disease and illiteracy are prevalent. The village is now applying to U.S. AID for money to build a badly needed health center.

I'll be here 2 more days and then back to Kokofu for some more poetry [research]. On Sept. 3rd I'm supposed to meet the C.U.S.O. (Canadian) volunteer for Acherensua and then on the 5th to meet Prof. Denteh [and then] to go to Kokofu again. On the 8th I'm supposed to go to U. of Ghana Accra for a Peace Corps Conference there. So I'm keeping a little busy.

*Asiwa is a village in Ashanti Region, near Lake Bosumtwi and not far from Kokofu.*

*US AID is the United States Agency for International Development.*

*C.U.S.O. is Canadian University Services Overseas. The new Canadian volunteer will replace Lawrie Altrows.*

*Jon and Ohene visit Professor Denteh, at the University of Ghana, to get advice on the apaeɛ project.*

**September 1, 1969.** From Mr. E. W. Owoahene-Akyampong in Kumasi, addressed to Mr. and Mrs. John R. (Cap) Thiem in Chattanooga.

Dear Sir John,

It may seem very strange to you to have heard from me. You know I am E. W. Owoahene, John's [Jon's] friend. I think you have arrived in Tennessee safely to see once more Mrs. [Thiem] and Judy. [Not] [l]ong after your journey to East Africa with Jon I met John [Jon] once more. In fact he told me a number of your adventures that you experienced in Kenya. Most interesting of all was your attempt with Kilimanjaro for a very high altitude and how you were able to descend 30 miles [in one] day. He also told me of the number of animals you saw, the other great mountains and kinds of lakes you saw. I hope you learnt more about Africa. Surely you might have also equally enjoyed [your stay] in Ghana and more especially in Acherensua where I am [stationed] with Jon now.

It might interest you to know that two days after Jon's arrival from Kenya, I took Jon to Asiwa, my father's village—a sizeable village near the Lake, south of Kumasi. No "Whiteman" or "Obroni" had ever been there. Jon was therefore greeted as a Royal visitor. Wherever we went children and others followed to see John [Jon]. We met with the celebrated men and women in the town. Jon also attended Church Service at the Presbyterian Church with me. He was given the opportunity to speak to the congregation and I interpreted [for] him. The townsmen were much friendly. Notable incidents are how Jon saved the life of my friend's son. He generously bore the expenses and the hospital fees. He also advised on how to obtain an U.S. AID [sic] for a Health Center. His visit was marked by hectic periods since he had no time to rest.

I remember Jon also entertained about 80 children to a soft drink party. Children could not leave him for their beds [to go to bed] and were sorry to miss him even during the nocturnal hours. It was a nice stay and journey we made.

We returned from Asiwa, the village, for Kumasi[,] where we are now 1/9/69. The stay with Jon and my parents was so unique that John [Jon] has been asked to return during the Christmas [holiday]. Therefore with good presents from Jon to my parents, I would like on behalf of all citizens to thank him. We hope he will stay in Ghana with these virtuous aspirations in life.

Please return some of the pictures you took with my wife and children to me. Remember me to Mrs. Thiem, and my pretty Judy whom I think Jon will give to me in marriage (Ha! ha! ha! ha!)

Till I hear from you too,
    it is,
        E. W. Owoahene-Akyampong

*In Ghana, dates follows British usage: the day precedes the month. Thus 1/9/69 is September 1, 1969.*

*"Jon saved the life of my friend's son": Jon gave first aid to a boy with a deep cut on his hand. The boy was being treated, ineffectually, with traditional medicine. The wound had been bleeding steadily for a number of hours, and the boy was shaking from loss of blood. Jon applied a tourniquet, and then, hiring a lorry, he took the lad to the nearest health clinic, about half an hour down the dirt track from Asiwa.*

*". . . my pretty Judy": Ohene later named one of his daughters Judy, after Jon's sister. Over the course of his adult life, Ohene fathered 16 children.*

**September 12, 1969.** Jon at the University of Ghana in Legon to his parents and sister in Chattanooga. Excerpts.

I've spent the last 5 days here at [the] University of Ghana at a Peace Corps conference. [. . .]

I've now met both the new volunteers coming to Acherensua. The Canadian is Nestor Kwasynscia [Kwasnycia] and the American is David Fitzjarrald. I like them both.

In about 3 days Nestor + I will go back to Acherensua to get ready for the school year.

**September 20, 1969 (date recorded).** Cassette tape transcription. From Cap and Ginny in Hamilton, Ohio, to Jon in Acherensua. Excerpts.

[Side Two, messages from Thiem relatives in Hamilton, Ohio]:
[Grandpa Rudy]: Hi Jon, this is . . . Grandpa. Your Mother and your Dad and your Dad and Judy [sic] made a surprise visit on us this afternoon. Sure glad to see them. We also enjoyed the [African] pictures Cap took. [. . .]
[Uncle Don, Cap's brother]: Hello Jon. Just saw your slides from your little trip and it looked like you had a real good time. You looked pretty

good. Cap looked pretty sick. And I understand you'll be home next year, next August, about. So when you come home we'd like to see you.
[Barb, Jon's cousin, age 19]: OK, Jon. Let's see. This is Barb. [laughs]. Wow. Gosh. OK.
[Davy, Jon's cousin, age 7]: Hi. I'm David Thiem.
[Aunt Lula, Don's wife]: Hello Jon. Well, we hope when you come home you'll come see us. Goodbye.

*Jon's parents paid visits with their tape recorder, and they asked relatives and family friends to record messages for Jon. The responses in these excerpts are typical. People do not usually offer more than a simple greeting. They are a bit tongue-tied. (The same baffled response was not uncommon among Ghanaians, though there was less hesitation when they spoke Asante rather than English.) Most Americans at this time were unfamiliar with speaking into a portable cassette recorder. It was a new technology. (Nor did they have much practice talking into telephone answering machines, a technology that did not take off until the early 70s.)*

**September 29, 1969 (date recorded).** Cassette tape transcription. Cap and Ginny Thiem in Chattanooga to Jon in Acherensua. Excerpts.

[Side One]:
[Cap]: Dear Jon, happy birthday from your father. I certainly wish I could be there to celebrate it with you, but as you know, that's impossible. [. . .] . . . I want you to tell Mr. Owoahene we enjoyed the words and the songs and all their expressions of gratitude to you as you went to the village of his parents. Tell him that I will be personally writing him a letter. I received his letter the other day. I appreciate all his kind words, and I remember fondly the meeting and the short while we had together.

[Side Two]:
[Ginny reads into the recorder a mini-biography of Jon she has written, concluding]: Happy Birthday, Jon, love Mom and Dad.

[Cap]: It's been a busy time since I've been back to America. I told you in one of the letters, I've been working yeoman's hours. In fact I've been putting in some 12 to 16 hours a day at the plant and at home, getting caught up. [. . .]

We often think of all the things that you've done as you worked your way up from a young boy to a young man where you are today. As I work and as I play and as I sit at home, I often think of those three weeks that seem like a dream rather than a reality that we spent together in Africa. I hope that you enjoyed them as much as I did. I believe I'll carry their memories for a long time. The fact is, some of them come back stronger, but I'm kind of like you, I go from one thing to the next, and they just pop back now and then. [. . .] I will seek out and find, I assure you, a telescope for . . . the Headmaster and I will write Mr. Owoahene. [. . .]

I have to laugh, when mother and I are talking, she'll ask me this or that, was your bed soft, how was your room fixed, and it seems that a lot of those details, which are quite important to the ladies, and I guess sometimes are trivia to us, are left unanswered. As I think about these things I try to relate them to you. I did enjoy very much your comment that it was like Christmas when you got back [to Acherensua from East Africa] and you were glad you saved the cookies [that Ginny baked]. I could almost see you in your gossamer room, shrouded by spider webs in the corner, sitting there reading, or listening to the tapes, and eating your Christmas cookies. [Ginny sends the recording of a TV interview with a member of SDS]

[Ginny's response to the tape Jon sent, recording events of his stay in Ohene's village, Asiwa]: We enjoyed Mr. Owoahene and the Presbyterian service, as well as the guitar playing and the singing . . . we'll always cherish the tape. [. . .] It's surprising how well they sang and the talent they have, too. Not everybody can sing like that. You ought to join in with him sometime and sing in Twi. We couldn't understand the Twi, but when you come back you can interpret it for us. [. . .]

The mail man just came to the door and he didn't have anything from you again. I'm getting kind of anxious. It's been a couple of weeks, although I was glad you sent the note from Accra. [. . .] All the neighbors are anxious to see the slides. [. . .] Well, Kofi, this tape is about to run out, so I'll say good luck, good health, good school year.

*Side One:*
*(For Ohene's letter to Cap see, September 1, 1969.)*
*Side Two:*
*". . . I've been working yeoman's hours." Cap's three-week trip to Africa set him back in his work. At the time he was area supervisor at the Dupont nylon plant in Chattanooga.*
*Ginny addresses Jon as "Kofi," his Asante name.*

**October15, 1969 (date recorded).** Cassette tape transcription. Ginny in Chattanooga to Jon in Acherensua. Excerpts.

[Side One]:
[On this tape Ginny recorded TV programs about the October 15th nationwide Moratorium against the war, as well as news reports about civil rights protests in Tennessee]
[Tape of a news cast on the curfew in Chattanooga]: "Ninety students stayed away from classes yesterday in protest over the School Board's decision to cancel the student votes on whether the school would drop its Confederate flag emblems and the song Dixie . . . ." [Brainerd High School, Chattanooga] [. . .] "Negro students in Memphis ended their boycott of city schools today and returned to classes. Memphis officials said today's attendance was normal after 62,000 students stayed away from classes yesterday. The NAACP which called the boycott to support demands for the resignation of three white school board members, called the day of protest a success."
[Ginny]: This is some current events of Chattanooga to keep you up to date of what's going on here. Jon, you always write and say everything sounds so peaceful in my letters, so I thought if I bring you some of this kind of thing, you'll know what's going on.

*On Moratorium Day (October 15th) there were protests and vigils in opposition to the war, which by this date had claimed the lives of around 40,000 U.S. soldiers, 8,000 more than a year earlier when Jon began his first term as a Peace Corps teacher. Many universities voluntarily closed. Ralph Slotten gives a report on Moratorium Day in Carlisle, Pennsylvania (Slotten to Jon, Early November 1969).*

**November 3, 1969.** Jon in Acherensua to his parents in Chattanooga. Excerpts.

As usual I've been very busy. Owoahene and I've [sic] been working on our Ashanti Poetry Project. Last weekend I went to Accra to get books + run errands for the school, plus there's the teaching.
[. . .]
In November there is to be a 2 day Mobilization. If the movement keeps up, Nixon will be forced to call the boys home. Three more years of the war he is saying now. I don't think Americans will tolerate it any longer.

**[Early November, before November. 22, 1969].** Ralph Slotten in Carlisle to Jon in Acherensua. Typed. Excerpts.

Dear Jon,
I have had your card from Nairobi on my desk for a couple of months as a reminder that I must write to you.
[. . .]
I cannot imagine what Africa must have done to you! You must be quite a different fellow than I remember you, after a year and a half of tribalism, teaching responsibility, and three hundred more books embedded in your cerebrum! I anticipate your return and the opportunity to know you again after the alterations .. .. ..
You and your father must have had a wonderful time in East Africa. India seems quite normal and possible to me—but Africa! That is something unthinkable!
[. . .]

I have been reconceiving my Religion 313 course . . . . I am gearing it to this mod generation's search for relevance! ("search for identity and community") and looking for myth and ritual motifs in American life . . . . I think much to my students' (initial) disgust, I am heavy on the past—what there is of an American past!

[. . .]

My seminar in myth and ritual this fall has been a disaster! Only a couple of students have any idea of what is coming off—Jill McClanahan, whom I believe you must know, is one of them. What a contrast to my glorious autumn in myth and ritual with one Jon Thiem to stimulate me.

We are up to our ears in New Democratic Coalition affairs (I am chairman!)—I am also chairman to COO (Conscientious Objectors Organization) and on Policy and Academic Program[s]! But I am a terrible committee member, and I am hoping that nobody will ever vote for me again if I do a bad enough job. [. . .] We had a very successful Moratorium in Carlisle on Oct. 15, which really turned into a Love-In—we had an Agape (Love-Feast) for about 60 marchers in our living room after the peace-hike—a regular happening, took off our shoes, sat on the floor sang folk-songs written for the Mass—Roman Catholics, Protestants, and Jews present, and both students and faculty.

[. . .] . . . I hope that time and space will not altogether smash our friendship. Martha often asks if I have written you, wanting to know what you are doing, thinking, and so on. [. . .] —When does your Africa term expire?

**November 17, 1969.** Jon in Acherensua to his parents in Chattanooga. Excerpts.

. . . I'm not interested at all in pursuing a career of public service or administration. When I majored in Political Science I had considered this course but in studying administration, etc., I realized that this was not the thing for me as either a course of study or career. My experience in the Peace Corps has reinforced this indifference towards a career of public activity, service or leadership. [. . .] . . . I have chosen an academic career in literature (on the university level) as a profession. The study and teaching of literature are things I enjoy doing. The Peace Corps has been bearable 1) because I've been able to teach literature even though on a rudimentary level 2) I have had ample time to study literature 3) I've had the chance to apply myself practically to the problem of collecting, translating, and commenting on Ashanti literature (my poetry project). Doing these things has increased both my competence and interest in the study of literature. I do not want to lose this impetus. But it is more than a question of impetus. It is a question of being successful in a field of academia in which I had little experience as an undergraduate (I was a political science major). [. . .] My excellence in this field [literary study] is first of all dependent on mastery of the tools of the field: linguistics . . . ; anthropology; French and Italian (in which my knowledge is only superficial) and Latin (of which I know virtually nothing). These are only the tools. I'm like a college graduate who is just beginning to learn math but who is applying to Engineering grad school.

[. . .]

Avoiding the draft. I'm not willing to do something I don't want to do just to avoid the draft. I wanted to join the Peace Corps not just to avoid the draft. If it had been only to avoid the draft I probably wouldn't have joined or if I had I would not have stayed.

I hope you will respect my feelings on these choices I've made. It's time I quit doing this thing and that thing if the things are unrelated to a bigger more continuous plan. [. . .] It's about time I stick to my guns and do one thing and one thing for long enough that I can tell if I'm going to succeed in it.

Right now I'm still busy on this poetry project which along with teaching has taken all my time and strength. [. . .] If I am lucky and it is [published] I'll be happy. If not I'll know what to do next time.

Thanks again for your suggestions.

*This letter is in response to a letter from Jon's parents. They have urged him to apply for the White House Fellows' Program—in part because it offered draft deferment.*

# LETTERS FROM GHANA

**November 22, 1969.** Jon in Acherensua to Ralph Slotten in Carlisle, Pennsylvania. This letter is a reply to Ralph's letter sent in early November. Excerpts.

I've developed lots of new notions (to me) about this strange Africa and also about myself, as I'm sure you have also concerning the places you've visited (and yourself). I'm glad I joined the Peace Corps: I definitely have decided to study literature, especially in the kind of program that can accommodate oral and popular literature. My studies with you were invaluable in opening my eyes to new sorts of "literary" phenomena and perspectives. [. . .]

.. .. .. .. Did I tell you I've been collecting oral traditions? They are heroic praise poems in the court of the Ashanti King (Asantehene)[.] To date I and Mr. Owoahene (the Religion master here) have collected about 23 [poems] totalling 180 lines. Most of our free time in the last 4 months has been spent transcribing, translating (a literal one) and annotating these things. They are one one of the few examples of traditional unsung poetry in Akan culture; none have been published that we know of. [. . .] I'm enclosing some rough drafts of a few of the Apaeɛ (as they are called) along with some tentative notes. [. . .]

The Ashantis were once great hunters, if not a hunting society. Today the animals have been killed off or driven away and the lands made into farms. In the Apaeɛ, however, animals and hunting are preponderant in the praise imagery. I've combed through my 4 volumes of Rattray's exhaustive and exhausting anthropological work on the Ashantis but have failed to find any reference about a "master of animals." The fetish priests (Okomfo) do, however, have certain powers over animals. There are some animals which are even given a human-like burial when they are killed (Bongo and elephants). [. . .] Human-like burial is a way to appease their spirits which might harm man otherwise. [. . .]

More about <u>The American Adam</u>: If your students are hostile to your course because of its emphasis on the past, make them read Chapter 1 . . . : it proves that being against the past is a basic American tradition. (Lewis's book is one of the most satisfying I've read on American culture.) I think personally I'm more past oriented, but living in quasi tribal surroundings has made me despise the practical, dismal effects of traditionalism. As an aesthetic oriented person I find tradition indispensable to the game of art; my objection is that tradition in Africa stultifys [sic] creativity in doing things, in relieving the burdens of ignorance and suffering. These last I think are terribly related. I'll have to wait until I see you again in America to discuss these things.

*Slotten's Ph.D. dissertation focused on the "Master of Animals" figure. In 1969, he was planning to do further work on the subject, hence Jon's remarks on animals in the apaeɛ and Akan tradition.*
    *The American Adam is an incisive study written by the scholar R. W. B. Lewis.*

[Early **December 1969**]. Jon to his parents in Chattanooga. Excerpts.

This weekend was simultaneously faulted and exalted by a visit, an official visit by our former ass't. headmaster, currently the honourable member of Parliament from the Asunafo constituency and ministerial secretary for Labour and Social Welfare. Such an important visit generated a lot of pomp and circumstance. I had the irritating privilege of giving the "vote of thanks" for Mr. Badu Nkwansah which forced me to get rigged up in my Haspel suit and the outlandish blue and white tie Dad left me. Afterwards we retired to the Headmaster's lawn for a lawn party, more "votes of thanks," heavily peppered mutton, beer, dancing to soul and highlife [music] etc. This was better than the lecture. David's (P.C.V.) girlfriend . . . (. . . from near Accra) was here and she
created a minor hit. Nestor (the Canadian) was away on his 350 c.c. motorcycle to visit friends in Dommahenkro [Dormaa Ahenkro].
    Last week we received visits from the Peace Corps staff and [from] Dr. Wittsenberg of Hwidiem hospital who delivered a hilarious lecture on "Abortions and Birth Control." . . . the Headmaster asked the Doctor (in front of 800 students of Acherensua Secondary School and Hwidiem training college) if a man would become pregnant if the woman were on top during sexual intercourse. The Doctor (without cracking a smile) enlightened him as to the "facts." Meanwhile life in Acherensua goes on.

Next week I go to Kumasi to see about the publication of our [Ashanti] poem[s] (which looks doubtful). [. . .] Time is flying.

*Mr. Badu Nkwansah, the former Assistant Headmaster, was elected from the Asunafo district to the new parliament in the first free election (August 1969) since Nkrumah had been overthrown by the military in February 1966. Before the election, Badu Nkwansah represented Asunafo at the Constituent Assembly which proposed the new constitution and generated rules for the election and the transition to democracy. See the cassette tape transcription of April 4, 1969, for a conversation between Badu Nkwansah, McClure and Jon. On Badu Nkwansah's exemplary career as a candidate for public office in the 1969 national election, see John Dunn, "Politics in Asunafo."*

**December 11, 1969.** Jon in Acherensua to his parents and sister in Chattanooga. Excerpts.

I'm invigilating (monitoring) an exam while I am writing this. I received your two letters Dad and enjoyed reading them. I'm glad you accepted my decision on the "White House Fellows." [. . .]

Thanksgiving we stayed here and had chicken and gave thanks. It was also Nestor's birthday. Right after that he was in a motorcycle accident and got his face badly scraped, now he's O.K.

Kofi (whom Dad met) is an alien (his parents are from Ivory Coast) and under the new Aliens decree he is supposed to be deported. I think he'll be able to stay, however, with our support.

[. . .]

I got a letter from McClure. He is teaching Chem. in an English School outside of Paris. Osei Adjei is now in Germany. This summer the 3 of us plan to meet somewhere in Europe.

*"He was in a motorcycle accident . . . .": Canadian volunteers were allowed to have motorcycles. Peace Corps volunteers were not, unless necessary for their work.*

# LETTERS FROM GHANA

"Kofi" is Kofi Ampofo, the Peace Corps cook's assistant and nephew. His parents are Ivoirian. The Aliens Compliance Act of 1969 resulted in the forcible expulsion, from December 1969 to April 1970, of about 150,000 "aliens"—largely Nigerian artisans and laborers who did not have work permits. See Gocking xxxi, 156-57. Kofi was not deported.

Osei Adjei was a master at Acherensua Secondary School.

**December 16, 1969.** Jon in Acherensua to his parents and sister in Chattanooga. Excerpts.

I was very happy to hear from you that I'm #342 [in the draft lottery]. It's almost certain I won't be called. David, the other volunteer here is #74. I sure was lucky. A good reason to be merry this Xmas.

Answers to Questions: As far as I know I never got Cora's or Kaye's cards or money.

I got [the] calendar but [the] box was opened + no hankies.

No cookies or candy and no $10 [for] Thanksgiving did I get. The mail hasn't been coming through. [There is a] New Postmaster + I have to pay NC 10.00 for customs duty. Inform all not to send money or gifts as they may either be stolen or I shall have to pay customs duty. [. . .]

I'm not planning to request deferment from my Draft Board.

[The] Letter you got from [the] Post Office clerk. Must be from Accra. David Fitzgerald's [sic] mother got one also from the same guy. Apparently he collects [the] addresses of P.C.V. mail. Don't worry. Send him a Xmas card.

*In the U.S. Draft Lottery (the drawing was on December 1, 1969) Jon received number 342, out of a possible 365, making it most unlikely he would be conscripted when he returned to the States. David's number 74 is low, making it more likely he would be. Peace Corps service is only a deferment from the draft, not a substitute for it. Returned volunteers, after having spent two years abroad, could be legally drafted. Some were, and some died in Vietnam.*

*"NC" is the Ghanaian currency: New Cedi.*

# LETTERS FROM GHANA

*Jon's parents have received a letter from a Ghanaian postal clerk they do not know. Many Ghanaians who could write English were eager to correspond with North Americans.*

**December 1969.** Excerpts from the manuscript *Apaeɛ: Ashanti Praise Poems. Recited from Oral Tradition by Kwasi Dum. Collected and Translated by Jon Thiem and E. W. Owoahene.* For more background on this work see *The Oral Poetry Project* section in the Introduction.

FOREWORD [excerpts]

The goal of this little publication is to introduce to Ghanaians and non-Ghanaians alike some examples of a high verbal art, in this case Ashanti oral poetry. We who have collected and introduced these poems have at various times studied and taught literature . . . Neither of us has had much formal training in linguistics or cultural history, yet we have tried in a general way to put these little gems into some sort of linguistic and cultural setting. We hope that at least the transcription of these poems, if not some of our commentaries, will be of value to scholars.

We owe our greatest debt to the reciter, Kwasi Dum, whose marvelous recitations, interest, and co-operation have sustained this project.
[. . .]
[The foreword expresses gratitude to Peace Corps Ghana staff members Bill Opel, Whit Foster, and Ira Okun, for their enthusiastic support of the project.]

Finally, we owe a lot of gratitude to the kind people of Sebedie and Kokofu, especially Nana Osɛe Assibey, paramount chief of the Kokofu traditional area, and Mr. B. K. Boama whose hospitality made this project a real pleasure.

E. W. Owoahene
Jon Thiem

December 1969
Acherensua Secondary School

# LETTERS FROM GHANA

Acherensua, Ghana

INTRODUCTION [excerpts]
[...]

Milieu and Performance [excerpts]

Apaeɛ are recited by the king's or chief's executioners (abrafo). At one time these men were also responsible for human sacrifices and other executions; today, they are mainly praise reciters. During durbars or festivals a number of these executioners stand near the king. If one becomes inspired he steps forward, assuming the formal recitation stance . . . , and points his ceremonial sword towards the king. The executioner then exclaims, "He is the one!" and begins reciting . . . . Meanwhile all activity has stopped. Everyone has become solemn and rapt with attention. The recitation completed, the durbar carries on with drumming and horn blowing until another executioner steps forth to recite another Apaeɛ. This ritual may be repeated a number of times.

The conduct of praiser and praised is very important. If the king smiles or is inattentive he may be forced to pay a fine to the reciter. Sometimes, as in Apaeɛ 23 of this collection, an executioner will recite a humourous [sic] or even off-colour Apaeɛ to test the king's self control. If, however, a reciter fumbles his lines he can be severely punished and in former times may have even lost his life.

During a recitation the executioner wears his robe or cloth wrapped around his waist in the style of a warrior rather than in the everyday style of having it fully draped over his shoulder. He carries a ceremonial sword along with *sɛpow—special* knives that in former times would be stuck through the cheeks of sacrificial victims to prevent them from cursing the king as they were being executed. On his head the executioner wears a leopard skin cap (krobɔnkyɛ).

Kwasi Dum: the reciter

The Apaeɛ here transcribed and translated were recited to us in June of 1969, in the village of Sebedie, a mile from Kokofu, Ashanti region. The reciter is known as Kwasi Dum. His real name, Kwasi Amoako-Asamoah, was changed to Kwasi Dum because his mother Afua Sɛɛwa (of Sebedie), bore him beneath an Odum tree while returning from Bekwai. He is now fifty years old and lives in Sebedie.

Kwasi Dum told us that he learned these Apaeɛ from his father, Agyei (from Esumeja), who was an executioner for the Ashanti king. [When Kwasi Dum was] a child his father repeated them to him so he learned them by heart. His father was also a priest and executioner for the god Ta Kora (an ɔbosom). Upon his father's death Kwasi Dum inherited these duties. On occasion he is called on to recite Apaeɛ before the Ashanti king and the paramount chief of Kokofu.

*Kwasi Dum recites apaeɛ, Sebedie, June 1969.*

Apaeɛ and Notes [excerpt]

Apaeɛ 14 [Osei Tutu's war deeds]

He is the one!
You did it, you did it,
You did it, you did it.
You did it, you did it, you killed Ankama
And his fetish the wind.
You killed Beyeeden,
You killed Mensomwo,
You killed Panin-a-ode-mmofra-bae,
You killed Panin Tukoo.
You are unique.
Oben Mmireku says don't kill him,
For he will serve your favorite wife.

[commentary]:

The tradition is that Panin-a-ode-mmofra-bae, a chief of Kaase near Kumasi, was killed by Osei Tutu. His successor, Panin Tukoo, invited Osei Tutu to the funeral. At the time there were only seven guns in Ashanti and they were owned by the chief of Kaase. Osei asked that he and his men be allowed to fire the guns in honor of the deceased. This request was granted, but instead of firing the guns into the air Osei and his men fired on Panin Tukoo and the elders of Kaase, killing them. The outraged Amakom chief, Akosa, led the people of Kaase in a war against Osei Tutu but because Osei had the guns he defeated them. Thus did Kaase come under the power of Kumasi.

War captives sometimes pleaded for their lives by offering to serve in a demeaning position, such as servant to the king's wives.

*The complete manuscript of* Apaeɛ: Ashanti Praise Poems. Recited from Oral Tradition by Kwasi Dum *is 62 typed pages. English versions of about half of the apaeɛ were published in the Winter 1978-1979 issue of the journal* Translation *(Columbia University). See Kwasi Dum, in* Works Consulted. *Other apaeɛ were published in a collection of poems by Bettie Anne Doebler, Ralph Slotten, and Jon Thiem, entitled* Nine Waves *(Sutter House, 2003).*

# LETTERS FROM GHANA

**January 2, 1970.** Jon at Legon to his parents and sister in Chattanooga. Excerpts.

Happy New Year. Just a quick note to tell you I'm at Legon (U. of Ghana) at a conference called the New Year School. Ohene and I went to his village (w/ Nestor) for a week and had a very good time climbing hills, seeing the lake, etc. This conference is very good. I've met a lot of people and various important Ghanaians have come to speak here. Our school recommences 16 Jan. 1970. Until then Ohene and I will probably go to Kokofu.

*This New Year School focused on Ghanaian development, a topic of great interest to Jon and Ohene. Further details on the visit to Ohene's village, along with a report on the conference at Legon, are found in the letter to Slotten dated February 4, 1970.*

**After January 30 and before February 19, 1970 (period in which recorded).** Cassette tape transcription. Jon in Acherensua to his parents in Chattanooga. Excerpts.

[Side One]:
The heat seems to bother me worse this year. And the doctor's wife at Hwidiem says the second year you are here the heat bothers you worse than the first year you are here. [. . .] Well, I think I'll turn this over and you can listen to the [school] debate discussion.

[Jon coaches students for an upcoming inter-school debate on the topic of whether chiefs should be educated]:
Jon: _____ as a matter of fact, chiefs are a dying institution. [. . .] More and more the government is taking over all of these things. And why is it dying? Why is chieftainship dying? [Jon asks the debate club students].
[Student]: _____ it can't contribute creatively to the government. [. . .]
[Jon]: As a matter of fact, our [debate team] opponents by asserting that chiefs should remain illiterate, are advocating the death of chieftainship, because chieftainship will not survive unless it keeps up with the times.

Then you can give an example of Nkrumah. What did Nkrumah do to chiefs? What did he do? [Student]: He got rid of them. [. . .]

[Side Two]:
[Jon, continuing to coach the students]: You have to emphasize that education brings literacy. With literacy you have the whole world of books, law books and things like that, open to you. And if a chief is illiterate he is not going to be able to understand the modern ways of government and defend his own institution. [. . .] O.K. [long pause] Now then, you are going to have to make a point. Is your argument going to be that the chiefs should be *required* . . . to be educated or that we are merely encouraging the education of chiefs? You want it to become a government law or just that chiefs ideally should be educated, but that there should be no law to that effect? [student reply, first part inaudible]:_____It should be encouraged. [. . .] [Jon]: O.K., well, make that point clear: we don't want to force this on the chiefs. I mean, it should be encouraged. [Long response by a student, hard to understand.] [Jon, summarizing the student's response]: O.K., we have to say . . . how much education we think is necessary. Say, secondary, or primary, or middle or university. [. . .] [student]: The rule of the Ashantis should be played by men of higher academic standards. [. . .] [Jon]: O.K. what about giving some examples
of contemporary chiefs who are educated? [a student responds at length with examples, but the response is inaudible due to a buzz in the recording].

*This is the last extant tape from Jon to his parents. Jon mentions in the tape that an investigation of corruption in the school's administration has been initiated (Side One). In another part of the tape Jon reports that the Acherensua debate team defeated the team from Sunyani Secondary School, where the debate took place. Mr. Owoahene and a British contract teacher were judges (Side One).*

**February 4, 1970.** Jon in Acherensua to Ralph Slotten in Carlisle, Pennsylvania. Excerpts.

The new volunteers here tell me that Peace Corps has instituted a rehabilitation program for returning volunteers: they keep implying that I may fail the minimum requirements for getting back to the States. There is a lot of joking about volunteers going gradually crazy (and not finding it out until they get back). A friend of mine this year went berserk and was sent home, but I've heard he's now recovered. We shall see.

Christmas I spent in a very isolated bush village with one of the masters at the school [Ohene]. Christmas in the bush is like a Ghanaian funeral: much rejoicing and drinking. The difference is there is plenty of food to eat. Christmas day we made a pagan pilgrimage to Lake Bosumtwi: the sacred lake of the Ashantis. It was a grueling 12 mile uphill climb. The village (called "under-the-orange-tree," which we couldn't find) lives mainly on the fish it gets out of the lake. This is not many, because Twi (the god or Bosom) forbids boats or metal objects to be used on the lake. So the people paddle around on flattened logs (like anemic surf boards) casting their nets here and there and usually getting very little. The day we went, there was no fish in the village.

# LETTERS FROM GHANA

*Fisherman on a wooden plank, Lake Bosumtwi, December 1969.*

After this we [Jon and Ohene] went to the University of Ghana to a conference on Ghanaian development. I participated in a seminar on tradition and social change. I discovered that Ghanaian intellectuals are very much opposed to traditional ways of doing things, in particular, the extended family system (a fascinating, complex, absurd institution I'll have to tell you about when I get back). I met there the grandson (nanaba) of the Asantehene (King of the Ashantis). [. . .] We discussed some of the commentaries on the praise poems I collected and he claimed a lot of them [the commentaries] were specious (though not, as he said, worthless). He was surprized [sic] about some things I came up with which are not supposed to be known. [. . .] P.S. I've included a photo of Kwasi Dum—my friend, reciter, and informant. Tell your kids if they don't behave Kwasi Dum will come get them (Ashanti mothers always tell their children that if they're not good the white man will come and take them away!)

# LETTERS FROM GHANA

*A "rehabilitation program for returning volunteers" did not exist, but this fantasy depicts volunteers' anxieties about debilitating culture shock on their return to America. They wonder: will they fit in after having lived two years in a West African milieu? Will they recognize their own society in the wake of the violence and protests that occurred in the period they were gone?*

*A "very isolated bush village": this is Jon's second visit to Ohene's village, Asiwa. Ohene, Jon, and Nestor spend Christmas there with Ohene's parents. Lake Bosumtwi, about five miles long, is the only natural lake in Ghana. Jon and Ohene found the village on the lake, but could not find the orange tree.*

**February 23 and 24, 1970 (dates recorded).** Cassette tape transcription. Cap and Ginny Thiem in Chattanooga to Jon in Acherensua. Excerpts.

[Side One, Feb. 23]:
[Cap complains of the poor quality of Jon's latest tape (post Jan. 30, pre Feb. 19) and of the fact that Jon has sent so few tapes]
[Cap about his visit to Africa]: I don't think I'll ever forget the trip. I don't want to get in the habit of just living in memory of that. [. . .] It was an expensive trip, but I think I got more of my money's worth out of those dollars than almost anything I've ever spent.
[Side Two, Feb.24]:
[Ginny]:
Jon, this is Tuesday the 24th. Just received your letter of February 17th. I'm glad you received the tapes and enjoyed them. And Mr. Owoahene's shirts . . . . I can't imagine what happened to those shirts. Dad sent them airmail. What I think I'll do is ask the Post Office why they were so long getting there. [. . .] We'll get the [canned] bacon down here at Kmart. I saw it Saturday, and it's 79 cents [a can]. I said to Dad, we'd have to send it air mail. He wasn't so keen on that. [. . .] I'll have Dad call Mrs. Moynihan . . . and find out Mike's address and what he's doing. [. . .] End of tape so I'll say goodbye. Love Mother.

# LETTERS FROM GHANA

**February to mid-March 1970 (likely period in which recorded).** Cassette tape transcription. Cap and Ginny in Chattanooga to Jon in Acherensua. Excerpt.

[Side Two]:
[Cap has acquired a telescope for Acherensua Secondary School, but has not yet found a good way of getting it over to Ghana]: I just hope that maybe one or two of the boys over the years would be inclined to pick up a scientific career based on the interest you could show through this. [. . .] So the telescope will come. I sit here and ask myself, was it worth all the work? But I guess it is.

**End of February 1970 (period in which recorded).** Cassette tape transcription. Ginny in Chattanooga to Jon in Acherensua. Excerpt.

[Side One]:
This is the story of my life around here. I'm constantly spending hours fiddling around with these tapes and articles.

**March 5, 1970.** Shabani Daudi in Moshi, Tanzania, to Cap Thiem in Chattanooga.

Dear Mr. John,

I thank you very much for your letter of 23/2/70 [Feb. 23, 1970] including the Colour [photo] you took [of] me at Arusha.

I hope this will not be the end of writting [sic] to each other.

Make sure that you come once again to Ngorongoro Creater [sic] and other Parks in Tanzania because by that time I know things will change here and your next trip will be of much interest.

Please pass my warm greetings to Jon and other friends over there.

I hope to hear from you by the next mail.

*Shabani Daudi was Jon and Cap's driver in Tanzania.*

# LETTERS FROM GHANA

**March 15, 1970.** Ohene in Acherensua to Jon's father, Cap Thiem, in Chattanooga.

Dear Mr. John,

I have received your letter of 9/2/1970 [February 9, 1970] and I was much pleased to have heard from you. My joy knew no bounds when I saw the beautiful pictures. Thank you very much. I hope that you also have copies of these pictures to keep to remember us with your family. I believe you really enjoyed your visit to Africa. Jon on his journey back from Kenya told me of your experiences and these might add to your joy. Mental pictures of you and Mr. Eugene Katona will always be framed in our minds. My family and especially Osei [illegible word], my elder son, will always ask of when Mr. Thiem's father will be back, on hearing the noise of an aeroplane. He will say: "Aruplay, baa-bye. Wokɔ a ka kyerɛ Misa Tim papa sɛ, mikyia wo ooo!" (Aeroplane, bye-bye. When you go, tell Mr. Thiem's father that I greet him ooo!)

The other pictures sent to Jon too have been received and Jon showed me a number of them. They were indeed beautiful. I thank you too for the beautiful shirts sent to me. I do not think I can thank you [enough] but I consider these as extra-ordinary marks of good-will from a famous friend. Remember me and my family to Mrs. Thiem and Judy (Miss). Will you do me a favor by sending to me the picture of your family (probably excluding Jon)? I believe that Jon will soon come back [to the States]. Hoping to hear from you again. Heartily [sic] greetings from my wife and children.

Wishing you all the best of luck.

With bonanza wishes,

E.W. Owoahene-Akyampong

*Ohene's "elder son," Festus Osei, is about two years old at the time of this letter. He never got over his interest in "aruplays." Currently, he works as a flight dispatcher at Kotoka International Airport, Accra. He and Jon are in regular contact.*

**March 23, 1970.** Jon in Kumasi to his parents in Chattanooga. Excerpts.

Got telescope books this morning. Hope Dave's girl will be bringing scope.

I just met John Asante (A.F.S. applicant) to get his completed application to deliver to Accra. Yesterday Dave and I spent all day working on it + typing the non-medical part.

I will be going to a teacher's conference at Cape Coast [Ghana] on 31st March. Before that I hope to go to Lomé [in Togo].

Well I've got to get to the store before it closes. Will write from Accra. [. . .]
(Standing in Post Office)

*John Asante, an Acherensua student, did well in an English essay contest sponsored by the U.S. Embassy. Jon and Fitzjarrald encouraged him to apply for a year of study in the United States through the American Field Service (A.F.S.) student exchange program. Asante was finally accepted and went to a high school in Modesto, California. (See also Dave Fitzjarrald's letter, July 11, 1970, Augustine Gyamfi's letter to Jon, June 1, 1971, and the first excerpt below from* The Achiscodian Times, *November 1970.)*

**March 29, 1970.** Easter Sunday. Ralph Slotten in Carlisle to Jon in Acherensua. Typed. Excerpts.

Dear Jon of Acherensua,

I apologize for my extreme slowness in responding to your last two excellent letters. Now at the end of spring vacation I am at last catching up on my woefully neglected correspondence with all and sundry.

Your life sounds so amazing and unbelievable that I hardly know what to say that will speak to your conditon. I was most interested in your translations of oral Akan literature. I spoke of it to Dr. Christian Gaba of the University of Ghana in Accra when he was here this past month, and he was also most interested. Unfortunately he is not an Akan-speaker and knew little about the subject.

[. . .]

[on his college students]: Nobody wants to do respectable academic research any more. Everyone wants to CREATE HIS OWN MYTH rather than study somebody else's; everyone is writing poetry, painting pictures, or just copping out on drugs. I have four students doing integrated independent research this fall—on various aspects of myth, ritual, symbol, and music in relation to Rock, Drugs, and contemporary American culture. One or two of them may come through with something significant, but I dread to think of what the other two will produce! They are very nice kids and I have a good and enjoyable relation with them, but they are light-years away from my generation—and by this time, I think, even from yours. They all seem so limp, patting their long hair, trying to sort out their thoughts from their bedrugged weekends, working through their identity crises! O for a good old-fashioned Hipster type with a rapier slash of wit and a razor sharp mind!

This year has been incredibly busy and full. Martha has been researching the McClintock Slave Riot in Carlisle of 1843 and has finally put her finishing touches on her paper, which she has delivered before the Cumberland County Historical Society, and hopes to get published. Amy is now a very tall and large 11 1/2 and my son Hugh turns 10 at the end of April. I have had some poetry published . . . .

[. . .]

I have sent letters of recommendation to Rutgers and Indiana and hope that all goes well with you. I will enclose a few specimens of my poetry, which I am sure compare ill with oral Akan literature.

[. . .]

Martha sends her affectionate greeting, to join mine. You are always welcome to make our home your headquarters when you wish to visit Dickinson or this part of the East, now that your parents have left you stranded for an Eastern pad!

*They "all seem so limp, patting their long hair, trying to sort out their thoughts from their bedrugged weekends . . . .": this statement captures Slotten's sardonic view of hippie culture and its lack of intellectual discipline.*

*"O for a good old-fashioned Hipster type."* Hipsters, unlike hippies, were noted for their detachment, anomie, and existentialist mindset. Norman Mailer's essay on the hipster, entitled "The White Negro" (1957) is the classic presentation of this countercultural type. Slotten knew this essay.

**April 6, 1970.** Jon in Accra to his parents in Chattanooga. Excerpts.

David's girlfriend came in today w/ the telescope. That was a fortunate coincidence. Still, it sounds like you had to pay alot of money. I + the school thank you. We're leaving it in Accra to have the school lorry come down specially to pick it up at the Peace Corps hostel.

I plan to meet Ohene Thurs. at Kokofu.
[. . .]
Everything's fine here but I'm tired of Ghana. Spent a lot of money on some art books here + a birthday present (dress) for Judy (seen [sent] to Miami U.)

*"a fortunate coincidence"*—in that Jon happened to be in Accra when Fitzjarrald's girlfriend arrived.

**April 12, 1970.** Jon in Acherensua to his parents in Chattanooga. Excerpts.

If I'm accepted at Indiana I think I'll go there for the following reasons: They have African studies which I can combine with literature, which Rutgers doesn't have. [. . .] Prof. Nilsson thinks Indiana would be a better choice for me than Rutgers. He implies that eastern universities are a bit unhealthy now. Too many racial and radical problems are distracting. [. . .]
Susan, Dave, [and] I took the left over money (thanks a lot for that) and had a fine meal at a French restaurant in Kumasi (wine and all). Susan was really impressed by the way you handled the whole deal, Dad. (I was too).

# LETTERS FROM GHANA

My poem manuscript has been typed and now I have to get permission from the Asantehene to publish. After that Peace Corps will handle [it] from there. It probably won't be published before I leave, though there is a slim chance.

*Professor Nilsson, who taught Political Science at Dickinson College, was one of Jon's major professors and gave him advice and encouragement about pursuing an academic career.*

*Susan is the name of Dave's girlfriend: she brought the telescope over from the States.*

**April 24, 1970.** Jon in Kumasi to his parents in Chattanooga. Excerpts.

We, 'Ohene' and I, are in Kumasi. Yesterday we went out to Bonwire and bargained for a double-weave Kente cloth: it will cost about NC 114: it's the best made. Adwini Asa (the exhaustion of all designs). It is being made on order and it should be done in about mid-June.
[. . .]
We saw the Asantehene's Secretary this morning and he said there should be no problem in publishing the Apaeɛ. (The Asantehene is now very sick. You have his picture in his Rolls Royce.)
[. . .]
Dave + Nestor are going to meet us about noon—today, and we all are going to celebrate Fitzjarrald's birthday which is Monday.

*Kente cloth is a colorful woven fabric; it has become a symbol of Ghana. Bonwire, a village of Kente cloth weavers, is about 12 miles east of Kumasi.*

*Kente cloth weaver, Bonwire, April 1970.*

**April 30, 1970.** Jon in Acherensua to Ralph Slotten in Carlisle. Excerpts.

I certainly enjoyed your poems. I showed them to Mr. Owoahene, my collaborator in Ashanti oral poetry, who was also appreciative. (It is a curious thing that he teaches religion, here.) He said he would like to write you so I'm giving him your address.

I'll apologize in advance for the shortness of this letter (which ideally was to have included an essay on "Length"). Instead I've copied out a handful of my own poems.

[. . .]

The only other poem that wants explanation is "Ahafo Dwarf." Ahafo is the name of the area where I live and is traditionally known as the Asantehene's hunting grounds. The stories about dwarfs in this neck of the woods are probably myths. They are not really folktales (as one might expect them to be) because the Ashantis don't take their folk tales seriously; they are usually seen as pleasing or entertaining lies or parables. Dwarfs are taken seriously and serve mainly an etiological end. First, they are used to explain why food left in the bush quickly disappears. They also account for the disappearance in the bush of children who [later] return. When a child is missing, food is put out in the bush (usually bananas, oranges + plantain). If the child reappears, it is said [that] the dwarfs (lonely, playful, hungry) kidnapped it to play with [it] and eventually swap [it] for food in a charming version of the "silent trade" . . . . If the child doesn't return, it is said that the Sasabonsam (tree devil, see Apaeε 1) fell on it and devoured it. Some scholars (see Rattray) believe the dwarfs are a racial memory of smaller autochthonic peoples (Bushmen or pygmy types) who died or were driven out as the Ashanti farmers began making farms in the rain forest. Their invisibility comes from their hunter's knack for camouflage, and whistling is of course a common communications trick among primitives. (An English master in our school insists there are 15 invisible, whistling dwarfs living near his house: I don't know how he ever counted them.) My poem tries to join these two aetiological motifs. It is a pleasant fancy to think there are a few pygmies lurking around, kidnapping children and returning them for food. Most Ashantis think very well of dwarfs and belief in them is nearly universal around here.

*The poems Jon sends to Slotten are among the first he has written, apart from limericks and humorous verse.*

**May 1, 1970.** Jon in Legon to his parents in Chattanooga. Excerpts.

May Day Greetings! David + I came down on the school bus yesterday and picked up the telescope this morning. We're now sitting in front of the university bookshop, waiting for it to reopen. Tomorrow we are getting up early and going to the Winneba Deer Festival (at Winneba on the coast) and the same day back to Acherensua.

I've been busy doing a number of things: buying stuff in Accra for "Ohene," writing memos for the Apaeɛ (poems), getting my Peace Corps termination physical (which is fairly exhaustive). When I get back [to Acherensua] the 5th form mock exam begins. So I'll have to grade all those. They were postponed because a 4th form (11th grade) student died: he was in the class of which I'm Form Master. I didn't know him very well; he was a poor student. He came to school straight after vacation, complained of sickness, and then became unconscious. He was taken to the hospital [in Hwidiem] + 3 days later he was dead. Death in this society is much more common than in ours. They also believe in a life after death . . . . I didn't go to the funeral [in another town] and am glad I didn't. The school bus that carried him home (his corpse) broke down on the way, so in the heat the corpse started to rot and stink badly. Owoahene went and said it was awful.

[. . .]

And Mike's address? I didn't get it yet.

**May 4, 1970.** Jon in Acherensua to his parents in Chattanooga. Excerpts.

We had no trouble setting up the telescope. We set the sighting scope by observing its shadow (from the sun) and then adjusting the position of the scope so that the scope's shadow was perfectly circular. This way we knew the scope was pointed directly at the sun. Sighting through the main scope we centred [sic] the sun their [there], and then centred the sun in the sighter scope. Yesterday evening we picked up Jupiter easily w/ the sighter scope (no moon). Even with the least powerful eyepiece, 3 of old Jupiter's moons were visible. (The Barlow was fuzzy but worked.)

We've been reading the astronomy books which are good guides. The subject is complex. I think I can calculate sidereal (star) time now. It's kind of interesting though. Our main problem is that the polar axis must be $7°$ off the horizon which (this is due to our position near the terrestial equator) puts all of the weight of the telescope on one side making the counterweight useless and the whole scope tipsy.

It's a fine piece of equipment but I don't think it will outlast the Peace Corps volunteers. [. . .] Soon I'll get the Head. [Headmaster] to write you + Dr. Volcheck, and I will too. Sorry about spending so much time on telescopes, Mother (They really are groovy.)

*Dr. Emil Volcheck, senior supervisor in the technical department of the Dupont plant (where Cap worked), procured the telescope, assembled it and checked it out. He also chose the astronomy manuals that were sent to Acherensua. When the scope arrived, Jon, with the help of Fitzjarrald and Kwasnycia, learned how to calibrate its position in relation to the movement of the stars. Jon would set the telescope up in the school grounds after the electricity was shut off in the evening and then view the stars and galaxies, often staying up after midnight. (See also the Headmaster's letter of thanks to Cap Thiem, May 26, 1970.)*

**"May Something, 1970" (after May 4th).** Mike Moynihan in East Lansing to Jon in Acherensua. Excerpts.

It has been years since I've heard anything from the "Heart of Darkness" in Western Africa. Naturally I'm pissed. I wrote to your mom about two weeks ago and received an eleven page (both sides) letter in return detailing the family activities since last summer. She even sent me an envelope already addressed + two airmail stamps so I would have no excuse for not writing you, except my own laziness. Which seems reason enough to me. I'm not in school now and haven't graduated yet. I almost got drafted twice but beat it for a while. I won't bore you with details of that. But I was forced to drop out of school. I'm going to start again this summer and take one course. And work some, I hope. Your mom said you were coming home about Aug. 1st, subject to change. If so I insist upon your beating your ass up here for a while. Then I'll talk some, but I'm too lazy to write a long letter now. "That art is greatest which denies art" (Jon Thiem—collected works). Silence, the ommission [sic] of the endless repitions [sic] of history of histories of stories based on histories (my own most mysterious one included), is that virtue I have strived for this past year. I write now in the interest of basic communication, such as dates, not in the interests of Art (whoever he is). Anyhow, I'm basically pissed at the world in general + [the] U.S. Military in particular right now. [. . .]

For some reason I have an intense and illusory desire to sit down over a couple beers and talk with you. Not events, but just perception[s] + attitudes that I need to bounce off of your rubbery mixture of cynical, philistinian humanism, just to see them come back at me in different form with your distinctive mental imprint upon them. [. . .] But at any rate that's why you must make it up here + let me introduce you to the finer points of the Midwest. Since you[r] mother also said you might be going to Indiana University. That's not too far from here (250 miles, maybe). That would be nice. I could hide out with you when the F.B.I. comes after me. We went on strike for a while here at school after the Kent State killings, but that too is a different story. Don't believe everything you hear in Newsweek; a lot of it is a crock of shit. The country is gonna [sic] go pretty soon if things don't begin to change in a hurry. Revolution will be a distinct possibility in 5 years if this stuff with Agnew, Mitchell, Laird, and Rogers keeps up. [. . .]

[. . .]

My newest roommate is just back from 2 years in Vietnam. He brought a kilo of Cambodian grass with him (pure + uncut) which cost about 4 dollars. It's really good stuff. Unfortunately I never smoke. I just watch the others get stoned. Don't ask why but I've never gone the dope route in any form. Some people would argue that I've been on it all my life, on the other hand. [. . .] I've been alive + well, the family is alive. [. . .]

What are you planning to do after PC service, both immediately + long range. Ain't much time left anymore. Oh, well. I feel no compulsion to dwell upon our mythical past. Seems distant + irrelevant, or at least a bit tedious tonight. Perhaps we've grown out of it, except as a sentimental memory. It no longer serves as a viable foundation for whatever has [followed] or may yet follow it. Too contradictory with the present. I know in some sense, particularly in Africa, you long, at times, for its reassurance + simplicity, for its naive beauty, just as we will one day long for college. I do too, I guess, perhaps even more. You speak of the facts of that past, and I think I only wish [for] the mood, the freedom + the childishness. Perhaps that's what you intend to convey with specific references; I don't know. But enough of this hogwash. I began with the intention of not beginning, thwarted myself, recognized my folly, + now end my mnemonic meanderings.

How was your trip to Mount Kilimijaro [sic]? What did your dad think of old Africa? [. . .] Your Mom said you had a monstrous letter you wrote but never mailed; Mail it! My ex- roommate of 4 years is in Malaysia now with the Peace Corps. He writes pretty often. At first he disliked it very much, but now I think he is beginning to enjoy + appreciate it somewhat. He is Eastern Religion oriented, which he says is best studied outside the orient. Too much Religious prejudice amongst believers. Anyway for now, take it easy.

*"Heart of Darkness" is an allusion to Joseph Conrad's story of the same name. Here Mike means that Jon himself is the heart of darkness, not Africa.*

*"I almost got drafted twice . . . .": Mike's application to join Peaces Corps was either lost or rejected. In the end, he was never drafted.*

*The "Kent State killings": on May 4, 1970, the Ohio National Guard shot four students dead and wounded nine others during an antiwar protest at Kent State University. One of the students who died was not part of the protest.*

*"Agnew, Mitchell, Laird, and Rogers" were, respectively, Nixon's Vice President, Attorney General, Defense Secretary and Secretary of State.*

*"My ex-roommate of 4 years is in Malaysia now with the Peace Corps." The ex- roommate is John Chamberlin. Jon met him for the first time in September 2012, in San Francisco.*

**Mid-May and May 18, 1970 (period in which recorded).** Cassette tape transcription. Judy in Chattanooga to Jon in Acherensua. Excerpt.

[Side One]:

[Judy Thiem reports to Jon on the protests at her campus in the wake of the Kent State killings. She is a student at Miami University in Oxford, Ohio]:
Here I am after all that riot. Well, it wasn't really [a] riot—campus trouble. We were closed down. Wow, we were off Tuesday for memorial services for the Kent State students that were killed. The next day we had classes. Thursday we had some rallies. And before you knew it there were three fire bombs and Shriver, our president, just closed the school down . . . .
[. . .]
We're really looking forward to you coming home.
[. . .]
Some of the schools reopened. Ohio University closed down, so it looks like they are out till summer session comes around. The trouble mainly now is outside radicals coming on the campuses, like Miami. The Panthers, the Weather girls. Who else? Kent State students. And they're the ones causing a lot of the trouble. [. . .]
[On her boyfriend John]: I showed him my African dress which I'm really proud of and Daddy wore his African top.
[. . .]
I enjoyed your letters which you have sent me and I hope you get my last one which was [sent] about 3 weeks ago.

*". . . outside radicals." Outsiders there doubtless were, but there were also "inside" radicals, along with middle-of-the-road students enraged by the Kent State massacre on May 4th. Ginny sent Jon a number of newscasts on the event. Miami of Ohio was closed down on May 7th and reopened May 17th.*

**May 21, 1970.** Jon in Acherensua to his father in Chattanooga. Excerpts.

As usual I've been busy with grading papers (and how I hate it). There've been disturbances in the school recently. The headmaster is being sacked at the end of this year. Last week he bribed some students to start a strike, beat up the masters, and set the Bursar[']s Office on fire.

The other students got wind that this was planned by the headmaster[,] so they set up a vigilante committee to prevent the strike. Riot police were later called in but they were unnecessary. The Headmaster's purpose was, it seems, to make the school look disorderly so as to put himself in a better light and also to destroy the records of his corrupt administration by firing [setting on fire] the Bursar's Office. He has stated publicly that he could care less about what happens to the school. Today the Board of Governors and the Brong Ahafo Region chief executive are here investigating. The students will of course do nothing to make the Headmaster look good, so it seems as if everything will turn out O.K. I put all this in your letter since it might disturb Mother to hear all this. (I live above the Bursar's Office). Anyway, there's nothing really to worry about.

About the <u>Kente</u>: I'm buying it for myself. I was planning to buy an <u>Adinkra</u> cloth for Mother when I learned that the school is presenting one to me on my leaving, as a gift (along with some traditional sandals). If that's the case, do you think I should still go ahead and buy another <u>Adinkra</u>?

*Jon does not report in this letter that students formed a human cordon for one night around the administration building, where the Bursar's Office and Jon's room were located.*

*Adinkra is another kind of cloth used in traditional robes; the design is a repeated series of abstract symbols stamped with black dye onto the cloth. The dye is applied with a small, carved calabash form.*

**May 26, 1970.** The Headmaster in Acherensua to John R. Thiem in Chattanooga. Typed.

Dear Sir,

<u>A TELESCOPE COMES TO ACHERENSUA SECONDARY SCHOOL.</u>

I write to acknowledge, with thanks and a deep sense of gratitude, receipt in April, 1970, of the telescope you sent across the seas as your personal gift to the Acherensua Secondary School.

When I mentioned the School's need for such an instrument to you at dinner at my house sometime last year (1969) on the occasion of your first tour to Ghana, little did I imagine that you would make it your special concern as a follow-up to your promise, to provide the school with one. Well you have honoured your word!

By your gift, the students of the school, staff, my children, wife and I are enabled to see, time and again, something more of the heavens than before, guided by your son, Mr. John [Jon] Thiem, Peace Corps teacher on the school's staff. Incidentally, Mr. Thiem is due to finish his teaching assignment in Ghana (Acherensua) next July, 1970. We take the opportunity to wish Mr. Thiem a safe return home.

And, believe me, as a school, we are very appreciative of your kind gesture of generosity to us—the provision of such an expensive telescope as a gift—I assure you that by that same gift, among other things, you and your son will long be remembered by the school.

Do please accept sincere thanks from a grateful school.
Yours very truly,
. . . . . .
(HEADMASTER).

**June 1970 (month in which recorded).** Cassette tape transcription. Cap and Ginny in Chattanooga to Jon in Acherensua. Excerpts.

[Side Two]:
[Cap]:
Let me make my closing remarks to Africa in my letter in the next day or two. And here's hoping that all the things you have to accomplish are being put by the side as you get them done and that you are not too hard pressed. I'm very proud of the job you've done in Africa and the way you stuck it out. And I'm just tickled to death for the change of climate and the change of atmosphere and the changes you'll soon see as you come back to the States. You deserve it. It's what you want. And I hope everything's going to be fine. Jon, we are really looking forward to seeing you. I just can't wait. I'll say good night.
[. . .]

[Ginny]:
Tell Mr. Owoahene goodbye for us and that we hope he'll enjoy his [tape] recorder as well as we have, and [that] he's well known over here in the States.
[Judy]:
Hi Jon. Waiting to see you. It's not long, I'll tell you. We're all getting hyper tense over here, waiting to see how you are. [laughs]

**November 1970.** "The Historical Background & Progress of the United Nations Student Association—Achisco Branch." Article from the *The Achiscodian Times*. The Editor is Kwadwo Nkrumah-Boateng. Typed. Excerpt.

The Society was founded in 1969 under the patronage of Mr. Owoahene. It was working progressively by the help of Senior E. R. Buckman. Later on Mr. Owoahene became less interested and so all the work concerning the society was done by seniors Buckman, Minta Boamah, Kwadwo Nkrumah Boateng and some members of the executive Board. During the re- opening of the 1970-1971 academic year it nearly collapsed, but by the help of the New President, Senior Kwadwo Nkrumah Boateng, Mr. Fitzjerrald D [sic], the patron, and senior Minta Boamah, the General Secretary, the society was revived. The number so far, for the members, is about 50.

The society during the last two weeks of the 1969-70 academic year organised a symposium [in] which Mr. Thiem, a Peace corp [sic], was the Principal speaker. The society also went to Bechem, St. Joseph's Training College, to celebrate the 25th anniversary of the United Nations. Thanks go to the treasurer for 1969-1970 who worked hardily [sic] to keep the society moving.

New members as well as master[s] are invited.
By Steven Mintah Boamah 5A (General Sec.)

**June 5, 1970.** Jon in Takoradi to Mike in East Lansing. The letter was written in the coastal city of Takoradi, where Jon is attending the Peace Corps Termination conference, but it was mailed from Kumasi. Excerpts.

I'm sitting on the balcony of a room in one of the plushest hotels in Ghana. It's the site of our [Peace Corps] termination conference. I've eaten more meat here in one day than I have in 2 months at home (Acherensua). The grease sticks to the fingers. The great pieces of meat stick in the stomach giving belly ache. A meaty shit is wholly different from a yam or rice one (staples).

The rainy season has come in at Acherensua. The egrets have migrated to dryer places. The school compound is going back to the jungle. Toenails grow faster. Outstanding are butterflies and stars. The former for their variety and profusion, the latter for their rarity and brilliance in the rainy season. There is small dust in the air at this time. The heavens are truly heavens.

[. . .]

My parents, perhaps indiscreetly, sent me your letter to them which I enjoyed all the more in that it was not addressed to me and [was] probably free of all the subtle biases a person has built up and used in writing another. Biases I'm not free of either.

I'll be happy to leave Ghana but I'm not very excited about going back to America.

Recently I've gotten worked up about Robert Frost whose poetry serves a[s] a sort of vacation in the country from my usual Nabokovian pursuits. (In Pale Fire Nabokov both parodies + admires Frost whose guise, there, is John Shade). Nabokov is of course the greatest genius of the English language of this century. There is for me a real ecstasy, a cosmical pleasure in reading him. He has made these 2 years bearable.

My lottery # I guess you know by now is 342. My deferment ends in early September. I think there's a good chance, though, I may be called. I was pleased to learn recently from the weighing scales in the Peace Corps office that my weight has been hovering around the unacceptable level for draft candidates. I've heard that if you're 5ft. 11 and you weigh under 128 lbs. they won't take you. This may be a fairy tale. Anyway, you might look into the possibility of renouncing beer, potatoes + other Irish staples.

# LETTERS FROM GHANA

From the tone of your comments it sounds as if you will go if you are drafted. I can't really blame you. Maybe I would do the same. Jail would be intolerable I've decided; Canada less so but still so. [. . .]

But Frost's example is perhaps the best instruction. Read his biography and his poems.

My other alternative is secondary [school] teaching. But that is a lot of work. The pay's pretty good, however, + here I've learned to live cheaply—my main pleasure expenses being books. It's costing me alot of money to send them back. (I'm using a Gideon bible for something hard to write on).

[. . .]

I didn't write you for a long time. I did write a letter but failed to mail it. For about 4 months I went into a bad depression which I'm now out of thanks to Frost et al.

<u>Next day</u> (Sunday)

I've arranged for my flight: 10th July to Rome via Abidjan. Air Afrique is putting me up at the Hotel Ivoire (finest hotel in all West Africa) w/ all meals paid. I'll probably stay in Italy about 2 weeks, then fly back home via Paris or maybe change my G.T.R. (Gov't. transport ticket) into a student ship ticket.

Anyway if you're not in Vietnam I should see you this summer at Rehobeth [Rehoboth] beach. I'll be there around 30 July and will probably spend the remainder of the summer eating. I'm also anxious to see what Tennessee has to offer (in the way of cuisine).

*". . . small dust" is Ghanaian English for "little dust." The rainy season generates rain clouds but the thunderstorms clear the air of the dust that fills the atmosphere in the dry season, Harmattan.*

*Jon's fear that he may be drafted (in spite of a high lottery number) stems from a report sent out by the Peace Corps Ghana office that some states would call all numbers issued in the draft lottery.*

*The resigned, impersonal tone of this letter reflects Jon's exhaustion.*

**June 15, 1970.** Jon in Acherensua to his parents in Chattanooga. Excerpts.

As usual I've been busy. Received your tape on the draft and enjoyed it very much. I basically agree with the protesters but I think they could be less violent and try more to persuade people rationally. For rationally speaking all reason is on their (our) side.

The Headmaster has been given notice to get out of the school in 1 week. His reticence in mentioning me is because he doesn't like me or many other members of staff, though on the surface we are cordial enough. The things he's done to the school are criminal and his punishment is beginning.

I hope to go to Accra soon, tomorrow or next day to complete my Peace Corps physical. Also some of my teeth need attending to—with the lack of water I've neglected their brushing.

I think I told you my trunk is on its way.
[. . .]
I was very happy to hear I was accepted at Indiana.
[. . .]
This summer I'm afraid I'm going to be cracking the books. The program there [at Indiana] is tough especially vis languages.

Thinking of you all and anxious to get home.

". . . his reticence in mentioning me," i.e. in the letter the Headmaster wrote to Cap Thiem thanking him for the telescope, May 26, 1970.

**November 1970.** "Akwaaba." Poem welcoming the new headmaster, published in the *The Achiscodian Times*. The Editor is Kwadwo Nkrumah-Boateng. Typed. Excerpt.

Akwaaba

Our New Headmaster is coming.
[. . .]
Our beloved master,
God sent to free Achisco,
Let deeds of darkness fly
And joyful praise! Osagyefo

# LETTERS FROM GHANA

And redeem Achisco.

by Michael Weridu Kusi

*"Akwaaba" means "welcome." "Osagyefo" means "savior." The "deeds of darkness" allude to the previous headmaster, dismissed in June 1970.*

**June 19, 1970.** David Fitzjarrald in Acherensua to Bob Hunnes in Champaign, Illinois. Excerpts.

There is no beer in Acherensua today, and my corn stalk in the courtyard has a potash deficiency. Faced with these almost insurmountable odds, I march forward spreading love, helping Ghana into the glorious era of development. Training the little minds of today who will become the pointy heads of tomorrow.

I have come into copies of the DI [*Daily Illini*] . . . . And inside are pictures of people getting beat up by the cops. What happened to the old days when people used to be amused by Frank Bellanger and Martin-Trigona. [. . .]

After a year in this open-air nut house I have finally adjusted. Our benevolent PC [Peace Corps] director, Mr. Blatchford, who, incidently, was caught by Newsweek photographers playing tennis with Spiro Agnew, has been making soft noises to get the Volunteers to stop protesting in front of American Embassies everywhere. "Our" magazine [the Peace Corps magazine] says they may take our money away. Then, no beer! any more.

[. . .]

If you (or anyone) gets a moment, explain what has happened to America. The News fiction weekly are always so full of bull shit.

*"Martin Trigona" is most likely Andy Martin (born 1945) who, according to Wikipedia, received his B.A.(1966) and a law degree (1969) from the University of Illinois.*

*President Nixon appointed Joseph Blatchford as the new Peace Corps Director in May 1969. In practice, Blatchford took a conciliatory line with the dissenting volunteers, but he did begin to replace Peace Corps administrators (including country directors) who were Democrats with Republicans.*

*Spiro Agnew, Nixon's Vice President, was popular with right wing Republicans for his pro-war rhetoric and his aptitude for name-calling. It seemed incongruous that the Peace Corps director would associate with him. Agnew was forced to resign in 1973 because of indictments for extortion, conspiracy, and bribery committed during his tenure in political office.*

*". . . explain what has happened to America" neatly expresses the incomprehension of volunteers at the violence directed against people exercising their rights to assembly and free speech.*

*"The News fiction weekly" is a reference to* Newsweek *magazine.*

**June 26, 1970.** David Fitzjarrald in Acherensua to Bob Hunnes, Champaign, Illinois. Written on Acherensua Secondary School (A.S.S.) stationery.

Glad to get your letter. Just a week ago I sent you a letter to the DI [*Daily Illini*] office. I was wondering then about you and the draft, and your affliction was good news.

Well, I've now spent one full year in Ghana (on June 29). Don't have a lot tangible to show for it.

To answer your questions about PC. The last issue of the Volunteer was full of BS about the recent protests by volunteers. They were saying, "If you keep on protesting, Congress will cut our money." It's hard to understand all this nonsense out here. Both the Congressmen and the PC overestimate the effectiveness of PC. First of all, we couldn't do much for American foreign policy if we tried. Granted, our mere presence means something. But out "in the field" one doesn't get the feeling he's working for Uncle Sam. As for AID [the U.S. Agency for International Development]. In Ghana the PC staff steers kind of clear of them. We use some of their money in projects. AID officials drive big cars and have air conditioners and don't do very much.

I may be getting apathetic over here, but in Ghana the hassle about AID and CIA is ludicrous. But it might not be in Afghanistan. It all boils down to, "Will I take money from these people to accomplish something 'good'?"

I don't know about other places, but I think that the idea that Volunteers are helping a lot is wrong. At the same time (that's a phrase I picked up from you), the experience for the Volunteer and the new perspective about the States you get is probably worth it. The Committee for Returned Volunteers is pretty radical. They're always saying the PC is an extension of US imperialism and should be abolished. Congressmen say all PC volunteers are draft-dodgers and it's a waste of money. One damning for one action and the other damning for none of that action.

Here in Acherensua we have a well-defined role as a teacher to fill. I'm no "super- vol," [super volunteer] and I just teach. It's frustrating and it's probably in the end a waste of time, for 95% of the students are hopeless cases. But the hassle is here and not in Accra or Washington. I don't have much to do with PC/Washington. Blatchford [Director of the Peace Corps] seems an ass.

Projects like the one you mentioned can be more rewarding than teaching. Also more frustrating. You get over into another culture and discover how American you really are. Ironically enough, it means you see how much you have in common with Tricky Dick [President Richard Nixon].

An experience in partial isolation makes the prospect of prison less and less palatable. I don't want to spend two years out here in the bush only to go back to queers attacking me in prison. But my idealism hasn't completely flown.

I remember the times when we both were straight and conservative, and when I thought you were too cautious and uncommitted. Now it's probably the other way around. I feel tired and all the moral fury and "acts of conscience" at home have a hollow hypocritical ring. My friends write and tell me things are all upside down, people are madly going to their own corners. Are there any signs now things are cooling off?

Possibly the McCarthy nonsense won't come. I wish I could be home and see what's happening. Sometimes when I'm climbing the walls here, or when I'm getting shit on by everyone, I think about the hassles at home and cool down. A fellow can afford to relax and be cool about things in America, but not about the things in Acherensua. But who's to say which is more important to me personally? Rationally I know the answer, but while I'm here the problems at home can still be approached "academically."

It's funny that after 6 years or so I still feel I can communicate with you. After this year, many of the people at the Big U seem to have microscopic vision. Their life doesn't extend beyond the Union and the Auditorium.

For all this hedging I'm still contemplating CO [conscientious objector status], Canada, and jail. Won't this war stop ever?

Still living with Nestor Kwasnycia, though he irritates me a lot sometimes. But he's learned how [to] make pizza (with Polish corned beef). We get lots of Eastern European products here; guess the trade started when Nkrumah was around. I'm trying to save the dough to get to Kenya and E. Africa this summer. Our charter flight was cancelled, and it's pretty expensive. Maybe I'll send you a card or something from Nairobi. A little more exotic than Acherensua. "Hey fellow, I've got a friend in Africa!" Wow! Wild, stalking cocoa trees. Bottle of Star beer and palm wine.

[. . .]

A year is a damn long time. I sure would like to go back to school, but what could I study? Physics is out. Maybe I should go back and be an engineer. My brother's doing a thesis on dust devils. Drives all over dry lakes filming dust devils.

Hope you like my A.S.S. paper. School is over when I get my exams [sic] grades after the 8th.

Keep in touch.
Fitzjarrald

"... the McCarthy nonsense" is a reference to the McCarthy era in the early 1950s when Senator Joseph McCarthy, through a Senate subcommittee, conducted investigations against alleged Communist infiltrators in the government, movie industry, literature, and the arts. Though unable to summon much hard evidence, he ruined a number of careers and lives. McCarthy himself was eventually censured by the Senate. Fitzjarrald implies that the suppression of dissent among Peace Corps volunteers smacks of McCarthyism, though he thinks that in the end it may not come to that.

"Hope you like my A.S.S. paper" i.e., Acherensua Secondary School stationery.

*At the Beer Bar in Acherensua: Jon, Nestor Kwasnycia, Dave Fitzjarrald, and two women friends from Hwidiem, 1969-1970.*

**July 11, 1970.** Dave Fitzjarrald to his parents. Excerpts.

I had a nice time on the 4th seeing Jon off at the airport (to Italy) and then mixing with Middle America at the American Embassy party. Free hot dogs and American beer.
[. . .]
    I've decided for certain to stay here next year, in case you haven't heard. The new volunteers arrived and went to Winneba [on the coast] on Tuesday. Here I am an instant veteran. I'm in good spirits, though Jon's

going-away celebrations in Accra cut into my reserves a lot. After Salary time on Aug 1, I'm off. I sort of envy Jon up there in Europe. We had to listen to Jon's Tales of Italy for the last 2 months. (He was there his Junior year in college). All those nice airplanes at the airport going places. The charter flight to E. Africa was cancelled, adding about $175 to the cost of the trip. So I don't know if I'll go. Up in the air.
[. . .]

Rainy season is here, our rain barrel is full, but we can't see the stars very off [often]. Can't have everything.

Do you think there is any future in my applying for conscientious objector status from the draft board? Alternate service. If I do that I would need 3 or 4 people at home to vouch for me. But it's a big problem—I suppose in Marshall [Illinois] these days it would cause as many problems for you as it would for me. I just don't know. The military seems completely contrary to my nature. I don't want to cause a lot of trouble, and I'm not averse to doing work, but for what purpose—what benefit—should I go kill people? Write and tell me what you think if you would. I don't think things will clear up by next year.

My main success for the year (mine and Jon's) is the student we sponsored for the American Field Service to spend a year in high school in the State[s]. He got selected to go and we've been hassling around with physicals and such. Then we got a letter saying he was out because he missed exams two terms because of illness. I guess they thought it was some chronic disease. I was calling people up in Accra, and badgering the Acting Headmaster here and finally got a letter from him off to New York today. So I hope to see my student—John Asante—off to the States early in August. He's real excited about it, and I guess I am too.

Nestor had an accident with his motorcycle, but he wasn't hurt. The cycle was and we've been "bloody short of transport."
[. . .]
I really appreciate hearing from all you folks at home.

*Jon left Ghana on July 3rd, not July 4th.*
*Fitzjarrald received a low number in the draft lottery, which made it more likely he would be drafted after his completion of Peace Corps*

*service. Hence his questions about applying for conscientious objector status. As things turned out, he did not get drafted.*

**November 1970.** "The News on the Hour." Article on John Asante published in the *The Achiscodian Times*. The Editor is Kwadwo Nkrumah-Boateng. Typed. Excerpt.

<u>THE NEWS ON THE HOUR</u>

This is Radio Achisco. The time is 0 AMT. Here is the news read by Pokazulu. The former news editor of the club, master Asante John, has flown to U.S.A. by air, as a result of his performance in a National Essay competition organised by the American Embassy in Secondary Schools. Master Asante will be away for one year. Whilst in the States, he will study English Language, American History, Journalism, Literature, Public Speaking and Typewriting.

The Executive Board on behalf of the members congratulate him on his achievement and wish him the best of luck in his studies.

**October 27, 1970.** Jon in Bloomington, Indiana, to Ralph Slotten in Carlisle. Excerpts.

Your delightful version of the "whistling dwarf" . . . plunged me back into the jungle and away from your fine Midwestern autumn. Here I've enclosed 2 more pieces. [. . .] The 2nd line in the Twi song [I translated] includes a pun not in the original but remains literal. It literally reads:

Death is like the halo of moon
That encircles the neck of man
I am a stranger
I do something and it is bad
But God will provide.

I brought you back a 'fetish' from Ghana (found on the farm of a friend). I can't send it, tho[ugh] it fits in my hand. If it should get into the wrong hands, anything could happen (eg. all the books north of the equator turn into locusts or vacuum cleaners). So when I see you I'll deliver it personally and as mystagogue teach you its powers, its rights, its diet. Until then you'll just have to make do with God.

*Slotten wrote a poem on "The Whistling Dwarf"; it was based on Jon's poem "The Ahafo Dwarf." See Jon's letter to Slotten, dated April 30, 1970.*

*The fetish (a small leather pouch) was found by Ohene on his farm plot.*

**November 1970.** "Achisco Module 2 in Space." Published in the *The Achiscodian Times*. The Editor is Kwadwo Nkrumah-Boateng. Typed. Excerpt.

The Achisco module 2 was blasted off last Saturday. The engineers in the space craft are Osei Kwadwo Albert (Captain)[,] Boamah Albert Asare, Isaac Nkrumah and WE BA. Captain Osei Kwadow has announced to the television viewers on the campus that they are due down in two hours if their broken tea-tank is not satisfactorily repaired.

They would land on the Achisco great ocean (the crocodile pond).

*Contrary to the assertion in "Achisco Module 2 in Space," there was no television in Acherensua, either at the school or in the village.*

**June 1, 1971.** Letter to Jon from Augustine Gyamfi, West African Exams Council, Accra. Sent to Jon's parents' address in Chattanooga. Excerpts.

Dear Mr. Thiem,

It might be somehow a surprise to you to get a letter from Ghana at this time; but if you could recall to the days when you were here and remember Augustine, this letter will no more be a surprise at all.

Now it is your old student A. Gyamfi writing to ask for a favour if only it is not beyond your control.

All is about a school I want to get from [sic] the States. A relative of mine in Britain has asked me to join him there to continue my education. He gave me a school and when all the necessary particulars had been processed, the 2 month British postal strike occurred. Therefore, by the time my particulars got to the school all students had been enrolled already. This, in fact, put me in a fix and . . . my uncle in Britain has asked me to try any other country I want to study [in], if I could get admission in a school. And you know that I know more about [the] States than anywhere else and have chosen to continue my education there. It is in view of this that I am writing to ask you to do me a favour by way of sending me adresses [sic] of schools, so as to write to apply for admission.
[. . .]

The course[s] I prefer most are Business administration, Accounting, Catering, Hotel management or Mental and General nursing.
[. . .]

From the adress [sic] it could be seen that I am in Accra. I am now employed with the exams council as clerical officer on a monthly salary of 40 cedis. Cosmos Acquah also teaches at Dr. J. B. Dankwa Secondary School at Nkawkaw. He uses [sic] to visit me and I have given your adress [sic] to him.
[. . .]

Since I came to Accra in last July, I have not been to Acherensua and I can't give you anything about our school; except that they have got a new Headmaster. Mr. Poku-Maboah has left the school for Opoku Ware Sec. School in Kumasi.
[. . .]

May I know if John Asante has ever paid you a visit. Till then, it is Cherioo and greetings to your family—especially your father and sister you used to talk about.

*Augustine Gyamfi was Prefect of Students when Jon taught at Acherensua Secondary School. For a conversation between Jon, Augustine and Cosmo, see the cassette tape transcription from early June 1969. John Asante and Jon Thiem never managed to meet up in the States.*

**March 3, 1983.** Ohene in Nigeria to Jon in Fort Collins, Colorado. Ohene's letter is sent from the Army Children Secondary School, Army Barracks, Epe, Lagos State, Nigeria. Excerpts.

Dear Jon,

I have received your Xmas Card . . . and I thank you very much sincerely for your remembrance and love. I was so pleased with the card because I heard of you once again. I thought I had lost contact with you and [that you] had left Colorado for an unknown place. I was very pleased with the family picture—Nat and Ben. smiling all the way and Mrs Queen of "The Praise Poems of the Ashantis" in her brightest 'royal' smiles. That was amazing. And now—your academic beard and all those changes in your physical appearance!!! In consequence, let me take the opportunity to congratulate you on your academic promotion to the office of Associate Professor and hope beats within me; for I am sure about it that Professor Emeritus would in future come your way. I am not addressing you in borrowed robes because I knew your merit and efforts in achieving an aim when you were with me in Ghana. More grease to your elbows.

I travelled home to Ghana in August 1982 to visit my family. I told Osei, my first born now in Form 3 of Tepa secondary School, that I had written to you. I had not received a letter back from you. He asked me whether you were still at your post. I could not confirm then, but uncertainly I remarked that you might be there. He was pleased to hear of you. He tells me he has forgotten the mental image of you . . . . He kept on looking at the last picture sent in 1980. All members of the family were very well. My wife had taken to trading and my sisters were local peasant farmers. They were all happy to see me. I shall re-visit them in August 1983 and hope to tell you more of them and conditions in Ghana as a whole when I return.

Has the storm of the snow subsided? You see Jon, I am not a good swimmer and fear the waves so I do not swim in the Ocean. I, however,

enjoy visiting the shore to take the breeze or share with the company of fisherman and holiday makers. There are 37 kinds of Beer in Nigeria and they sell cheaply. I often take it, with my favourite being Gulder, Star, or Harp. Sometimes when a little tipsy, I long for home and [to] be with my family, especially to see my little daughter 1 1/4 yrs old who was named after my junior sister. I fall into moments of thought and the desire to leave finally, but when back to normalcy I look ahead to the fortune I would want to seek and the future I would want to store [up] for my family. O, when shall all these end and man [be able] to take life pretty easy?
[. . .]

The experience in Nigeria is that their economy is fast falling apart because of the oil glut. Things are becoming expensive these days. Let me take the opportunity to inform you that Nigeria has driven away all illegal aliens. This affected about 1 million Ghanaians. In all[,] these aliens numbered about 2 million. All affected Ghanaians have since left. I do not know what other problems the Ghana government is going to face as a result of this exercise but we still hope for the best. Who knows whether Ghana is not going to become like the ancient Jews of the Diaspora? Mismanagement of our past leaders and especially the Soldiers have destroyed . . . Ghana, [once] the pride of Africa. Now we live in abject poverty and misery—where there is nothing!!! To send just one (1) tin of sardine[s] to Ghana is hailed as if some one has just bought a new mercedes benz 250. I foresee no salvation. If at all[,] it would be ages ahead. But we will do the best we can before our time comes to an end.

Unfortunately I have not visited Kwasi Dum (Apaeε) for the past 4 years. He was getting older when I last saw him and I can't predict his life or death. I will try to go to him in August. I shall write back to you when I return and tell you of my interview with him. The Kokofu-hene at that time [you were in Ghana] is dead. A new one had been installed. He is the uncle of my ex-wife.

Acherensua was as it had been for long. Many people have died including the wooden- truck driver and your friend 'Okyeame.' At a later time after David and Nestor had left, Mr. Kuffuor became the Headmaster. Now it is headed by a new man I do not know at all. Before I left for Nigeria, the only old teacher who was there was Mr. Ababio (the one who came from Ntotorofo-junction road, Acherensua). In my last visit in 1980, I was surprised to see new people altogether. The new generation from 1969-80 had grown and I did not know them. I was happy to learn that astronomy was still being learnt because of the device [telescope] given by your father. Your name shall never depart in the annals of the school's history.

When I travel back to Ghana, I will show your picture to my family and people at Asiwa (my village) who know you, and the comments they would make, I shall communicate with you. I am very sure they would be pleased to hear of you.

Where are David Fitzjarrald, Nestor Kwasnycia? Any wind of them?

It has been a long time since I heard of your father. Surely Judy and mother are doing very well, I suppose? Remember me to them.

Remember me also to your wife Barbara, Nat and Ben. Write back soon. Best of luck to you. "Ohene"

*Ohene's letter, written thirteen years after Jon left Ghana, is a fitting epilogue to this collection.*

*In 1983, Jon is literature professor in the English faculty at Colorado State University. Nat (born 1977) and Benji (born 1979) are his and Barbara Thiem's children. Ohene refers to Barbara as "Mrs Queen."*

*". . . I am not a good swimmer . . .": Epe, Nigeria, is on the coast, so Jon had asked Ohene in his last letter if he swam in the ocean.*

*"Nigeria has driven away all illegal aliens." Nigeria expelled aliens without work permits on January 17. Ohene, who witnessed the expulsion of Nigerians from Ghana in 1969, now witnesses the expulsion of Ghanaians from Nigeria in 1983. As a* legal *alien, he is not subject to the expulsion orders. The need to take back a million of its citizens deepened the economic crisis in Ghana.*

*"Mismanagement of our past leaders and especially the Soldiers have destroyed . . . Ghana": on December 31, 1981, the military had again seized power, putting an end to the Third Republic (1979-1981). At the time of this letter, the military dictatorship, led by Jerry Rawlings, still rules. Economic conditions are dire.*

##

# LETTERS FROM GHANA

## "POST SCRIPT"

How will the letters collected here be received in the future? In an age of total digital communication?

Within the space of one generation, the handwritten letter has nearly vanished. Because of the technologies that have replaced it, communication has become more efficient and continuous. It has also become more impersonal and less individualized. On Facebook, a message is typically posted to *all* one's friends. The content of the message is not directed to, or specially shaped for, a particular individual, but rather for a group. The whole point of social media is to enable people to send instant simultaneous messages to a bunch of people. And the messages bear all the marks of having been composed for a group. As McLuhan would say, the medium becomes the message.

The intimate, unsettling things about myself that I might tell *one* friend in a letter, I would not tell to a group. The letter writer creates a *special* persona for each individual he or she is addressing. Today, this special (and sometimes secret) persona is being replaced by a more public one. The result is a collectivization of discourse. This is great for reaching a lot of people. It is great for networking and for doing business. But the tone and contents of these communications are no longer those of the personal letter.

Until the 1980s, the personal letter was a vital medium, especially in times when circumstances separated people. Few alternatives were available. Between March 1944 and March 1945 (the last year of World War II), 374 million letters were sent abroad from England alone (Hartley 193, note 2). This figure does not include letters sent *to* England by military personnel overseas. Immense numbers of letters were written during World War II, among them the wartime correspondence of Cap Thiem and his parents, and the letters sent to Cap by Ginny Pitcher, his fiancée.[1] These letters present the correspondents in all their quirky individuality and give us a glimpse of how each one related to the other on a personal basis.

# POST SCRIPT

Today the personal letter will seem a relic of the past.[2] While the children born immediately after World War II—the "Baby Boomers"—once wrote letters, the Boomers' children have written few, apart from Thank You notes. The children of the children of the Boomers may no longer learn cursive writing, the script in which untyped letters were executed. Schools are beginning to drop this skill from their curriculums.

The question arises: will the generation born in the first decades of the 21st century be able to *read* the ancient letters in cursive that they stumble on in attics, basements, and self storage units? Probably not, unless the letters are converted to print form, or read to them by an aged relative—if one is available.

Readers of the letters collected here will be users of email or other forms of electronic messaging—a boon for people who feel the compulsion to be in daily contact with other people. Letters have drawbacks. They lack instantaneity. Stamps and writing materials are costly. Trips to USPS mail boxes or post offices are an inconvenience.

There is, however, this to consider: letters on paper have a better chance of getting handed down to the next generation than emails do. In theory, there is no reason why emails cannot be saved. The question is, will it happen? The *effortlessness* of electronic communication presents us with both the curse of too much information and the blessing of easy deletion. These conditions will work against preservation.

What aspects of ourselves will persist in the future, outside of countless pictures, public records, and the archives of the National Security Agency? Where will later generations find windows into *our* souls and circumstances?

# POST SCRIPT

## NOTES to "Post Script"

1. Letter-writing was a Thiem family tradition. Rudy Thiem, Jon's grandfather, wrote letters to Hazel Howe during his military training in the First World War, and then later to his son Cap when Cap was in military training during the Second World War. A selection of the Thiem family correspondence from the latter period has been published under the title *War Letters 1943-1944* (compiled by Jon Thiem). Hazel Thiem and Ginny Thiem, even more than their husbands, were indefatigable correspondents.

2. Jon and Ohene continued to exchange letters until Ohene's death in 2008. Jon and Ohene's son Festus Osei communicate via email—the sign of a global shift away from letters.

# ADDENDUM

Apaeɛ for Owoahene

He is the one, He is the one!
Owoahene, whose name we beat on the akwadum drum.
Wo ye sa ye sa. Wo ye sa ye sa.
You did it. You did it.
Owoahene, death knocked at the door,
And you whispered, "Ohene is not at home."

He is the one! He is the one!
Ohwintimpreko who plucks the ripe and the unripe.
Kokote Kwaako, Bush Pig of Acherensua
who empties the wine pot in one gulp.
Black Cobra Siako who never eats frogs and does not go hungry.
Bird of the Desert Kyenkyeboafo
Who brings foo foo from the clouds, that the women may eat.
Ohene, you bring foo foo from the clouds, that the women may eat.

He is the one! He is the one!
Obrofotefo the Interpreter
whose speech is like a net.
Ohene, we say you love words.
You say, you do not love words.
But are you not the Obrofotefo
whose speech is like a net?

The ancestor who could not write says 'thank you!'

Jon Thiem
November 2006

# WORKS CONSULTED

Adepoju, Aderanti. "Patterns of Migration in West Africa." Manuh ed. 24-54.

Alden, Peter C. et al. *National Audubon Society Field Guide to African Wildlife.* New York: Alfred A. Knopf. 1995.

Amin, Julius. "The Perils of Missionary Diplomacy: The United States Peace Corps Volunteers in the Republic of Ghana." *Western Journal of Black Studies* 23.1 (Spring 1999): 35-46.

American War Library. *Vietnam War Deaths and Casualties by Month.* n.d. Web. 16 November 2012. Source: Comptroller, Secretary of Defense.

Amoako, Joe. "Ethnic Identity, Conflict, and Diasporic Constructions in the New World: the Case of Asante." Konadu-Agyemang, Takyi, and Arthur 107-119.

Annin, Collins. "Empowering Poor Communities for Change: The History and Role of Civil Society in Poverty Reduction in Ghana." *Poverty, Education and Development.* Ed. Francis Godwyll and So Young Kang. New York: Nova Science Publishers, 2008. 65-84.

Anyidoho, Akosua. "Techniques of Akan Praise Poetry in Christian Worship: Madam Afua Kuma." *Multiculturalism and Hybridity in African Literatures.* Ed. Hal Wylie and Bernth Lindfors. Trenton, NJ: Africa World Press, 2000. 71-86.

Apter, David E. *Ghana in Transition.* 1963. Rev. ed. Princeton, NJ: Princeton University Press, 1972.

Arhin, Kwame, ed. *The Life and Work of Kwame Nkrumah.* Trenton, NJ: African World Press, 1993.

Arhin Brempong, Nana. "Chieftaincy, An Overview." Odotei and Awedoba 27-41.

Astley Maberly, C. T. *Animals of East Africa.* Nairobi: D. A. Hawkins Ltd., 1965.

"Audio Cassette." *Wikipedia.* 16 November 2012. Web. 17 November 2012.

Austin, Dennis. Introduction. Austin and Luckham 1-14.

Austin, Dennis and Robin Luckham, eds. *Politicians and Soldiers in Ghana: 1966-1972.* London: Frank Cass, 1975.

Baffour, Takyi K. "Africans Abroad: Comparative Perspectives on America's Postcolonial West Africans." Okpewho and Nzegwu 236-254.

Barbier, Mary Kathryn. "Introduction." Wiest, Barbier, and Robins 1-13.

Birmingham, David. *Kwame Nkrumah: The Father of African Nationalism.* Rev. ed. Athens: Ohio University Press, 1998.

Boafo-Arthur, Kwame. "A Decade of Liberalism in Perspective." *Ghana: One Decade of the Liberal State.* Ed. Kwame Boafo-Arthur. Dakar: Codesria Books, 2007. 1-20.

Bowen, Gordon L. *Public Opinion and the Vietnam War.* n.d. Web. 17 November 2012.

"Brief History of the School." *Achisco Akunini.* 13 June 2010. Web. 17 November 2012.

Brinkley, Alan. "1968 and the Unraveling of Liberal America." Fink, Gassert, and Junker 219-236.

Calvocoressi, Peter. *World Politics Since 1945.* 9th ed. London: Pearson Longman, 2009.

# WORKS CONSULTED

Casely-Hayford, Leslie. "Gendered Experiences of Teaching in Poor Rural Areas of Ghana." Fennell and Arnot 146-161.

Chazan, Naomi. *An Anatomy of Ghanaian Politics: Managing Political Recession, 1969-1982.* Boulder: Westview Press, 1983.

Corbin, Amy. *Sacred Groves of Ghana.* 1 June 2008. Web. 16 November 2012.

Coyne, Christopher J. *Doing Bad by Doing Good: Why Humanitarian Action Fails.* Palo Alto: Stanford University Press, 2013.

DeBenedetti, Charles. *An American Ordeal: The Antiwar Movement of the Vietnam War Era.* Syracuse: Syracuse University Press, 1990.

Dum, Kwasi. *Apaeɛ: Ashanti Praise Poems. Recited from Oral Tradition by Kwasi Dum.* Comp. and tr. Jon Thiem and E. W. Owoahene. 1970. Typescript. Sixty-three pages.

---. "Apaeɛ: Heroic Poems of the Asante Court." Tr. Jon Thiem and E. W. Owoahene. *Translation* 6 (Winter, 1978-79): 222-228.

---. "Six Apaeɛ in Praise of Osei Tutu, King of the Asante." Tr. Jon Thiem and E. W. Owoahene-Akyampong. *Nine Waves. Poems by Bettie Anne Doebler, Ralph Slotten, Jon Thiem.* Lititz, PA: Sutter House, 2003. 156-158.

Dunn, John. "Politics in Asunafo." Austin and Luckham 164-213.

Fennell, Shailaja and Madeleine Arnot, eds. *Gender, Education, and Equality in a Global Context.* London: Routledge, 2008.

Fink, Carole, Philipp Gassert, and Detlef Junker, eds. *1968: The World Transformed.* Cambridge: Cambridge University Press, 1998.

Ghana Statistical Service. *2000 Population and Housing Census Data Analysis Report.* 2005. Web. 17 November 2012.

Gocking, Roger S. *The History of Ghana.* Westport CT: Greenwood Press, 2005.

Graff, Harvey J. *The Labyrinths of Literacy.* Rev. ed. Pittsburgh: University of Pittsburgh Press, 1995.

---. *Literacy Myths, Legacies, & Lessons: New Studies on Literacy.* New Brunswick, NJ: Transaction Publishers, 2011.

Grubbs, Larry. *Secular Missionaries: Americans and African Development in the 1960s.* Amherst: University of Massachusetts Press, 2009.

Haar, Gerrie ter. *How God Became African: African Spirituality and Western Secular Thought.* Philadelphia: University of Pennsylvania Press, 2009.

Hartley, Jenny. "'Letters are *everything* these days': Mothers and Letters in the Second World War." *Epistolary Selves: Letters and Letter-writers 1600-1945.* Ed. Rebecca Earle. Aldershot, UK: Ashgate, 1999. 183-195.

Herring, George C. "Tet and the Crisis of Hegemony." Fink, Gassert, and Junker 31-53.

*Historical Dictionary of Ghana.* Ed. David Owusu-Ansah. 3rd ed. Lanham MD: The Scarecrow Press, 2005.

Hobsbawm, Eric. *The Age of Extremes: A History of the World, 1914-1991.* New York: Pantheon Books, 1994.

Hoffman, Elizabeth Cobbs. *All You Need is Love: The Peace Corps and the Spirit of the 1960s.* Cambridge: Harvard University Press, 1998.

Horn, Gerd-Rainer. *The Spirit of '68: Rebellion in Western Europe and North America, 1956-1976.* Oxford: Oxford University Press, 2007,

# WORKS CONSULTED

"ICT Centre for Acherensua Secondary School Inaugurated." *Achisco Akunini.* 13 June 2010. Web. 17 November 2012.

Konadu-Agyemang, Kwadwo, Baffour K. Takyi, and John Arthur, eds. *The New African Diaspora in North America.* Lanham, MD.: Rowman and Littlefield, 2006.

Kuma, Afua. *Jesus of the Deep Forest (Kwaebirentu Ase Yesu).* Ed. and tr. Kofi Ron Lange and Jon Kirby. Accra: Asempa Publisher, 1981. Quotations from the typescript were kindly sent to me by Kofi Ron Lange.

Lange, Kofi Ron. *Style in Kwaebirentuw Ase Yesu.* n.d. Typescript. 1-11

Langguth, A. J. *Our Vietnam: The War 1954-1975.* New York: Simon & Schuster, 2000.

"List of Countries by Literacy Rate." *Wikipedia.* 16 November 2012. Web. 17 November 2012. Ghana statistics are from the 2010 Ghana Census.

McNamara, Robert. *In Retrospect.* New York: Times Books-Random House, 1995.

McWilliams, Wayne C. and Harry Piotrowski. *The World Since 1945: A History of International Relations.* 7th ed. Boulder: Lynne Rienner, 2009.

Mailer, Norman. *Miami and the Siege of Chicago. An Informal History of the Republican and Democratic Conventions of 1968.* New York: World Pub. Co., 1968.

---. *The Armies of the Night.* New York: New American Library, 1968.

---. "The White Negro." 1957. *Advertisements for Myself.* 1959. New York: G. P. Putnam-Berkeley Publishing Corp., 1966. 311-331.

Manuh, Takyiwaa. "Ghanaians, Ghanaian-Canadians, and Asantes." *Africa Today* 45 (July through December 1998): 481-494.

---, ed. *At Home in the World? International Migration and Development in Contemporary Ghana and West Africa.* Accra: Sub-Saharan Publishers, 2005.

Masur, Matthew. "Historians and the Origins of the Vietnam War." Wiest, Barbier, and Robins 35-53.

Miescher, Stephan F. "Becoming Ɔpanyin." *Africa After Gender?* Ed. Catherine M. Cole, Takyiwaa Manuh, and Stephan F. Miescher. Bloomington: Indiana University Press, 2007. 253-269.

Nkrumah, Kwame. *I Speak of Freedom: A Statement of African Ideology.* New York: Praeger, 1961.

Odotei, Irene K. and Albert K. Awedoba, eds. *Chieftaincy in Ghana: Culture, Governance and Development.* Accra-Legon: Sub-Saharan Publishers, 2006.

Okpewho, Isidore. "Can We 'Go Home Again'?" Introduction. Okpewho and Nzegwu 3-14.

---. *The Epic in Africa: Towards a Poetics of Oral Performance.* New York: Columbia University Press, 1969.

Okpewho, Isidore and Nkiru Nzegwu, eds. *The New African Diaspora.* Bloomington: Indiana University Press, 2009.

Pach Jr., Chester J. "Tet on TV." Fink, Gassert, and Junker 55-81.

Rathbone, Richard. *Nkrumah & the Chiefs.* Accra: F. Reimmer, 2000.

## WORKS CONSULTED

Reid, Ian C. *Guide Book to Mount Kenya and Kilimanjaro.* Nairobi: The Mountain Club of Kenya, 1963.

Rice, Gerard T. *The Bold Experiment: JFK's Peace Corps.* South Bend, IN: University of Notre Dame Press, 1985.

Rothmyer, Karen. "The Peace Corps at 50." *The Nation* 292.12 (March 21, 2011): 9.

Senadza, Bernardin. "Education and Inequality in Ghana." *Journal of Economic Studies* 39.6 (2012): 724-739.

Smith, Esther Y. "Apaeε: Praise Poetry of Akan Kings." *Southern Folklore Quarterly* 39 (1975): 171-186.

Sutherland-Addy, Esi. "Projecting Royalty: the Evocative Power of the Poet at Court." Odotei and Awedoba 247-258.

Takyi-Amoaka, Emefa. "Poverty Reduction and Gender Parity in Education." Fennell and Arnot 196-210.

*The Fog of War.* Interviews with Robert McNamara. Dir. Errol Morris. 2003. Film.

Thiem, Jon. "Reading and *Rereading:* A Twenty-first Century Perspective." Rereading Faces: Matei Calinescu and the Fates of Comparative Literature. University of Western Ontario. London, Ontario. October 21, 2011. Address. Also at www.jonthiem.com/reading-and-rereading

---. Comp. and ed. *War Letters 1943-44.* Boulder, Colorado: Lulu.com, 2010.

Twuum-Baah, K. A. "Volume and Characteristics of International Ghanaian Migration." Manuh, ed. 55-76.

U.S. Department of Commerce. *Ghana. Country Demographic Profiles.* 1977. Google Books. Web. 16 November 2012.

"Vietnam War Casualties." *Wikipedia.* 6 November 2012. Web. 17 November 2012.

Wiest, Andrew, Mary Kathryn Barbier, and Glenn Robins, eds. *America and the Vietnam War: Re-examining the Culture and History of a Generation.* New York: Routledge, 2010.

Wilks, Ivor. *Forests of Gold: Essays on the Akan and the Kingdom of Asante.* Athens: Ohio University Press, 1993.

Yankah, Kwesi. "The Making and Breaking of Kwame Nkrumah: The Role of Oral Poetry." *Ghanaian Literature.* Ed. Richard K. Priebe. New York: Greenwood Press, 1988. 43-57.

# TIMELINE

**1957**
March 6   The Gold Coast becomes the independent state of Ghana. Kwame Nkrumah, chairman of the Convention People's Party and prime minister, is made head of the new government. Martin Luther King, Jr., attends the celebrations.

**1958**
July   The Preventive Detention Act gives Nkrumah powers to silence and intimidate opponents.
Sept.   The government arrest and internal banishment of the Okyenhene, Ofori Atta II, king of Akyem Abuakwa (Kibi)—the key part of a campaign to break the power of the traditional chiefs.

**1960**
July   Ghana is declared a republic; Nkrumah wins the presidential election and becomes Head of State under the constitution of the First Republic.

**1961**
March   The Peace Corps is created by executive order of John F. Kennedy.
April   Sargent Shriver, first head of the Peace Corps meets with President Nkrumah in Accra.
Aug. 30   Ghana becomes the first nation to receive Peace Corps Volunteers.

**1964**
Feb.   Ghana becomes a one-party state governed by Nkrumah's Convention People's Party (CPP)

**1965**
Oct.   Jon, in Carlisle, Pennsylvania, together with several other students and his political science professor, demonstrates against the escalation of U.S. military involvement in the Vietnamese civil war. The protest takes place in front of the Carlisle draft board office.

**1966**
Feb.   Kwame Nkrumah visits China with the goal of arbitrating an end to the Vietnam War.
Feb. 24   Military and police officers seize control of the government while Nkrumah is in China; he is deposed.

**1967**
Oct. 21   Jon joins around 30,000 other war protesters at the March on the Pentagon.
Nov.   In this month 1,018 U.S. soldiers die in Vietnam (American War Library). Defense Secretary McNamara writes a memo to President Johnson admitting the failure of the government's Vietnam war policy.

**1968**
Jan. 30   The first Tet Offensive in Vietnam begins, a coordinated effort of the North Vietnamese and the Viet Cong.
Feb. 29   Defense Secretary Robert McNamara leaves office.
Feb.   In this month 2,293 U.S. troops die in Vietnam (American War Library).

# TIMELINE

March 16   The My Lai massacre. A U.S. army unit (of the 23rd Infantry Division) murders between 300-500 unarmed villagers, largely women, children and old men. (This event becomes known to the U.S. public only many months later.)

March 31   President Johnson announces he will not stand for re-election.

April and May   Student protests and sit-ins at Columbia University.

April 4   The assassination of Martin Luther King Jr. He was an advocate of withdrawal from Vietnam.

June 5   The assassination of Robert F. Kennedy, the day he won the California presidential primary; he proposed the withdrawal of U.S. forces from Vietnam.

June 15-Aug 16   Jon is in Peace Corps training, Columbia University.

Aug. 16   Jon sends a letter to his draft board requesting appeal of its decision to reject his Peace Corps deferment.

Aug. 20-21   The Soviet invasion of Czechoslovakia.

Aug. 21-22   Jon and the other Peace Corps trainees who were at Columbia fly to Ghana via London and Amsterdam.

Aug 22.   Arrival in Accra, Ghana.

Aug. 24-Sept. 4   In-country training at Kibi (Kyebi), Ghana. Jon meets the Okyenhene, King of the Akyem Abuakwa people.

Aug. 26-29   At the Democratic National Convention in Chicago, televised news reports show police beating unarmed war protesters with clubs.

Sept. 6   Jon arrives in Acherensua and begins to prepare for teaching English at Acherensua Secondary School.

Nov.   By the beginning of this month, 32,000 U.S. soldiers have died in Vietnam (McWilliams 219).

Dec. 23-31   Jon and McClure travel to northern Ghana, Upper Volta, and Ivory Coast.

**1969**

Jan. 1-Jan 10   Jon and McClure continue their West African travels.

Jan.   Cap Thiem moves from Wilmington, Delaware to Chattanooga, Tennessee. Ginny and Judy Thiem follow some weeks later.

June 14-15   Jon, McClure, and Ohene visit Kokofu; Jon and Ohene record oral poems (apaeɛ) recited in Asante Twi by the "fetish priest" Kwasi Dum.

July 6-7   Volunteers Altrows and McClure leave Acherensua for good.

July 20   The U.S. Apollo 11 mission lands the first humans on the moon.

July 25   Cap Thiem arrives in Accra and meets Jon; dinner with McClure, who is still in Accra.

July 26-28   Trip to Kumasi, capital of the Ashanti Region.

July 28   Travel to Acherensua; dinner with the Headmaster. Visit to the settlement of a fetish priest.

July 29   Return to Kumasi.

July 31   After a brief stay in Kumasi, back to Accra.

Aug. 1   Cap and Jon fly from Accra to Nairobi, Kenya (via Lagos and Entebbe).

Aug. 3   The Kilimanjaro climb, in Tanzania.

# TIMELINE

Aug. 6-14  Visits to Ngorongoro crater, in Tanzania, Nairobi National Park, Mombasa, and Nairobi, in Kenya.
Aug. 15  Cap flies from Nairobi back to the States.
Aug. 18  Jon is back in Accra.
Aug. 21-Sept. 1  Jon and Ohene visit Kokofu/Sebedie and Ohene's village, Asiwa.
Aug. 29  The first free national elections in Ghana since the military seized power on Feb 24, 1966; Mr. Badu Nkwansah, Assistant Headmaster, is elected to the new National Assembly.
Sept. 3-4  Jon and Ohene are in Kokofu and Kumasi.
Sept. 5  Jon and Ohene visit the University of Ghana to consult with Prof. Denteh on the apaeɛ project.
Sept. 8-12  Jon attends the Peace Corps conference at the University of Ghana.
Sept.-Dec.  Intensive work on the apaeɛ: transcription, translation, research, and commentaries.
Sept. 30  After four years of military rule, the inauguration of the Second Republic under President Kofi Busia.
Nov.-Dec.  Enforcement of the Aliens Compliance Act: the new government expels around 150,000 foreign workers from Ghana.
Dec.  Completion of the apaeɛ manuscript.
Dec.  Drawing of numbers in the U.S. draft lottery: Jon receives the lottery number 342, which makes conscription unlikely.
Dec. 25  Jon's second visit to Asiwa with Ohene and Nestor Kwasnycia; visit to nearby Lake Bosumtwi, sacred to the Asante people.
End of Dec.  Jon and Ohene enroll in a conference: "The New Year School" at the University of Ghana.

**1970**

Jan. 1-7  Jon and Ohene attend "The New Year School" and participate in sessions on Ghanaian development.
Feb.  A formal investigation of the Headmaster is launched.
March 28  Jon and Steve Rendig, another Peace Corps volunteer, visit Lomé, Togo.
March 31  Jon is in Cape Coast for a teachers' conference.
April 6  The telescope that Cap Thiem donates to Acherensua Secondary School arrives in Accra.
April 23  Ohene and Jon visit Bonwire to order a custom-made Kente cloth robe for Jon.
April 24  Jon and Ohene visit the Asantehene's secretary in Kumasi to ask for permission to publish the apaeɛ.
May  The death of the Asantehene Prempe II (b. 1892); Fitzjarrald and Jon pick up the telescope in Accra for transport back to Acherensua; Jon submits the apaeɛ manuscript to the Peace Corps office; investigation of the school's headmaster draws to a close; student unrest, due to rumors that the administration building is going to be burned down to destroy records.
May 4  At Kent State, Ohio, four unarmed students are shot and killed by the Ohio National Guard during an antiwar protest.

# TIMELINE

June 4-6   Jon attends the Peace Corps termination conference in Takoradi, on the coast. Mid-June to June 30   Jon is in Acherensua for the last time; at the end of the month the Headmaster of the school is dismissed.

July 4   Jon flies to Rome via Abidjan.

Circa July 5-July 30   Jon is in Italy and France; he meets up with McClure, who is teaching in Paris.

Circa July 30   Jon flies from Paris back to the United States.

Aug.   Jon visits his family in Rehoboth Beach, Delaware, and Chattanooga, Tennessee.

Sept.   Jon enters the Ph.D. program in Comparative Literature at Indiana University, Bloomington.

# GLOSSARY

*For the historical entries below, I have frequently relied on David Owusu-Ansah's magisterial* Historical Dictionary of Ghana *(2005).*

*1-A*  a selective service classification denoting eligibility for compulsory military service
*1-Y*  a selective service classification for males with a medical condition, making them available for military service only in times of urgent need
*4-F*  a selective service classification providing exemption from military service for medical reasons
*Abidjan*  capital of Ivory Coast, the country on Ghana's western border
*Abrafo*  an executioner; in the Asantehene's court, the abrafo recites apaeɛ
*Accra*  the capital of Ghana
*Achebe, Chinua* (1930-2013)  Nigerian novelist and author of *Things Fall Apart* (1958), a novel which Jon taught in Ghana and later in the United States
*Acherensua*  the name of a village and district secondary school in the Brong-Ahafo region
*Adinkra*  a traditional cloth embellished with abstract prints and used in robes
*Afrifa, A. A.* (1936-1979)  Ghanaian officer who took over as chair of the military government in 1969, after the resignation of General Ankrah
*Ahafo*  part of the Brong-Ahafo region; Ahafo means "Asantehene's hunting grounds"
*Aidoo, Ama Ata* (b.1940)  Ghanaian playwright, poet, and short story writer; Jon taught her play *The Dilemma of a Ghost* (1965)
*A.I.D.*  the U.S. Agency for International Development
*Akan* (or Twi)  the language spoken by several related ethnic groups; Asante (or Ashanti Twi) is one of the major dialects; Akan also refers to the shared culture of several interrelated ethnic groups, including the Asante, Fante, Brong, and Akyem Abuakwa
*akpeteshie*  a clear strong alcoholic liquor distilled from palm wine or cane sugar juice
*Akwaaba*  Asante for "welcome"
*Ampofo, Kofi*  the teenage assistant to Opong, the Peace Corps cook in Acherensua; he is Opong's nephew; in 1969, he is in danger of deportation because he is the son of parents living in Ivory Coast
*Ankrah, Joseph* (1915-1992)  Ghanaian general who chaired the military junta that overthrew Nkrumah; he was forced to resign in 1969, after accepting bribes *apaeɛ* traditional oral poems recited to honor the king in Akan royal courts

# GLOSSARY

*Armah, Ayi Kwei* (b. 1939)   Ghanaian novelist and author of *The Beautiful Ones Are Not Yet Born* (1968)

*Asante* (formerly Ashanti)   the largest ethnic group in Ghana, about 19 percent of the population; the Asante belong to the Akan culture, along with the Fante, Brong, and other peoples; Asante (or more frequently Ashanti) is also the name of a region and the name of the Akan dialect spoken by the Asante people

*Asantehene*   the Asante King, titular head of the Asante people; his seat is in Kumasi; Prempe II (b. 1892) was Asantehene from 1935 until his death in May 1970

*Ashanti*   traditional anglicized name for the Asante people and language, and also of the administrative region whose capital is Kumasi

*Asiwa*   village near Lake Bosumtwi in the Ashanti region, south of Kumasi; Ohene's hometown

*Auden, W. H.* (1907-1973)   English-born poet and essayist; he visited Dickinson College

*Barth, John* (b. 1930)   U.S. novelist and short story writer; his essays on postmodern and magical realist narrative were highly influential

*Biafra*   the self-designated name of several provinces that seceded from Nigeria; the secession led to the Biafran war, which was in full swing in the late 1960s

*bilharzia* (also schistosomiasis)   a parasitic disease of the tropics contracted from bathing or swimming in ponds and rivers

*Bonwire*   a village in the Asante region, near Kumasi, specializing in the weaving of Kente cloth

*Borges, Jorge Luis* (1899-1986)   Argentine short story writer, poet, essayist— one of the founders of postmodern fiction

*Brong-Ahafo*   administrative region west of the Ashanti region; the capital is Sunyani

*Brong, the*   an Akan people

*bush, the*   another name for the rain forest or any rural area

*cassava*   a starchy tuber (manioc); it is a staple food in Ghana and an ingredient of foo foo

*cedi* (or new cedi)   the basic unit of Ghanaian currency—about one dollar at the official exchange rate in the late 1960s

*chop*   West African English for "food"

*chop house*   an eating establishment

*coco yam*   a tuber and one of the staple foods in Ghana; an ingredient of foo foo

*CPP*   the Convention People's Party, the political party founded by Kwame Nkrumah

# GLOSSARY

*Cronkite, Walter* (1916-2009)  television news anchor, whose reports Cap and Ginny regularly send to Jon on audio cassette tapes

*C.U.S.O.*  Canadian University Service Overseas; it is similar to the Peace Corps

*Dickinson College*  in Carlisle, Pennsylvania; Jon graduated from there in 1968, with a degree in political science/international relations

*Destool*  among the Akans a chief or king may be destooled, i.e. dethroned

*Dum, Kwasi*  priest of the god Ta Kora, abrafo, and reciter of apaeɛ; a resident of Sebedie, near Kokofu

*Durbar*  in West African English, a festive reception or meeting of chiefs and kings

*enstoolment*  the Akan equivalent of enthroning a king or chief; the term refers to the official stool upon which the personage sits

*Ewe*  an ethnic group in the southeastern part of Ghana

*expatriot*  Jon's intentional misspelling of "expatriate"—a pun

*Fante*  an Akan people living on and near the coast of Ghana

*fetish priest* (okomfo)  a celebrant in the traditional religion who possesses powers emanating from the supreme being Onyame, including the power to summon a spirit for curing sickness

*fifth form*  the final year of a Ghanaian secondary school student (in institutions without a sixth form), roughly equivalent to 12th grade

*first form*  the first year of a Ghanaian secondary school student

*foo foo* (or fu fu)  paste made of mashed cooked yam, cassava and plantain and served in the form of a ball with a sauce or in a soup; the national dish of Ghana

*Ga*  an ethnic group concentrated in Accra and the surrounding area

*Golden Stool, The*  a gilded stool that symbolizes the unity of the Asante nation and the authority of the Asantehene—it evidently appeared in the time of Osei Tutu and Okomfo Anokye in the late seventeenth century

*Griot*  a traditional bard or singer of tales, especially associated with the ancient African civilization of Mali; Jon also uses the Anglo Saxon term *scop,* an oral poet

*Harmattan*  refers to the dry season, generally from November or December through March; arid winds (the Harmattan) blow out of the Sahara; the days are hot, the nights cool, the air thick with dust

*Hausa*  the name of an ethnic group, largely Muslim, and a language widespread throughout West Africa; Hausas are often itinerant traders found especially in northern Ghana

*Highlife*  the distinctive dance music of Ghana, sung to words and played by a large band

*high table*  a formal arrangement (originating in Britain) for seating diners of high status, such as teachers, honored guests, etc., traditionally at a table

# GLOSSARY

placed higher than other tables; Jon ironically refers to those not so honored as "low table"

*hipster* a counter-cultural type of the 1950s and 1960s, the epitome of 'cool' and existential chic; Norman Mailer memorably related the hipster ethos to African American attitudes and styles in his essay "The White Negro" (1957)

*Ivory Coast* (Côte d'Ivoire) the country on Ghana's western boundary; the two nations share similar ethnic groups, weather, and vegetation; the capital is Abidjan

*Kente cloth* a colorful woven fabric that has become a symbol of Ghana; it appears as the background design on the cover of this book; the main Akan center for weaving Kente cloth is at Bonwire, near Kumasi; Kente robes are worn on ceremonial occasions

*Kibi* (Kyebi) the capital of Akyem Abuakwa and seat of the Okyenhene, about sixty miles north of Accra; Jon did his "in-country training" there

*Kofi* a common Ghanaian name; the nickname Jon adopted

*Kofi Ampofo* the Peace Corps cook's young nephew and assistant

*Kokofu* a village south of Kumasi, near Lake Bosumtwi; the seat of the Kokofuhene; it was one of the original villages of the Asante confederation and in Asante tradition, the original homeland of the Asante people

*kramofo* Akan word for Muslims

*Kumasi* capital of the Ashanti region of Ghana, three to four hours by mammy wagon from Acherensua

*"Kwasi Obroni"* i.e. "Kwasi White Man," a generic name for whites; Kwasi is a common given name in Ghana

*Laye, Camara* (1928-1980) West African writer from Guinea who wrote in French, author of *The African Child* and *The Radiance of the King*

*Legon* suburb of Accra and location of the University of Ghana *Lomé* the capital of Togo, the country on Ghana's eastern border *lorry* a freight truck, or a truck fitted out (with benches in the back) for carrying passengers

*Mac* Jon's name for his tape recorder (after Marshall McLuhan)

*McLuhan, Marshall* (1911-1980) Canadian communications theorist, who postulated that the form or structure of media has a more powerful influence on social relations than media content; he predicted the coming of the Internet

*Mailer, Norman* (1923-2007) U.S. novelist, essayist, journalist, and polemicist

*mammy wagon* another name for a passenger lorry (truck); it was fitted out to carry passengers, 15-20 comfortably, but often up to 30; with stops, it averaged about 25-30 mph

# GLOSSARY

*mmoatia*  the dwarves of Akan folk tradition; they are mischievous, capable of making themselves invisible, and able to communicate with each other by whistling

*mpaninfo*  the elders, plural of opanyin, village elder or elderly person

*Nabokov, Vladimir* (1899-1977)  U.S. novelist (Russian-born and raised) and lepidopterist; his literary work spans the periods of modernist and postmodern fiction

*N.C.*  New Cedi, the currency of Ghana

*Nkrumah, Kwame* (1909-1972)  Ghana's president from 1957-1966; he was the first head of state to admit Peace Corps volunteers

*Nkwansah, Badu*  he was, successively, assistant Headmaster of Acherensua Secondary School, representative to Ghana's Constituent Assembly, elected representative to the National Assembly, and Ministerial Secretary for Labour and Social Welfare in the Kofi Busia government

*nsafoɔ*  palm wine, a white foamy alcoholic beverage made of the fermented sap of palm trees

*ohene*  Akan word for chief or king

*Ohene*  the nickname of Jon's Ghanaian colleague and friend E. W. Owoahene-Akyampong

*okomfo*  "fetish priest"

*Okomfo Anokye*  a fetish priest closely allied to Osei Tutu I

*Okyeame*  the spokesman or interpreter of Akan kings and chiefs, who are not supposed to address people directly

*Ofori Atta II* (1899-1973)  the Okyenhene

*Okyenhene*  king of the Akyem Abuakwa people, who are Akans; his stool is in the town of Kibi (Kyebi)

*omanhene*  paramount chief, the king of an Akan state

*opanyin*  an old person; also, a village elder, or a mature man who has earned great respect for his achievements and generosity

*Opong*  the cook for Peace Corps and CUSO volunteers at Acherensua Secondary School

*Osagyefo*  honorific term meaning savior; in the apaeɛ an epithet of King Osei Tutu; a popular name for Kwame Nkrumah

*Osei Tutu* (c. 1660-1717?)  the first Asante king (Asantehene); founder of the Asante confederation; he occupied the Golden Stool and is the main figure in the apaeɛ collected by Jon and Ohene

*Oware*  a traditional Ghanaian "board" game; the "board" may be two parallel rows of small cavities in the ground into which, during the game, seeds (the counters) are dropped by the two players; or the board may be carved wood with a similar set of cavities

# GLOSSARY

*Owoahene-Akyampong, E. W.*   Jon's colleague and co-translator; also known as "Ohene"; he is the Bible master at Acherensua Secondary School

*plantain*   a large banana-like fruit; a Ghanaian staple and ingredient in foo foo

*palm wine*   in Akan nsafoɔ; a white foamy alcoholic beverage made of the fermented sap of palm trees

*paramount chief* (Akan: Omanhene)   king of an Akan state

*PC*   Peace Corps

*PCV*   Peace Corps Volunteer

*peto*   an alcoholic drink made from corn (maize)

*Prempeh II* (1892 -1970)   Asantehene from 1930-1970

*rainy season*   the coolest time of year in Acherensua, lasting from April to July, with a second period from September through November

*sasabonsam*   the malevolent tree demon in Akan folklore

*S.D.S.*   Students for a Democratic Society, a radical political organization of the 1960s and early 1970s, non-violent (except for the Weatherman faction)

*Sebedie*   village near Kokofu; the home of Kwasi Dum, fetish priest, abrafo, and reciter of apaeɛ

*Sundiata, the epic of*   an orally-transmitted African narrative celebrating a hero of the empire of ancient Mali; the epic was passed down by griots (oral singers of tales)

*Sunyani*   the capital of the Brong-Ahafo region, north of Acherensua

*Tamale*   capital of the Northern Region of Ghana; it has a large Muslim population

*Tet Offensive, the* (Jan.- Feb. 1968)   A surprise military campaign that demonstrated the strength and tactical daring of the Viet Cong and the North Vietnamese army, which invaded five of the six major cities in South Vietnam, penetrating Saigon itself, with attacks on the U.S. embassy and the Presidential palace

*Togo*   nation to the east of Ghana; the capital is Lomé

*Tristram Shandy* (1767)   title of a humorous, digressive novel by Laurence Sterne

*Twi*   traditional name for Akan, the language of the Akan peoples; it includes Asante

*UP*   United Party, the political party in opposition to Nkrumah's Convention People's Party (CPP)

*Upper Volta*   the country on Ghana's northern boundary, in the Sahel region, south of the Sahara; today it is called Burkina Faso; the capital is Ouagadougou

*Volta River Dam*   a large-scale project, completed in 1965; it created an immense reservoir (Lake Volta) in eastern Ghana, used for generating hydroelectric power; it was financed in large part by Kaiser Aluminum to smelt (non-Ghanaian) bauxite

# GLOSSARY

*Vonnegut, Kurt* (1922-2007)   U.S. novelist and short story writer; he made extensive use of science fiction conventions and postmodern metafictional devices

*zongo*   quarter of a town where "foreigners" and Muslims live

*zongofo*   Akan word for "foreigners," sometimes applied to Muslims

*Jon in East Africa, August 1969.*

## ABOUT THE AUTHOR/EDITOR

Jon Thiem is professor emeritus of English and Comparative Literature at Colorado State University. He has lived in Colorado for the last 35 years.

After Peace Corps service in Ghana (1968-70), Thiem went on to Indiana University where he received his doctorate in Comparative Literature in 1975.

His essays have appeared in *Comparative Literature, The Journal of the History of Ideas, Cadmos, Sincronie, Translation and Literature, The Dictionary of Literary Themes,* and in the collection *Magical Realism: Theory History Community* (Duke University Press).

Selections of his poems are included in *Book of the Mermaid* (Sutter House, 2001) and in *Nine Waves* (Sutter House, 2003).

Thiem is the author/co-author of several books. *Lorenzo de' Medici: Selected Poems and Prose* (Penn State Press, 1991) was short-listed for the Columbia Translation Center Prize. *Real Life: Ten Stories of Aging* (University Press of Colorado, 1994) is an anthology of world fiction, co-edited with philosopher Patrick McKee.

*Rabbit Creek Country: Three Ranching Lives in the Heart of the Mountain West* (University of New Mexico Press, 2008) was written in collaboration with his research assistant Deborah Dimon. It examines the interwoven lives of three early twentieth-century settlers in the Colorado mountains. *Rabbit Creek Country* was a Finalist for the Colorado Book Award in 2009.